Exploring the Political Economy and Social Philosophy of F. A. Hayek

Economy, Polity, and Society

The foundations of political economy—from Adam Smith to the Austrian school of economics, to contemporary research in public choice and institutional analysis—are sturdy and well established, but far from calcified. On the contrary, the boundaries of the research built on this foundation are ever expanding. One approach to political economy that has gained considerable traction in recent years combines the insights and methods of three distinct but related subfields within economics and political science: the Austrian, Virginia, and Bloomington schools of political economy. The vision of this book series is to capitalize on the intellectual gains from the interactions between these approaches in order to both feed the growing interest in this approach and advance social scientists' understanding of economy, polity, and society.

This series seeks to publish works that combine the Austrian school's insights on knowledge, the Virginia school's insights into incentives in non-market contexts, and the Bloomington school's multiple methods, real-world approach to institutional design as a powerful tool for understanding social behaviour in a diversity of contexts.

Titles in the Series:

Interdisciplinary Studies of the Market Order: New Applications of Market Process Theory, edited by Peter J. Boettke, Christopher J. Coyne, and Virgil Henry Storr
Knowledge and Incentives in Policy: Using Public Choice and Market Process Theory to Analyze Public Policy Issues, edited by Stefanie Haeffele
Exploring the Political Economy and Social Philosophy of James M. Buchanan, edited by Paul Dragos Aligica, Christopher J. Coyne, and Stefanie Haeffele
Exploring the Political Economy and Social Philosophy of F. A. Hayek, edited by Peter J. Boettke, Jayme S. Lemke, and Virgil Henry Storr

Exploring the Political Economy and Social Philosophy of F. A. Hayek

Edited by
Peter J. Boettke, Jayme S. Lemke,
and Virgil Henry Storr

ROWMAN &
LITTLEFIELD
INTERNATIONAL

London • New York

Published by Rowman & Littlefield International Ltd.
Unit A, Whitacre Mews, 26-34 Stannary Street, London SE11 4AB
www.rowmaninternational.com

Rowman & Littlefield International Ltd. is an affiliate of Rowman & Littlefield
4501 Forbes Boulevard, Suite 200, Lanham, Maryland 20706, USA
With additional offices in Boulder, New York, Toronto (Canada), and Plymouth (UK)
www.rowman.com

British Library Cataloguing in Publication Data
A catalogue record for this book is available from the British Library

ISBN: HB 978-1-78660-563-4
PB 978-1-78660-564-1

Library of Congress Cataloging-in-Publication Data Available

ISBN 978-1-78660-563-4 (cloth : alk. paper)
ISBN 978-1-78660-564-1 (pbk. : alk. paper)
ISBN 978-1-78660-565-8 (electronic)

∞™ The paper used in this publication meets the minimum requirements of American National Standard for Information Sciences—Permanence of Paper for Printed Library Materials, ANSI/NISO Z39.48-1992.

Printed in the United States of America

Contents

Introduction

Exploring the Political Economy and Social Philosophy of F. A. Hayek

Peter J. Boettke, Jayme S. Lemke, and Virgil Henry Storr

The interdisciplinary chapters in this volume explore and engage the political economy and social philosophy of Friedrich Hayek from a wide variety of contexts and from many disciplinary perspectives. The contributors come from law, economics, philosophy, anthropology, political science, and history. Consequently, the range of topics covered in this volume is extraordinarily wide, running the gamut from immigration, to white supremacy, to ancient agricultural practices, to the nature of what it means to be free. Together, these contributions demonstrate the continued significance of Hayek's research program to a large variety of disciplines.

AN OVERVIEW OF F. A. HAYEK'S CAREER AND RESEARCH PROGRAM

Friedrich August Hayek was born on May 8, 1899. Hayek was educated at the University of Vienna and in the tradition of the Austrian School of Economics. He received his first doctorate in 1921, and his second in 1923. Hayek had served in the Austrian military during World War I, and after the war he finished his formal education at University of Vienna. Based on a recommendation from Friedrich Wieser, Hayek was hired to work with Ludwig von Mises, first as a special assistant on the economic analysis of the Treaty of Saint-Germain-en-Laye for the Austrian government. Later, Mises would establish the Austrian Institute for Business Cycle Research and Hayek would be appointed its first director. In between, through sponsorship from Mises, Hayek would travel to the United States to study at New York University and develop expertise in the modern statistical analysis of trade cycles, and to consult with Wesley Claire Mitchell at Columbia and the National Bureau of Economic Research..

Upon his return to Vienna, Hayek would continue his collaboration with Mises in developing what became known as the Austrian Theory of the Trade Cycle, as well as continuing his own independent research in technical economic theory, monetary economics, capital theory, and public policy. In 1929, Hayek published *Monetary Theory and the Trade Cycle*, and then in 1931, he delivered a series of well-received lectures that were later published as *Prices and Production.* The lectures earned Hayek an invitation from Lionel Robbins to join the faculty at the London School of Economics as the Tooke Chair of Economics and Statistics. Hayek taught at the LSE from 1931 to 1950. He also served on the faculty of the University of Chicago from 1950 to 1962, and then the University of Freiburg from 1962 to 1968. After retiring in 1968, he spent a year as a visiting professor at UCLA while working on *Law, Legislation and Liberty*, and then accepted an appointment at the University of Salzburg from 1969 to 1977. After leaving Salzburg, Hayek returned to Freiburg, where he would spend the rest of his life. His final book was *The Fatal Conceit*, published in 1988.

In addressing Hayek's work, scholars face a considerable challenge, as his biographer Bruce Caldwell has repeatedly stressed. His first published works came in the 1920s and his last published work in 1988. It is not just that he published over seven decades that creates a problem, it is also that his work ranged from technical economics to theoretical psychology; from epistemology and the methodology of the social sciences to legal, political, and social philosophy. He also contributed to economic history, public policy analysis, and contemporary affairs. He was awarded the Nobel Prize in Economic Science in 1974, and he also received the Companions of Honors Award from Queen Elizabeth in 1984, and the US Medal of Freedom from G. W. Bush in 1991. Ironically, he was a man for the ages and a man for his age. His article "The Use of Knowledge in Society" was recently picked as one of the top twenty articles ever published in the *American Economic Review.* But his *The Road to Serfdom*, published in 1944, thrust Hayek from an academic economist and philosopher into the role of an international intellectual celebrity.

In this volume, we emphasize the breadth of his influence across academic disciplines, or we should say *potential* contributions and influence because many of these papers are introducing aspects of Hayek's thought into disciplinary conversations where previously they were absent. Rather than focus on Hayek the man and his personal biography, this volume is more focused on Hayekian *concepts* and *analytical constructs* and how they might aid the scientific and scholarly conversations in disciplines as diverse as anthropology to legal philosophy.

Despite the range of Hayek's writings and the chapters in the volume, there is a remarkable coherence. From his early work on the problem of imputation to his later work on the institutional framework, the critical coherence can be found in the notion of the coordination of human activities through time. In economic affairs, the production plans of some must mesh with the consumptions demands of others. In legal affairs, the law must provide the predictable framework so as to create expectations and guide human decision making and interactions in mutually beneficial ways. The evolution of mores and the implicit rules of just conduct similarly frame human interactions so as to provide the predictable background so individuals can realize the gains from social cooperation.

This coherence is perhaps inevitable given the doggedness with which Hayek pursued a particular set of questions throughout his lifetime. In brief, Hayek was absorbed with the idea that the knowledge that is available to us is always limited, and this limitation has a significant impact on both our actions and the results we will achieve when we attempt to engage in social and political organization. This emerged as a significant theme in his work with the publication of "Economics and Knowledge" in 1937, and continued to drive much of his inquiry through his final book, *The Fatal Conceit*, published over fifty years later.

Hayek's insights about knowledge become even more important once it is recognized that nothing in the social world occurs in isolation. There is no such thing as a distinct economic political, or social, sphere—they are inextricably intertwined. This is perhaps most discussed in the literature in the context of spontaneous ordering, which is the idea that the uncoordinated actions of many people can aggregate up to an effect greater than intended, and that—depending on the context—these emergent phenomenon can be orderly, in the sense of aligning expectations and facilitating coordination. This kind of systemic process thinking has continued to be a significant reason why Hayek's scholarship is so influential, both within economics and in other disciplines. As such it is perhaps no surprise that the Nobel Prize he shared with Gunnar Myrdal in 1974 was awarded in part for his "penetrating analysis of the interdependence of economic, social and institutional phenomena" (The Royal Swedish Academy of Sciences 1974).

The chapters in this volume pick up the core concepts and constructs from Hayek, critically examine them, and deploy them to address issues in various fields of study. Genuine interdisciplinary conversation, of the kind attempted in this volume, is difficult. We believe that creating space for it here will be significantly beneficial to both existing scholars of Hayek and to scholars in a wide range of interconnected social science disciplines who have yet to fully explore the implications of Hayek's social philosophy and political economy for their own areas of interest. The individual contributions are intriguing and thought-provoking, the joint effort constitutes an exciting exploration into the continuing relevance and evolutionary potential of the ideas developed by one of the most active and original minds in the social sciences and humanities of the twentieth century.

AN OVERVIEW OF THE VOLUME

The first set of chapters in this volume explores and extends Hayek's insights on reason and the nature of knowledge. The most well-known application of Hayekian knowledge theory is to questions of centralized economic planning. Exactly what kind of knowledge does economic coordination require, and what are the implied limitations for the would-be planner? The contributors to this volume, however, explore questions about the significance of local knowledge, the limitations of human reason, and the bounded epistemic capacity of experts in a variety of theoretical and applied contexts.

In chapter 1, "The Disciplinary Role of Market Prices: A Hayekian Critique of Chinese Socialist Governance," Adam Frost brings an applied historical perspective to Hayek's (1945) theory that price systems are a means of coordinating the actions of disparate market participants who may never meet, but whose actions nonetheless affect each other's well-being. Frost addresses the tragic and complicated question of how the Great Famine of 1959–1961 was allowed to become so severe. Nearly 45 million died of starvation, yet Mao Zedong's powerful Chinese Communist Party government seems to have taken nearly a year to fully appreciate the severity of the famine. Frost argues that although violence, ideological blinders, and the suppression of free speech are all important factors in understanding the phenomenon, there is another important consideration that has often gone unappreciated: that by shutting down local markets, Mao's regime suppressed a price mechanism that would have revealed skyrocketing demand for basic foodstuffs, alerting officials much more quickly to the severity of the shortages and potentially discouraging the export of agricultural products that were needed more desperately by the Chinese population than the Chinese Communist Party's foreign customers.

In chapter 2, "Justice Theorizing and Local Knowledge," Gregory Robson applies Hayekian knowledge theory to the task of moral and political theorizing itself. Robson asks, what kind of knowledge does a theory of justice require, and how does the nature of the knowledge required limit justice theorists in their quest to understand the guiding principles of a society in which all receive their fair and just moral due? This question is further complicated to the extent that such theories are "action-guiding," meaning they are expected to guide actual behavior by helping individuals correctly identify their moral responsibility in particular situations. Robson argues that our moral duties are sufficiently context dependent that in many cases the theorist will not have enough knowledge of the particular characteristics of the individuals involved to be able to say what should be done in a specific instance, particularly in light of the fact that individuals often have to balance many potentially conflicting duties and obligations.

In chapter 3, "The Silent Role of Emotions in Hayekian Political Economy," Brianne Wolf explores the relevance of emotion for Hayekian political thought and for political economy more broadly. Although Hayek rarely refers explicitly to emotions, Wolf argues that emotions are an important if implicit component in his social theory. Scottish Enlightenment thinkers such as Adam Smith and David Hume, she explains, treated the emotions we experience when interacting with each other as important considerations in being able to understand social systems, and even as valuable forces for personal and social improvement. As such, given how heavily Hayek draws on Enlightenment thought, it would be puzzling if he viewed emotion as irrelevant, or as better done without. Wolf argues that although Hayek does speak critically of allowing emotion to dictate policy, there is room within Hayekian theory for understanding emotions as ameliorating some of the limitations on social organization otherwise suggested by his consistent emphasis on the limits of reason and critique of rational constructivism. Throughout the chapter, Wolf explores the ways that emotion is and is not relevant to Hayekian theory, both providing context for comments that are critical of emotion and suggesting the possibility that making room for emotion could help social theorists achieve a better understanding of the evolution of social institutions that emerge "spontaneously" rather than through the explicit exercise of reason.

In chapter 4, "Justificatory Failures and Moral Entrepreneurs: A Hayekian Theory of Public Reason," Brian Kogelmann considers the justificatory failure critique of public reason liberalism. In short, the justificatory failure critique claims that if a rule can only be justified when all individuals accept its validity, then there are no rules that will actually be justified in any plausibly realistic conception of society. In response, Kogelmann argues that if we take Hayek's concerns about epistemic capacity seriously, then the full range of potential sets of rules is not understood well enough to enable a claim that no justifiable set of rules exists. Further, Kogelmann draws on Hayek's discussion of the fact that some institutional settings will be more conducive to the discovery of previously unknown sets of rules than others, suggesting that the way forward for the public reason project is through the incorporation of some version of institutional analysis.

The next set of chapters explores the implications of Hayek's ideas for contemporary debates over the nature and implications of different theories of political rights and organization. Hayek's political theory was first articulated in *The Road to Serfdom* and then subsequently developed most explicitly in his later treatises, *The Constitution of Liberty* and *Law, Legislation, and Liberty*. In this branch of his work, Hayek sought clarity on the fundamentals of how the individual members of a society interact with and relate to each other. The tensions Hayek identifies in the social and political world—law vs. legislation, general rules vs. arbitrary dominion, freedom vs. coercion—are applied to issues of contemporary relevance in social science by the next set of authors.

In chapter 5, "The Case for Opening Borders: A Hayekian Critique of Discretionary Immigration Controls," Liz Hemsley applies Hayek's distinction between arbitrary and general rules to contemporary debates over immigration and national sovereignty. Hemsley notes that many forms of immigration control are arbitrary, meaning that they establish different sets of rules regarding entry, ability to work, and citizenship for different populations. These are distinct from general forms of border control that apply equally to all, such as a requirement that all who have been exposed to tuberculosis must be quarantined. Hemsley argues that arbitrary forms of immigration control are inherently more problematic than general controls because different people are treated unequally under the law. In addition, Hemsley explores the implications of Hayek's political theory for the argument that countries have the right to determine their own immigration policies in service of their own national interests, and that arbitrary coercion may be a necessary part of this national self-determination.

In chapter 6, "A Liberal Response to Group Rights," Samantha Godwin considers Hayek's relevance to contemporary theories of identity politics. Godwin suggests that theories that consider rights to be a function of group membership bear analytical similarities to the earlier theories of collectivism that Hayek was responding to in much of his work. One particularly significant similarity is the extent to which theories of both collectivism and group rights consider rights as attaching at some level beyond that of the individual. Further, Godwin argues that theories of group rights do not overcome the limitations of more atomistic versions of liberalism in the way that some of their advocates suppose them to, showing this through critical interpretation of a variety of different types of group rights claims.

In chapter 7, "The Social Basis of Ultimate Legal Rules: Hayek Meets Hart," Mikołaj Barczentewicz brings Hayek into conversation with the legal theory of H. L. A. Hart. An important component of Hart's theory is that legal systems are undergirded by a "rule of recognition" that determines whether or not a group will accept a particular exercise of legal authority. This is significant in part because it suggests that the ultimate basis of legal authority is not in the designs of those who would wield that authority, but in a tacit set of commonly shared beliefs that emerge throughout the history of a civilization. Similarly, Barczentewicz argues, Hayek considered the commonly held attitudes of a group to serve as a kind of limit on political authority. Further, these attitudes are believed to emerge over time in ways not completely understood to the participants in the social order, and certainly without those participants ever having intended any particular outcome. Barczentewicz continues this comparison of Hart and Hayek throughout the chapter, in the process illuminating productive tensions and possible convergences that suggest opportunity for further incorporation of Hayekian theory in constitutional law and other legal scholarship.

In chapter 8, "F. A. Hayek and the Administrative State," Daniel Gibbs articulates the theory of bureaucratic organization implicit within Hayek's broader political theory. Gibbs argues that for Hayek, the features of the democratic structure within which the administrative arm of a government operates will be critical to understanding the behavior and choices of public administrators. The nature of the separation of powers within a democratic system is particularly critical to disciplining the growth of the scope of the administrative state. Without an effective separation of powers, there is a tendency toward an expansion of administrative authority that will make that authority increasingly ungovernable and unresponsive to control by democratic means. Gibbs concludes from this investigation that Hayek's work will be useful to contemporary scholars of public administration who engage in institutional analysis in an effort to understand how the administration of a government can retain an appropriate degree of professionalism and distance from the whims of shifting political winds.

The final set of chapters in this volume speaks to Hayek's theories regarding the spontaneous or emergent nature of complex social phenomena such as markets, languages, and cultural norms. This conversation raises important questions about the relationship between intentional action and the consequences that result from those actions without having been explicitly intended. Further, the emergent character of many social institutions suggests that the identification of the conditions under which emergent processes can be reliably expected to be conducive to order and cooperation will be a critical project for those interested in the possibilities and limitation of social organization.

In chapter 9, "Explaining Culture in Hayek's Cultural Evolution," Matthew Martinez situates Hayek's theory of cultural evolution in the context of contemporary research in evolutionary psychology. After articulating Hayek's views on cultural evolution, and on the limited applicability of theories of biological evolution to the study of human societies, Martinez explores the extent to which Hayek's work is commensurable with the contemporary literature in evolutionary psychology. The chapter also considers what can be learned by connecting Hayek's theory with contemporary research on the relationship between culture and the biological components of cognitive processes. For example, the emergence of norms such as honesty, fairness, and respect for property rights may be better understood by taking account of the interaction between biology, culture, and the mind. Martinez's analysis suggests that the recent trend in evolutionary psychology toward explanations that are methodologically individualist and cultural in nature rather than gene-centric has lent a new relevance to Hayek's work on cultural evolution.

In chapter 10, "A Hayekian Perspective on the Domestication of Maize," Crystal Dozier employs anthropological research on the origins of teosinte—the wild ancestor of domestic maize—to explore the extent to which human nutrition and eating practices are emergent rather than the result of intentional design. Anthropological evidence suggests that teosinte was a wild grass with small kernels covered in tough inedible shells, and as a result was a highly inefficient source of calories compared to other wild plants accessible at the time. So how did this unappealing grass come to be one of the most valuable sources of low-cost calories in the modern world? Dozier suggests the sweet-stalk hypothesis, which posits that humans began to chew and grind the stalks of the plant both for their sweet taste and for their value in making a kind of early wine, kept humans and teosinte in sufficient proximity to enable cultivation once the kernel of the plant mutated in a way that made the kernel as well as the stalk a desirable food source. The implication of the chapter is that some of the most fundamental of human practices, such as the early domestication of plants for food, were shaped by the unintended consequences of actions undertaken for completely different purposes. The use of teosinte was an action, but its cultivation into a modern food source was an emergent property of other human social behaviors.

In the final chapter of the volume, "Bad Spontaneous Orders: Trust, Ignorance, and White Supremacy," Caleb Harrison argues that the extent to which a social system facilitates trust should be a critical margin for evaluation, and then explores the difficult question of what happens when an emergent order undermines rather than facilitates trust and cooperation. In order to do so, Harrison considers systems of white supremacy, arguing that systems of white supremacy can be conceived of as spontaneous in that they are systematic and self-perpetuating even in the absence of explicit, direct control. Harrison connects this claim to the idea that trust is a critical component of any socially beneficial order by suggesting that it is the erosion of trust, a problem that is further exacerbated by the fact that systems of white supremacy make it easy for those in the more powerful group to be ignorant of the conditions faced by those in the less powerful group, that make these particularly spontaneous orders so perverse.

On the whole, the contributions to the volume challenge both Hayek's work and conceptions about his work in unexpected ways. The surprising diversity of connections between Hayek's body of work and contemporary research across the social sciences suggests an opportunity for scholars working in a variety of fields and from a variety of perspectives to continue to work together, challenging each other and generating new conversations intended to explore questions in ways that transcend traditional disciplinary limitations.

REFERENCES

Hayek, F. A. 1945. "The Use of Knowledge in Society." *American Economic Review* 35 (4): 519–30.

The Royal Swedish Academy of Sciences. 1974. "The Prize in Economics: Press Release." October 9. https://www.nobelprize.org/nobel_prizes/economic-sciences/laureates/1974/press.html.

Part I

EPISTEMIC LIMITATIONS

Chapter 1

The Disciplinary Role of Market Prices

A Hayekian Critique of Chinese Socialist Governance

Adam Frost

In the middle of the twentieth century, the People's Republic of China suffered the largest famine in human history. The famine was not the result of natural forces, but of human engineering. In 1958 the Chinese Communist Party (CCP), under the direction of Chairman Mao Zedong, launched the "Great Leap Forward," a mass-political campaign aimed at transforming China's agrarian economy, practically overnight, through rapid industrialization and socialist collectivization. But, instead of achieving massive gains to productivity as was envisioned, the overzealous policies and brutal systems of extraction pressed the rural Chinese population into hunger, sickness, and starvation. Though the exact death toll remains unclear, scholars have estimated that the Great Famine (1959–1961) claimed as many as 45 million lives.[1] But even more surprising than the sheer quantity of deaths was the fact that this man-made disaster seems to have gone on for well over a year without China's central government being fully aware of its magnitude or scale.[2] Tens of millions of Chinese starved while the state, largely ignorant of their suffering, continued to tax farmers and export grain abroad.

More than a half-century later, scholars still struggle to explain how a famine of such massive scale and scope was ever possible. Historian Frank Dikötter (2011) and journalist Yang Jisheng (2012) have each taken great pains to assign the blame squarely with China's Great Helmsman, Mao Zedong. Both scholars inculpate Mao for his dictatorial style of rule, his misguided utopianism, and the violent state apparatus that he presided over and designed.[3] Other China scholars, such as Gail Hershatter (2011), have focused more on the role of ideology in the production of misinformation, arguing that it was the competitive frenzy to achieve increasingly unrealistic production targets combined with the social pressure to blindly pursue utopian goals that ultimately precipitated systemic food shortages. While these scholars have each deepened our understanding of the multivalent factors that contributed to the Great Famine as well as the social and political contexts in which it occurred, they have largely failed to address the more fundamental question of why the Chinese state, in its supposedly expansive capacity, was not fully aware of the existence of widespread famine within its sovereign territory. If Maoist China was, as these scholars suggest, a Foucauldian society in which state power permeated the most basic of human activities, why then did the central government lack information about the dire conditions in rural society?

Economist Amartya Sen (Sen and Drèze 1989) perhaps came closest to tackling this knowledge problem in the development of his entitlement approach. Sen argued that China's Great Famine, like other major catastrophes, resulted from dire maldistributions of resources made possible by a lack of free press and democratic institutions. If China had been democratic rather than socialist, Sen's theory goes, then people would have spoken up, information would have flowed, and there never could have been a Great Famine. For, as Sen (2000) boldly claims, "no substantial famine has ever occurred in a democratic country—no matter how poor."

Yet, even if we accept Sen's argument as true, the absence of democracy alone seems an insufficient answer. In the example of China's imperial past, we find that even though the structures of governance put into place by paternalistic rulers were far from democratic, officials were acutely aware of the many famines that occurred within their governed territory. Their Maoist counterparts, it seems, were not. Even though the Chinese empire lacked a free press, democratic institutions, and modern communication technologies, it was not until the mid-twentieth century that China faced this type of knowledge problem. Clearly, something changed.

In this chapter I will argue that the root cause of the inability of the Maoist state to understand the changing conditions of Chinese society can be found in neither the charismatic despotism of Mao Zedong nor the oppressive authoritarianism of Maoist politics. Rather, it arose from the suppression of agrarian markets and the gradual breakdown of competitive systems of information aggregation. Drawing upon Hayek's notion of competition as a procedure for the discovery of information, I will attempt to show that the Maoist state effectively blinded itself to the food shortages caused by its own misguided actions by eliminating the primary mechanism for knowledge discovery: market prices.

FAMINES, KNOWLEDGE, AND PRICES

In the premodern world, food shortages were a universal fact of life. In even the most advanced of civilizations, agricultural productivity was relatively low, and the accumulation of surpluses was limited by transportation and spoilage. Any drought, flood, or civil disturbance could easily exhaust grain stores and push agrarian populations to the brink of subsistence. However, these frequently recurring declines in absolute food availability did not directly translate into famine. Generally speaking, if shortages were identified in time, then they could be ameliorated by market or state actors before they led to extreme hunger, sickness, and starvation. Dire famines tended to occur only when there was a concurrent breakdown in the information systems that guided public and private grain circulation. In other words, the central problem of famine management and prevention was a knowledge problem.

As Hayek showed us, human knowledge exists in a diffuse state, dispersed among all actors in society. Knowledge, Hayek (1945) argued, cannot be "given to anyone in its totality" because each constituent member of a social system possesses unique "knowledge of the particular circumstance of time and place." And because this type of informal knowledge cannot be readily rendered into statistics, it is impossible for a single agent "to survey more than a limited field, to be aware of the urgency of more than a limited number of needs." For this reason, Hayek cautioned governing agents against exercising judgment on behalf of a great number of people. Decision making should be decentralized, left up to the multitude of individuals who know best their particular needs and circumstances (Hayek [1944] 2008, 44).

From this understanding of the nature of knowledge, Hayek arrived at an even deeper insight about the use of knowledge in society: the most efficient mechanism by which individual agents can receive and communicate information is the price system. In a market economy, prices are an emergent property of the dynamics of preferences and scarcity. As individuals compete over finite resources, they are compelled to operate in social cooperation to achieve their ends. To buy a loaf of bread, have a tractor repaired, or travel on a train, an economic actor must engage in mutual benefit with a multitude of other actors who are working to obtain other goods and services. Prices serve as a mass communications system, disseminating relevant information to all the members of an economic system, thus enabling them to act as a coordinated whole (Hayek 1945). The market process is thus a disciplinary process, because it forces individual market participants to orient themselves toward the interests of others and thus creates the social function of the market economy (Hayek [1968] 2002).

In addition to communicating knowledge horizontally, among the participants in an economic system, prices also enable the aggregation and vertical transmission of preferences. In society, preferences exist within individuals, and they generally go unrevealed until such time as those individuals engage in transactions. Transactions influence prices, and prices thus reflect preferences. Because prices keep account of changing individual preferences and communicate these changes in an informational form, it renders local society legible. Governments and other institutional actors can thus look to prices to better understand what is happening in the economy. And, if monitored closely, prices can provide important feedback on the effects of government action in local society. As we shall see, nowhere was the price system's capacity for information discovery more important than in the realm of famine prevention and management.

MENCIUS AND MARKETS

Throughout China's long imperial past, governing regimes took highly active approaches to managing grain. This was partly because in the Confucian political economy, the legitimacy of rulers was intrinsically tied to the welfare of their agrarian subjects. Emperors held the Mandate of Heaven only so long as they continued to fulfill certain obligations to society, the foremost of which was "nourishing the people." Hunger and famine, it was thought, were not caused by natural or economic forces, but by improper governance. If an emperor placed too great a tax burden on his people, removed them from labor during the agricultural season, or otherwise allowed them to fall into poverty and hunger, then Heaven would rescind its Mandate, and the people would be justified in overthrowing their imposter-king.

The great Confucian philosopher Mencius (372–289 BCE) once chastised a ruler for failing to adequately provided for the welfare of his people. Mencius said: "When men starve along the roadside, you fail to recognize that it is time for [grain] distribution. When people die, you say, 'It is not of my doing. It is the fault of the harvest.' In what way is this different than killing a man with a blade, all the while saying, 'It is not of my doing! It is the fault of the weapon'? Stop blaming the harvest!"[4] A generation later another Confucian philosopher, Xunzi (313–238 BCE), made the relationship between governance and famine more explicit, arguing that: "If [a ruler] follows the Way without deviation, then nature cannot cause misfortune. Flood and drought will not cause famine, heat and cold will not cause illness, and evil spirits will not cause misfortune . . . [Famine and suffering] cannot be blamed on Heaven."[5] Present in two thousand years of philosophical texts, this simple idea became the ideological cornerstone of the imperial state.

Applying this Confucian principle to practical governance, imperial regimes fixated on solving what they viewed as *the* perennial threat to the welfare of agriculturalists: short-term deficits in the grain supply. To militate against shortages, China created what would become premodern history's largest and most networked granary system. During times of plenty, local officials across China taxed surplus grains and stored them in warehouses for disbursement during periods of hardship. Though the specific mechanisms by which they carried out these goals changed significantly over time, the goal remained the same: keeping the people nourished. From a practical standpoint, ensuring the subsistence of agriculturalists helped the state militate against the persistent threat of food riots.[6] These efforts also had the enormously beneficial (yet largely unintended) consequence of making rural citizens more willing to move away from subsistence farming and toward specialization in handicrafts or the monocultural production of cash crops.

Yet within the Confucian political economy, it was not enough for the government to simply ameliorate food shortages. Rather, a moral leader was one who maximized the welfare of agrarian producers. Confucian thinkers held, rightly or wrongly, that peasants were overly local in their thinking and had limited time horizons. The common man, they believed, lacked the ability to apperceive how his present actions would bear upon his future self, his descendants, and greater society. When building a dam to irrigate their fields, for instance, farmers did not rightly consider how it would affect the water supply of the village a hundred kilometers downstream. Or when taking their crops to market at the close of a harvest, they did not properly calculate how much more they might earn by waiting until winter to sell. It was, therefore, the role of a Confucian state to adopt on behalf of its subjects a wider temporal and spatial perspective, designing institutions that could bring the decisions of individuals in harmony with greater social good.

The key institution developed to maximize the welfare of agriculturalists was a market-stabilizing system originally proposed by Mencius, the so-called "ever-normal granaries." Ever-normal granaries were part of a national buffer stock scheme that attempted to smooth cyclical fluctuations in grain prices (i.e., keep them "ever-normal") through directed purchases and sales (Will, Wong, and Lee 1991). In ordinary times, granary administrators actively traded grain on rural markets, buying when prices were at their yearly lows and reselling a portion of their reserves when prices were at their height.[7] It was hoped that through such acquisitions the government could both elevate minimum grain prices after the spring and autumn harvests, thus protecting farmers from unscrupulous speculators, and militate against sharp price spikes in winter, thus ensuring that people could afford enough to eat year-round. In periods of critical shortage, when it was determined that prices in a given area were beginning to approach socially unacceptable levels, granary administrators further intervened through subsidized disbursements of grain in an attempt to secure the food rights of the poor.

Ever-normal granaries also operated on the logic that by smoothing grain prices and rendering them predictable, they could exert a stabilizing influence over the broader economy. As Bai Juyi and Yuan Zhen, two renowned ninth-century scholar-officials, reasoned: "If the accumulation and distribution of grain attain their proper measure, and the relative strength and weakness of the currency varies according to the season, then the value of all the myriad commodities will achieve stability in and of themselves. And the four classes of people [i.e., literati, agriculturalists, artisans, and merchants] will all profit in their respective enterprises."[8] Through the institutional stabilization of grain prices, it was hoped that there would be fewer cyclical downturns left farmers hungry, artisans out of work, and merchants without goods to trade.

However eager to promote the welfare of their citizenry, rulers and granary administrators were entirely overzealous in their market interventions. Throughout much of the history of the imperial granary system, there existed an ever-present tension between the desire to address social problems through bureaucratic means and the recognition of the desirability of non-intervention. By the second millennia CE, China had developed a highly commercialized domestic economy that circulated commodities across its vast empire.[9] Even in poor and remote regions, where mountains and marshes limited the ability of oxen-drawn carts to access local markets, itinerant traders carrying goods on shoulder-poles brought commerce to rural communities. Chinese scholar officials were thus wary not to disrupt markets' vital role in the distribution of grain and other goods. As the historian Helen Dunstan has argued, while the imperial state often viewed merchants with suspicion, "it was generally accepted that redistributing grain surpluses was primarily the task of merchants" (Dunstan 2006, 15). A handful of pro-market statesmen called for even greater reliance on market forces in the work of famine relief. They argued that for areas with a high degree of commercialization, instead of combating critical food shortages through the stockpiling of grain, the state should instead disburse quantities of silver to famine victims and allow private grain merchants to meet their needs (Dunstan 2006, 446–47).

But even more centrally, the Chinese officials were aware that market signals conveyed otherwise unknowable information about the conditions in local society. Though administrators frequently failed in their attempts to stabilize grain prices, by warily monitored prices they could at least identify potentially disruptive changes in supply and demand. This was especially important as market outcomes were not always maximally desirable for rural society: Chinese officials recorded numerous instances in which historically impoverished regions experienced net outflows of foodstuffs during periods of mass starvation. Income inequality between the rural countryside and the coastal regions was such that poor peasants could sometimes be priced out of grain by their more affluent urban counterparts, even when the alternative was starvation.[10] This problem only grew with the commercialization of the economy, as ever-more producers became specialized participants in inter-regional markets.[11] Therefore, by observing grain prices, officials could detect when markets were moving food away from the people who needed it most and respond accordingly.[12]

Conversely, large spikes in grain prices also alerted officials to breakdowns in the system of commercial grain circulation. In late imperial history it was not uncommon for local populations to respond to food shortages by creating blockades and preventing grain shipments from leaving the affected area. From the perspective of locals, such acts seemed rational. Large land owners and wealthy elites were known to sometimes hoard grain during periods of scarcity and use their monopolistic positions to demand elevated prices from those less able to provide for their own subsistence or stockpile foodstuffs. However, as contemporary elites noted in their accounts of famines, the unintended consequence of such actions was that grain also could not easily enter from neighboring markets. Famine conditions thus deepened once local stores were exhausted. By monitoring regional grain prices and identifying breakdowns in commercial circulation, the Qing government could respond by eliminating obstructions to grain shipments and coercing grain hoarders to sell off their holdings at or below market prices.

The imperial state implicitly recognized the power of markets to reveal information, and officials regularly looked to market prices as the principle indicator of food shortages.[13] Though state institutions were deeply embedded in China's commercial grain markets, granary officials recognized the distorting effects that government purchases had on grain prices and were wary to not disrupt competition or distort prices to too great an extent.[14] By allowing markets to operate and using market signals to identify food shortages, imperial governments thus rendered the needs of society legible. It was through this process of harmonizing Confucian principles with market forces that Chinese dynasties were able to successfully promote the welfare of peasant-agriculturalists and foster stable population growth that outpaced that of Europe and much of the rest of the world.

MAO OVER MARKETS

By the fall of the empire in 1911, imperial systems of grain management had largely been dismantled. A half century of internal rebellions and foreign aggression had depleted national resources and pressed the Chinese people into conditions of bare subsistence. Throughout the 1930s and 1940s, political turmoil and protracted warfare further crippled commerce and curtailed the flow of goods (Myers 1970, 280). In the war-torn north, a series of dire famines collectively claimed the lives of tens of millions of Chinese. Peasants across China were forced to live on what little they could grow, steal, or beg for in cities. Social pressures mounted as governments struggled to allocate scare financial resources between famine relief and military spending (Edgerton-Tarpley 2008, 93). By the late 1940s, China had been reduced to a poor agricultural economy, with roughly 90 percent of its 550 million people living in abject poverty.

The Chinese Communist Party ascended to power on the back of the claim that the Communists alone would rectify the hunger and poverty that had enveloped China. Their solution to China's economic problems: socialist transformation. Instead of co-opting market forces as had been done in late imperial times, the Communists would attempt to subjugate them to the political imperatives of Maoism. They believed that by freeing the exploited proletariat, subsuming rural markets into systems of rationing and distribution, and supplanting competitive prices with state-fixed prices the country's total productive output would rise, thus increasing the standard of living for Chinese citizens.

The first step in socialist transformation was freeing peasants from the "feudalist" system of agrarian production. Beginning in 1946 and lasting until 1953, Chinese land reform radically altered the political and economic structure of the countryside. Peasant households were assigned class status, with the poor, middle, and rich peasants encouraged to engage in class struggle against those labeled as landlords. The period of concentrated violence that followed resulted in the executions of a million or more individuals.[15] Massive expropriations of land, property, farming tools, and draft animals were transferred to poorer peasant households, providing an immediate one-off boost to agricultural productivity (Fairbank 1992). However, such gains would prove fleeting.

As the following decade would reveal, the Communists' redistributive efforts were less an attempt at restoring a struggling economy than they were a political platform for extending state power into the countryside. Between 1952 and 1954, the CCP initiated the first stages of socialist collectivization. Rural families were organized first into "mutual aid teams" consisting of five to fifteen mutually supportive households, and later into "elementary agricultural cooperatives" made up of twenty to forty households. By the end of 1954, more than 400,000 Agricultural Producers' Cooperatives had been established nationwide, encompassing 11 percent of all rural households. Two years later, roughly 96 percent of all rural Chinese were organized into cooperatives. The driving economic principle behind collectivization was that agriculturalists could benefit from economies of scale (such as sharing farming tools and draft animals) and better coordinate their production and consumption.

From a political perspective, collectivization also enabled the government to exert greater control over rural production and more effectively extract resources from the countryside. By grouping families together into administrative units and inserting in these units party representatives, the CCP was able to redirect local production into channels that were believed to be of greatest benefit to the state, such as grain and cotton production. Furthermore, by having a direct presence in villages, officials could better monitor output and ensure compliance with taxation. In contrast with the Nationalists whose power never extended far outside of urban centers, the Communists were able to impose a high tax regime over the vast agricultural countryside.[16]

At the same time as the party expanded its influence over rural production, they also sought to exert more direct control over commerce. For nearly a millennium in China's highly integrated commercial economy, the vast majority of agriculturalists had produced crops and handicrafts not only for their own subsistence, but also for exchange on commercial markets. Every farming family was essentially a small enterprise that took market forces into consideration when making decisions about what to produce, how to invest capital, and how to allocate labor. However, this universal engagement with markets in rural China was severely curtailed in 1953, when the CCP, following the example of the Soviet Union, established a state monopoly over the wholesale trading of grains. Thereafter, farming households were assigned minimum procurement quotas based on the size of their lands and their total number of laboring bodies. Whatever they produced above these quotas, they were required to sell to government agencies at lower-than-market prices. In 1954 this state monopoly was expanded to include cotton, pork, oil seeds, and other essential commodities.

To further subjugate market forces, the Maoist state went to great lengths to obviate the need of currency, especially in the rural countryside. After abolishing former currencies and doing away with a millennium old bimetallic system of exchange, the CCP strictly limited the total amount of cash in circulation. In the agricultural sector, taxes were collected in-kind rather than in cash.[17] At the same time, rural workers' wages were set little above what was required to buy salt, soy, and vinegar, thus forcing people to barter for most of their goods (Solinger 1984).[18] After 1955, the Maoist state began also remunerating rural households for their labor in-kind, disbursing fixed quantities of grain, oil, vegetables, cloth, and the like. These actions served the dual purpose of constraining rural citizens from engaging in unsanctioned commerce and forcing farmers to employ themselves in monocultural production.[19] By the end of the 1950s, the rural cash nexus had been destroyed and most rural Chinese had been forcibly disassociated from formal markets.

Taken together, these extractive institutions formed the core of the Maoist development state. Enforced through the organizational structure of collectives, procurement quotas and state-mandated prices diverted the majority of agricultural surplus. Massive amounts of expropriated grain and cotton were shipped to the USSR in exchange for new technologies, expertise, and machinery. Even larger quantities still were transferred to the cities to feed a growing class of urban industrial workers. Rural farmers were exhorted to work tirelessly on behalf of the state, the fruits of their labor being used to fuel economic growth, while they themselves were left with just enough to subsist. It was largely through the control and exploitation of agriculturalists that China bought its industrial revolution. Maoist statesmen reasoned that if their systems of extraction could be maintained for a period of ten, or perhaps fifteen, years, then China would be able to "catch up" developmentally with the Western European powers.

However, not all went according to the Plan. Unsurprisingly, peasants did not enjoy sharing their personal property with the collective or having the majority of their produce taken by the state. Faced with the prospect of being forced to pool their land, tools, and animals, many of the more affluent rural households chose instead to feast. Draft animals, like oxen and mules, were slaughtered for their meat. Fruit and shade trees were chopped down for lumber and kindling. Anything consumable that could not be buried underground or otherwise hidden was consumed.

The suboptimal use of resources and resultant fall in productivity alarmed CCP leaders. In January 1955, the central government issued an urgent order to prevent the further slaughter of draft animals. In some areas officials reduced procurement quotas. Political centrists like Zhou Enlai and Liu Shaoqi began cautioning against "rash advance" and called for a more reasonable pace of economic transformation. But the damage had already been done.

By late 1955 shortages of foodstuffs and basic commodities enveloped China's vast countryside, and the consumption levels of many farmers had begun to fall back to that of pre-revolutionary times. A year later the CCP witnessed its first recorded incidence of mass starvation in the southwestern province of Guangxi. In their reports to the central government, a handful of local officials boldly lay the blame for the famine on the state monopoly over grain purchasing and marketing. Officials in the affluent coastal province of Jiangsu voiced similar complaints, arguing that the lack of markets and over extraction had deprived peasants of food, clothing, and cooking oil.[20] These leaders were summarily purged. Despite the growing cracks in the veneer of socialist prosperity, the CCP, under the powerful influence of Mao Zedong, pushed forward with the project of socialist transformation.

ENGINEERING FAMINE

From the CCP's initial ascent to power until the mid-1950s, China had followed a developmental trajectory based on the Soviet model of urban industrialization. Agricultural products were extracted from the countryside and used to fuel the growth of factories and the expansion of the urban working class. Machinery and technological expertise were imported from Russia and similarly paid with the agricultural surplus of rural farmers. Like in the USSR, in China the CCP created five-year blueprints for the future development of the economy, they reoriented the nation's productive capacities toward the production of steel, and they measured progress through the fulfillment of aggregate production milestones. However, after the death of Stalin in 1953, China's developmental model began to diverge from that of the Soviet Union in a number of significant ways.[21]

First, Soviet-style central planning did not play as central a role in the Maoist economic system. Under the powerful influence of Chairman Mao, the CCP fashioned a unique system of anti-expert, decentralized planning. The governance of the economy was directed by local leaders who were in turn subjugated to the political mandates issued by the center. Broad political objectives were issued by party leaders, often in the form of easily transmittable slogans, without explicit rules for how to carry them out in local contexts or evaluate their efficaciousness. Cadres were however provided with strong incentives to carry out such directives, and even stronger incentives to at least make it appear as if they had done so. This vision of a decentralized economic administration was not a repudiation of the theoretical underpinnings of central planning. Rather, it was an attempt to reinvent central planning within the conceptual framework of mass-line politics.[22]

Second, the Maoist economy never truly implemented rational economic calculation. Like the Soviet Union, Maoist China did maintain a centralized statistical system of reporting and analysis. Agricultural statistics, for example, were compiled from annual statistical reports on agricultural production conducted at the county-level and were supplemented with intermittent special surveys on labor, livestock, sown acreage, and income distributions.[23] However, unlike the USSR, in China the centralized statistical system was not managed by trained statisticians, but by party cadres and "the masses" (Riskin 1987, 219). As agricultural production became increasingly politicized under the leadership of Mao Zedong, local governments gained increasing autonomy over their methods of statistical surveying and data computation. When not fabricating agricultural production statistics to serve short-term political ends, the over-burdened and under-skilled representatives of local governments often made gross extrapolations based on limited data.[24] In other data categories, such as population totals, figures were simply replicated year after year. By the late 1950s the State Statistical Bureau had wholly lost control over statistical services in China.

The definitive break with the Soviet model came in 1958 when Mao unveiled his utopian scheme to "leap forward." Central to Mao's plan was the idea that China could simultaneously revolutionize its agricultural and industrial sectors by having rural workers not only grow food for the entire population, but also directly participate in industrialization. In the countryside, the CCP would implement "scientific practices" into agricultural production, with the aim of achieving much higher levels of output with fewer labor inputs, so that the majority of rural labor could be diverted into the production of steel.[25] Rural ingenuity, Mao thought, would trump technical expertise, as rural workers could innovate solutions to problems as they arose in their situated circumstances.

In an attempt to enact Mao's plan and realize further productive gains from scale and efficiency, the CCP abolished agricultural markets and reorganized rural communities into People's Communes. It was believed that by completely disbanding rural markets, the marketing and distribution of agricultural products could be rationalized within the system of state planning. Similarly, by reorganizing natural villages into administrative communes, rural production could be more easily monitored and controlled. With communal mess halls and service centers, no longer would workers need to squander time on things like buying food or rearing children. With less labor needed to maintain households, even more peasants could be mobilized to build and run "backyard steel furnaces."

This utopian vision was implemented in its entirety and with devastating results. During the subsequent wave of patriotic hysteria, reported production figures of grain and iron soared to new heights, even while actual per capita food production fell to historical lows. In the state-controlled media, stories spread of model communes growing fields of wheat so thick that the standing stalks would bear the weight of children. Many formerly cultivated fields were left fallow in expectation of the massive gains to agricultural output. In places where seeds were sown, agricultural labor was insufficient to reap what harvests there were to be had. Across China "excess" crops were left in the fields to rot. Farmers were far too busy melting down their pots and pans in backyard steel furnaces to produce low-grade pig iron.

It was not long before the communal dining halls began to run out of food. Peasants, having had their cookware melted down and having been disallowed to retain personal stores of food, were immediately faced with acute hunger. Rural protestors once again bucked against collectivization and demanded that local cooperatives be disbanded. In late 1958 two large "counterrevolution insurrections" in Yunnan had to be put down forcibly by the military. Elsewhere in China people abandoned their homes in search of food. In the province Anhui alone some 1.3 million people were made destitute in early 1958.[26] Hundreds of thousands more were captured by local militia, imprisoned in "repatriation stations," and forcibly sent back to their famine-stricken homes. Trapped in the countryside, empty-stomached peasants gnawed the bark from trees and ate "Buddha's soil" (powdery earth) until their bodies finally succumbed to anemia and scurvy.

Even as the death toll began to mount, Chinese society and the Chinese state remained ignorant of the true scale or scope of famine. Without markets to transmit information about scarcity from one locality to the next, knowledge remained hyper-localized. In villages across China people starved without knowing that other people in other villages were starving too. The government was equally unaware. To be sure, isolated reports of food shortages did begin to make their way to the eyes and ears of central government officials. But negative reporting posed a serious political risk. Most cadres preferred to remain silent about local conditions rather than chance incurring the wrath of their superiors. Without a functioning mechanism of knowledge aggregation, it was impossible for the central government to identify the systemic nature of the problem. In one of history's darkest tragedies, the Maoist state continued to expropriate grain from the countryside and export it abroad, even while millions of Chinese citizens died of malnourishment and famine-related disease.

It was only in October 1960—after Mao Zedong was delivered a report on the mass starvation taking place in Xinyang, Henan—that special investigative teams were sent out across China to report on local conditions. Their findings and the preliminary death tallies revealed that the reports of starvation were not isolated occurrences, but manifestations of pandemic famine. Confronted with incontrovertible evidence, the central government issued an emergency directive calling for the abatement of grain procurements, the return of semi-private plots of land, and the lifting of the ban on farmers engaging in sideline occupations. The following spring grain was finally imported from Western countries. Around the same time, rural and urban markets were restored, and officials once again began actively monitoring the market prices of grains and other commodities.[27]

However, these measures proved to be far too little and too late. An estimated 30 to 45 million individuals died of starvation or hunger-related sickness before the famine was un-engineered. As historian Lillian Li put it, "It is one of history's most deeply ironic tragedies that a government that came to power on the basis of its promise to address hunger only succeeded in making it a more central and urgent issue" (Li 2007, 4).

While Maoist development differed from that of the USSR, as history proved, the Maoist regime to still fell prey to a fatal pretense of knowledge. During the era of High Maoism, politics guided the majority of economic activity in China. The Maoist economy was embedded in a system of mass-line politics in which local political decision making took precedent over central rational economic calculation. The decentralized, politics-first approach to economic governance greatly inhibited the capacity of the Maoist state to collect and aggregate local knowledge. The socialist government left itself only with political apparatuses with which to "see" society. And when these apparatuses were rendered ineffectual by perverse incentive structures, the market institutions that had guided the actions of past regimes were no longer there to prevent leaders from creating unimaginable human suffering.

A HAYEKIAN CRITIQUE OF MAOIST CHINA

Whether by coincidence or conscious design, Friedrich Hayek's *Road to Serfdom* was first translated into Chinese in 1962, the exact year when China was exiting the worst famine in human history. Characterized as a subversive text "filled with poison," *Serfdom* was restricted for circulation among the highest-ranking party members, and was to be used for the purpose of critiquing "modern bourgeois reactionary economic theories." Hayek and his ideas were seen as a threat to socialism. According to the book's Chinese translator, Hayek was motivated out of a "deeply ingrained hostility toward socialism and all progressive tendencies," which led him to make conclusions based on ideological commitments rather than historical evidence.[28] Yet contained within the pages of Hayek's text was a powerful framework for making sense of the catastrophic events that unfolded in the Maoist economy.

Unlike the imperial regimes of China's past which co-opted market forces in order to understand the society they governed, the Maoist state made decisions on behalf of its subjects based on a fatal pretense of knowledge. Communist leaders believed that the preferences and needs of society could be immediately knowable and discoverable outside of a system of competitive markets. In the realm of grain distribution, it was simply assumed that the presence of famine would become known to the state through individual or statistical reporting. However, as history revealed, instruments designed by the state to gather knowledge are highly susceptible to political forces. When China became engulfed in the political hysteria of the Great Leap Forward, there were no market mechanisms to provide information that might otherwise have served as a check against misguided political action.

A preoccupation with statistical aggregates, Hayek presciently cautioned, leads leaders to make false assumptions of stability. A real economy experiences ceaseless churn, as innumerable individual decision makers act upon "knowledge that cannot be entered into statistics," to attend to the multitudinous unanticipated needs of society (Hayek 1945). The price system then communicates this vital, unascertainable information across time and space. If, for example, there is a shortage of grain in a given region, then the excess in demand over supply will cause grain prices to rise. This is true irrespective of the initial cause of shortage. Consumers can respond to these rising prices by rationing their current reserves for future consumption or substituting calorie sources. Grain merchants can alter their trade routes in anticipation of new profit opportunities. Even in cases of severe market failure, when grain is actively exported from an area experiencing a critical food shortage, information about the scale and scope of the shortage is still conveyed through rising prices. It is one of the great marvels of prices that since they reflect information which exists in a diffuse state, they can accurately represent diffuse phenomena.

In the Chinese socialist economy, however, prices played a passive role. Like the Soviet Union, the Maoist state first set the prices for strategic resources and grains, and eventually expanded state-pricing to the vast majority of goods in society. The primary function of prices was not to guide production, but rather to aid in calculation, accounting, and control. Unlike in the Soviet technocracy, however, in socialist China there were no attempts to rationalize the price of grain, or use prices to equilibrate supply and demand. In the case of the single most important commodity—grains—the Maoist state first established fixed prices in 1953 and did not adjust them again until 1957. Afterward, official grain prices remained almost unchanged until the death of Mao Zedong in 1976.[29]

As such, Maoist prices neither revealed information about relative scarcity, nor signaled individual subjective preferences. At best, they were reflections of the moral judgments of communist officials who determined how much goods *ought* to cost socialist consumers. At worst, they were the products of political calculations designed to maximize the amount of surplus extracted from rural producers. In either case, prices could not function as a mechanism for knowledge discovery.

In the late 1950s, when critical food shortages did arise from the gross miscalculation of aggregate output and general misallocation of resources in the Chinese economy, there were no longer any market signals with which the Communist Party could discover the systemic changes taking place. In the early stages of the Great Leap Forward, there were a handful of anecdotal accounts of hunger and reports of localized starvation that made it to the ears of political leaders. But without an effective mechanism for aggregating knowledge, it was impossible for them to know the extent or representativeness of these cases. State statistics failed to provide this necessary information; as a political tool, they were fully susceptible to the same hysteria that they might have otherwise belied. Without knowledge of the changing conditions of society, the Maoist government pressed forward with its utopian schemes. Reduced production was allowed to give rise to food shortages; food shortages were allowed to devolve into famine; and famine was allowed to expand into an unprecedented human catastrophe.

If Maoist China had not dismantled the market-oriented institutions that guided the actions of imperial regimes of the past, it is unlikely that the events of the late 1950s and early 1960s could have unfolded in the same way. As peasants were pulled away from agricultural production, the unchanging demand for grain would have exhibited an upwards pressure on local grain prices. If state officials were monitoring said prices, then they would have had to immediately question the accuracy of exaggerated production figures. Any anecdotal reports of hunger and food shortages would have immediately been situated within the macro-context of rising grain price data. In other words, while the elimination of market prices did not directly cause the Great Famine, it did severely curtail the ability of Chinese officials to understand the scale and scope of grain shortages in society, and thus inhibited them from taking effective action.

The economic anthropologist Karl Polanyi once warned us that societies are placed in great danger when their leaders attempt to subjugate politics to market forces. But as the case of China's Great Famine shows, it can be equally dangerous for politics to totalitize markets. Throughout China's long imperial past, rulers looked to prices as a principle indicator of food shortages. Although they actively intervened in grain markets in an attempt to maximize the welfare of agrarian producers, they also appreciated the limits of their power and were wary not to disrupt the unique ability of markets to reveal information about the conditions of local society. The Maoist government, however, was not as circumspect in its dealings with the economy. The gradual elimination of the price system in the 1950s inhibited the capacity of the Maoist government to understand society. And because leaders never succeeded in creating an alternative mechanism for aggregating local knowledge, radical utopian schemes were left unchecked as they devastated China.

To expand then upon Hayek, it is not only that competition is a discovery procedure, but that the fruits of competition—market prices—can exhibit a powerful disciplinary force over utopian schemes to direct human action.

NOTES

1. Frank Dikötter places the total number of deaths at 45 million. Yang Jisheng estimates that 36 million individuals suffered early deaths, while an additional

40 million failed to be born during the famine years. According to official Chinese population statistics, the total national population in 1961 was roughly 13.5 million less than the population of 1959.

2. Few scholars, with the notable exception of Frank Dikötter, claim that the Chinese Communist Party knowingly allowed its governed people to starve. Rather, they blame the Maoist regime for establishing authoritarian systems of governance that allowed the famine to occur. As James Scott summarily put it, "while it seems clear that Mao did not intend the deaths of the famine's victims in the way that Hitler did the deaths of the Jews after Wannsee, he presided over a violent state apparatus whose schemes murdered them as surely as if they had been lined up and shot." See James Scott, "Tyranny of the Ladle."

3. Frank Dikötter in particular argues that Mao Zedong took no serious action in the first half of 1959 after hearing about the first major reports of famine. However, as Felix Wemheuer points out, Mao wrote multiple letters to party members calling for the lowering of production targets, cracking down on false reporting, and punishing those officials who expropriate peasants' personal belongings. However, such adjustment policies were ultimately stymied in an environment of increased political radicalism following the Lushan Conference of 1959. See Felix Wemheuer, "Sites of Horror."

4. Author's translation of excerpt from the *Mencius*.

5. Author's translation of excerpt from the *Xunzi*.

6. As the historical sociologist R. Bin Wong has shown, throughout the Qing dynasty, spontaneous uprisings in response to food shortages and rising prices were a frequently recurring phenomenon. Crowds of poor, hungry peasants often gathered in market squares or in front of government offices to protest elevated grain prices. In times of enduring scarcity, tensions could escalate into riots, with peasant mobs ransacking public granaries or the homes of local elites in search of private stores of grain. See R. Bin Wong, "Food Riots."

7. Generally speaking, restocking purchases were made in local or neighboring markets at market prices. However, in some instances, especially during periods of systemic shortage, granary administrators procured grain directly from landowners at below-market prices. If the proceeds from the spring sales exceeded the costs of the fall procurements (and the costs of spoilage and transportation), then the surplus would be held in silver and saved for periods of shortage.

8. Author's translation of excerpt from "On Stabilizing the Price of Commodities" in the *Forest of Problems*.

9. On this point sinologist Thomas Metzger (1972) has shown that the late imperial Chinese economy was highly dynamic and commercialized. The "dynamism of the private sector," he argued, was reinforced by strong property rights, supportive state fiscal policies, and a shifting class structure.

10. This phenomenon was not unique to China. Historical scholarship has shown that even in times of famine, grain can continue to be actively exported from regions suffering from critical food shortages. Some Irish nationalists, for example, have accused the British of committing genocide for actively exporting grain out of Ireland during the Irish Potato Famine (see Cormac Ó Gráda 1999). Citing examples from India, Ireland, and Chad, Sen and Drèze point out that "the history of famines in fact contains abundant

examples of export of food through private trade from famine-affected regions to elsewhere." See Amartya Sen and Jean Drèze, *Hunger and Public Action*, 90.

11. R. Bin Wong has also argued that as greater amounts of grain were channeled into redistributional trade networks, grain was increasingly siphoned away from "customary circulation" by which local elites resold or lent grain to the local poor on a largely charitable basis.

12. As Helen Dunstan has shown, the Qing state generally upheld the right of merchants to transport grain away from any community from which they purchased it. However, in cases where popular sentiment turned strongly against merchants and government intervention could be framed as an attempt to curb the power of wicked monopolists, then state action might be authorized. See Helen Dunstan, *Conflicting Counsels*, 249–53.

13. In local gazetteers, late imperial Chinese officials commonly recorded spikes in grain prices along with anecdotal accounts of hunger and starvation, citing both as evidence of famine.

14. Throughout the late eighteenth century, for instance, there were efforts to find alternative means of replenishing granary reserves (such as diverting taxed grain surpluses) so as to reduce the quantity of restocking purchases made in local markets.

15. While Mao Zedong estimated that about 800,000 people were killed, R. J. Rummel argues that the death toll was at least 4.5 million. See Rudolph Rummel, *China's Bloody Century*, 223.

16. Rural farmers paid a three-tier system of taxation, made up of a "government grain tax" at a statutory rate of 15 percent of their produce, a large government procurement quota (selling grain to the state at below-market prices), and additional corvée labor obligations in the agricultural off-season.

17. The Maoist state strictly limited the amount of money in circulation. The average payout in the countryside was thirteen yuan per year, an amount that barely covered purchases of basic goods like salt, soy, and vinegar.

18. As Dorothy Solinger has shown, under Chinese socialism, both individual households and businesses used commodities, rather than currency, as the primary medium of exchange. Commodities took on new power and expanded functions, as they came to facilitate the majority of informal exchanges.

19. If producers had to pay their taxes in rice or wheat, it was all the more difficult for them to divert their labor into the production cash crops or some other "non-essential" (and not easily taxable) commodities.

20. In a major 1958 speech, Mao Zedong blamed the opposition of local Jiangsu officials on their class backgrounds. Mao said, "Thirty percent of the [local officials] raised a terrible fuss on behalf of the peasants, saying that the state monopoly for purchasing and marketing 'monopolized' too much. And what was the background of these cadres? They were well-to-do middle peasants. . . . Well-to-do middle peasants like to hoard grain but don't like to surrender it; they want capitalism, so yowl about the hardship of peasants." Quoted in Yang Jisheng, *Tombstone*, 105.

21. During this period China's relations with the USSR became increasingly hostile. Mao Zedong viewed himself as Stalin's true successor and the rightful leader of the international socialist movement. Tensions therefore radically escalated when

Nikita Khrushchev, in his "secret speech" of 1956, denounced Stalin for having created a cult of personality and having violated the central ideals of communism.

22. In his analysis of Soviet-style central planning, Mao Zedong concluded that the greatest threat to the functioning of the planned economy was too great a degree of centralization. Mao distrusted expert knowledge and actively opposed the bureaucratization of the state. Mao felt that many economic decisions were ill-served by central planners issuing edicts from offices in Beijing. Mao's solution was not to limit the scope of government intervention in the economy, but rather to expand the decision-making capacity of local governments. Mao criticized economic experts who failed to recognize the potential in harnessing the knowledge and enthusiasm of local farmers and workers in the project of socialist transformation. These individuals, Mao reasoned, understood much better than central planners the particular circumstances that shaped local economic development.

23. Local governments were required to compile annual statistical reports on agricultural production and submit them to the State Statistical Bureau by February of each year. In practice, the majority of counties submitted their data several months late. Beginning in 1956, local governments were further required to conduct recurring surveys of the basic conditions of Agricultural Producer Cooperatives, which included data on population, labor power, income distribution, total sown acreage, head of livestock, and harvested volume. See Nai-Ruenn Chen, *Chinese Economic Statistics*, 54–56.

24. For example, to estimate total agricultural output for a given commune during a harvest, local administrators would (1) visually estimate total sewn acreage, (2) designate certain plots of land as "model areas," (3) take sample cuttings from each of the model areas to calculate sample yield, (4) compute total output by first extrapolating the sample yield to the whole of the model areas and then extrapolating this figure again to arrive at the output for the estimate of total sewn acreage. See Cho-ming Li, *Statistical System of Communist China*, 123–24.

25. Farmers were coerced into adopting pseudo-scientific farming techniques like close-planting and deep-plowing that contradicted local knowledge and personal experience. Many of these practices were modeled after the pseudo-scientific ideas of Soviet agronomist Trofim Lysenko. See J. Becker, *Hungry Ghosts*.

26. Mao's extremely callous response to initial reports of grain shortages was to say: "Tell the peasants to resume eating chaff and herbs for half the year, and after some hardship for one or two or three years things will turn around." See Huang Kecheng, *Autobiography*, 277 quoted in Yang Jisheng, *Tombstone*, 337.

27. We find evidence of this in the gazetteers of the Bureau of Market Management. The central government reinstated markets as a means of combatting systemic shortages of essential commodities. When they did so they were surprised to learn how far market prices had deviated from official state prices. They continued to adopt a relatively relaxed approach toward the management of markets until late 1963, when average prices had finally fallen to roughly half of late 1962 levels.

28. Teng Weizao took particular offense to Hayek's characterization of fascism and communism as being twin branches of socialism that shared their origins in the nationalization of means of production and central economic planning. "Fascist and

Nazi domination," Teng wrote, "is the darkest form of bourgeoisie dictatorship," the antithesis of proletarian democracy. Nazis used plans to "intensify the exploitation of workers and to prepare for imperialistic wars" while Marxist planning was intended to "continuously increase the people's material and cultural standards of living." See Teng Weizao (1962).

29. It should be noted that state planners did debate the idea of loosening price controls at least three times in the first three decades of the PRC: first in the mid-1950s, then the early 1960s, and again in 1978.

REFERENCES

Becker, J. 1996. *Hungry Ghosts: Mao's Secret Famine*. New York: Henry Holt.

Chen, N. 1967. *Chinese Economic Statistics: A Handbook for Mainland China*. Chicago: Aldine.

Dikötter, F. 2011. *Mao's Great Famine: The History of China's Most Devastating Catastrophe, 1958–1962*. New York: Walker.

Dunstan, H. 1996. *Conflicting Counsels to Confuse the Age: A Documentary Study of Political Economy in Qing China, 1644–1840*. Ann Arbor: Center for Chinese Studies, University of Michigan.

———. 2006. *State or Merchant? Political Economy and Political Process in 1740s China*. Cambridge, MA: Harvard University Press.

Edgerton-Tarpley, K. 2008. *Tears from Iron: Cultural Responses to Famine in Nineteenth-Century China*. Berkeley: University of California Press.

Fairbank, J. 1992. *China: A New History*. Cambridge, MA: Belknap Press of Harvard University Press.

Hayek, F. A. [1944] 2008. *The Road to Serfdom: Text and Documents: The Definitive Edition*. Edited by Bruce Caldwell. New York: Routledge.

———. 1945. "The Use of Knowledge in Society." *American Economic Review*, 35 (4): 519–30.

———. [1968] 2002. "Competition as a Discovery Procedure." *Quarterly Journal of Austrian Economics* 5 (3): 9–23.

———. 2014. *The Collected Works of F. A. Hayek: The Market and Other Orders*. Vol. 15. Edited by Bruce Caldwell. Chicago: University of Chicago Press.

Hershatter, G. 2011. *The Gender of Memory: Rural Women and China's Collective Past*. Berkeley: University of California Press.

Li, C. 1962. *The Statistical System of Communist China*. Berkeley: University of California Press.

Li, L. 2007. *Fighting Famine in North China: State, Market, and Environmental Decline, 1690s–1990s*. Stanford, CA: Stanford University Press.

Metzger, Thomas A. 1972. "Finance in Ningpo: The 'Ch'ien Chuang,' 1750–1880." In *Economic Organization in Chinese Society*, edited by W. E. Willmott. Stanford, CA: Stanford University Press.

Myers, R. 1970. *The Chinese Peasant Economy: Agricultural Development in Hopei and Shantung*. Cambridge, MA: Harvard University Press.

Ó Gráda, C. 1999. *Black '47 and Beyond: The Great Irish Famine in History, Economy, and Memory*. Princeton, NJ: Princeton University Press.
Riskin, C. 1987. *China's Political Economy: The Quest for Development Since 1949*. Oxford: Oxford University Press.
Rummel, R. 1991. *China's Bloody Century: Genocide and Mass Murder since 1900*. New Brunswick, NJ: Transaction Publishers.
Scott, J. 1998. *Seeing Like a State: How Certain Schemes to Improve the Human Condition Have Failed*. New Haven, CT: Yale University Press.
_______. 2012. "Tyranny of the Ladle." *London Review of Books* 34 (23): 21–28.
Sen, A. 2000. *Development as Freedom*. New York: Anchor Books.
Sen, A., and J. Drèze. 1989. *Hunger and Public Action*. Studies in Development Economics. Oxford: Oxford University Press.
Solinger, Dorothy J. 1984. *Chinese Business under Socialism: The Politics of Domestic Commerce, 1949–1980*. Berkeley: University of California Press.
Teng Weizao. 1962. *The Introduction to the Communist Party of China's Translation of F. A. Hayek's The Road to Serfdom*. Translated by Matt Dale. Self-Published, Amazon Kindle, https://www.amazon.com/Introduction-Communist-Translation-Serfdom-Translated-ebook/dp/B00CTB63NQ/ref=sr_1_3?ie=UTF8&qid=1528848748&sr=8-3&keywords=introduction+to+road+to+serfdom.
Yang, J. 2012. *Tombstone: The Great Chinese Famine, 1958–1962*. New York: Farrar, Straus and Giroux.
Wemheuer, F. 2011. "Sites of Horror: 'Mao's Great Famine.'" *China Journal* 66: 155–64.
Will, P., R. B. Wong, and J. Lee. 1991. *Nourish the People: The State Civilian Granary System in China, 1650–1850*. Ann Arbor: Center for Chinese Studies, University of Michigan.
Wong, R. 1982. "Food Riots in the Qing Dynasty." *Journal of Asian Studies* 41 (4): 767–84.

Chapter 2

Justice Theorizing and Local Knowledge

Gregory Robson

Political theorists often aim to develop theories of justice that guide citizens and members of organizations to act in ways that make a society more just.[1] For example, Marx famously said—in words now inscribed on his tombstone—that "[p]hilosophers have only interpreted the world in various ways; the point, however, is to change it" (2000, 171–74).[2] And John Dunn says, "The purpose of political theory is to diagnose practical predicaments and to show us how best to confront them" (1990, 193). Yet justice theorists also acknowledge, rightly, that the principles, proposals, and directives they defend cannot be implemented (i.e., realized in practice) without considerable further thought by agents on the ground.[3] The complexity of real life seems to impose obvious epistemic limits on such action-guiding theorizing. What is less obvious, though, is exactly why and to what extent it does.

The thesis for which I will argue is that Hayekian epistemological insights into the nature and limits of political economy help to explain why justice theorists face the epistemic challenges they do, and where these limits are. This thesis differs markedly from alternative theses such as: justice theorists cannot say anything valuable about the content of justice (a claim that seems plainly mistaken); justice theorists can say nearly everything there is to say about justice (a claim that is mistaken in part for reasons to follow); or justice theorists face epistemic limits so severe that theorists should leave determinations of justice's requirements primarily or even solely to agents on the ground (a claim that is at least not obviously true, as theorists seem capable of formulating defensible general principles of justice). My thesis is far more modest than such claims. For I will argue, again, that Hayek's insights into political economy can help to *explain* why justice theorists face the epistemic limits that they do, and approximately where these limits lie. The basic reason we will explore for why incurable ignorance is a major challenge for justice theorists who try to guide action is that agents and organizations have, broadly speaking, many important features that are epistemically inaccessible in principle to the theorist. Theorists are constrained because they inevitably lack local knowledge of facts that bear on what justice requires, in much the same way that, as Hayek observed, central planners lack (and cannot get) the dispersed knowledge they need to allocate resources efficiently.[4]

The knowledge problem that justice theorists face concerns theoretical determinations of how citizens ought to treat one another, and how political institutions ought to treat or affect citizens as the institutions evolve, establish precedents, and foster newly emerging capacities. These two claims concern interpersonal and institutional justice. An example involving interpersonal justice provides an initial sense of the epistemic difficulties that action-guiding theorists face. An individual's life includes (in part, *is*) a complex of historical, cultural, personal, religious, political, and other aspects. So when, for instance, two individuals with their own, unique lives cross paths, and the agents form more than a merely superficial relationship with each other—how can a theorist say with any specificity, presumably from thinking abstractly in their study, how *these* (concrete, particular, actual) individuals ought to interact, beyond rehearsing fairly standard claims about, say, the individuals' moral duties to avoid widely recognized injustices? There *are* moral truths about how such individuals should treat each other. However, these will often be truths that theorists cannot fully articulate without first being familiar with the individuals in question. My aim is not so much to say that theorists should know such truths, as to insist that, in not knowing them, theorists lack knowledge relevant to what justice requires.

Aristotle rightly holds that theorists ought to search "for that degree of precision in each kind of study which the nature of the subject at hand admits" (1962, 5). Applying Hayek's insights about economic planners' epistemic limits to the subject of justice theorizing will give us a better handle on why justice theorists usually cannot offer precise guidance that agents or organizations on the ground can put into practice without relying on a heavy dose of their own practical wisdom. Theorists can reasonably defend general principles—for instance, honor others' legitimate expectations, respect people's property, don't free ride—that often apply in actual cases, but saying which principles matter in real cases rather than just "in general" is no easy task. So, while theorists do try to say things like "person A in situation B should not C," theorists obviously cannot tell us everything. It is worth finding a principled way of determining when, and explaining why, justice theorists run up against epistemological limits in their efforts to articulate how social arrangements can be made more just.

ACTION GUIDANCE, LOCAL KNOWLEDGE, AND JUSTICE

By an "action-guiding theory" I mean a theory that says how organizations or individuals can act or behave, or public policies be structured, in ways that are more moral or rational. *Action* comes in different kinds and degrees, occurs along various dimensions, and involves different people and organizations. Action-guiding theories can be found in political theory and ethics, and perhaps the clearest instances of action-guiding theorizing are what we find in applied ethics.[5] *Guidance* likewise has different kinds and degrees, and can involve recommendations, advice, suggestions, requests, and much else.[6] Action-guiding theorizing can provide: (i) criteria for evaluating current institutions and actions and for retrospectively evaluating whether changes to them have been for better or for worse; or (ii) particular proposals about how we ought to change our existing institutions and actions. My account aims to explore why theorists often cannot guide action in the second way.[7]

I use "justice" to refer to what people are owed or due (*suum cuique tribuere*, as Justinian put it) not just politically but in their nonpolitical interactions as well. Depending on one's view of the content of morality and justice, including how they relate to one another, some readers may want to think of my account as a commentary on morality *tout court* rather than justice alone. Fine by me. Additionally, by "local knowledge" I mean knowledge of *particular* agents or groups, including knowledge that bears on what they ought to do in their own, particular circumstances. (Consider: A theorist can know that someone normally ought to respect others without knowing whether the person ought to respect others *now*, if the theorist knows neither who the others are nor how they have actually behaved toward the person in question.) If justice theories consist of blends of normative and descriptive claims, then local knowledge is knowledge of facts about particular individuals and communities and the particular ways, if any, in which they may be given their due. You can get important information about persons by knowing that they are, as Aristotle says, rational animals; however, this information cannot give you "local" knowledge of a *particular* person's justice-relevant preferences, desires, interests, and so on.[8]

A final clarification: When I say that justice theorists face an "in-principle constraint" on their ability to guide the action of agents and the behavior of organizations and institutions (roughly, rule-governed bodies), I mean that it is an inherent and enduring feature of political life in complex societies that theorists' capacity to draw on local information will be limited.

Those, then, are the preliminaries. Let us turn now to Hayek's knowledge problem and its analogue for action-guiding political theorists.

HAYEK'S KNOWLEDGE PROBLEM

Hayek (2014, 93–104) famously challenged economic theories that claim that central planners ought to be primarily responsible for allocating economic resources. He argued that even a team of the most preeminent living economists could not allocate resources efficiently without consulting market prices, since evolving prices embody information that the price system brings into existence about the preferences of economic actors.[9] In centrally planned economies, planners face an insuperable knowledge problem when they try to allocate resources. They lack the kind of crucial, ever-changing information that market economies convey bottom-up via the price signal. Prices are necessary for efficient allocation (on any of various conceptions of efficiency), so planners cannot allocate resources from the top-down in the right quantities and at the right times to people and organizations with a wide range of needs and preferences.

In "The Use of Knowledge in Society," Hayek says that in economies "in which the knowledge of the relevant facts is dispersed among many people, prices can act to co-ordinate the separate actions of different people" (2014, 99). Similarly, in "The Pretence of Knowledge" he observes: "It is indeed the source of the superiority of the market order . . . that in the resulting allocation of resources more of the knowledge of particular facts will be utilized which exists only dispersed among uncounted persons, than any one person can possess" (2014, 366). So prices both result from and represent information about a vast number and array of economic activities that influence the supply and demand of goods. Prices also serve important *signaling* roles. They can, for instance, convey to economic agents that a certain good is scarce or abundant. A dramatic rise in the price of tin signals that tin is being valued more, perhaps due to a sudden restriction in supply. Profit, too, is an economic signal. A more profitable market sector signals opportunities for firms to enter. A less profitable one discourages entry.

Market prices accordingly "embody" or "reflect" *local* (i.e., dispersed or distributed) information about what you, I, and innumerable others desire vis-à-vis the distribution of an almost unimaginable amount and variety of economic goods. (As we will see, this sort of knowledge is similar to local knowledge of the sort to which justice theorists lack access.) As demanders of economic goods, we (often unwittingly) drive prices to reflect information about our preferences for goods as embodied in what we are willing to pay.[10] This information is also "local" in that, for instance, consumers sometimes have an intuitive sense of their willingness to trade off between goods, a sense which is inarticulable in practice and perhaps even in principle. Similarly, seasoned entrepreneurs often have an intuitive, nonverbalizable sense of the promises and perils of market opportunities. Many entrepreneurs know of good or bad opportunities when they see them. But they cannot always say precisely what makes them so.

Suppose, as is plausible, that such information about entrepreneurs and consumers is not propositional but largely a matter of their inarticulate "know-how." On this assumption, the information cannot be adequately represented in the linguistic vehicles we call sentences. Central planners, though, need to make their plans in a way that somehow incorporates such knowledge, and to communicate those plans in sentences (or formulae similarly incapable of embodying inarticulate knowledge). Thus, planners cannot include vital information about market actors in their allocation decisions. This is why, for Hayek, not even a supercomputer could allocate resources efficiently. It could not tap into the torrent of local, largely nonverbalizable information that price-based market processes continually rely on throughout the allocative process. Absent market processes, no such information would have been made. Consumers rarely consider fully such matters as how to weigh goods relative to each other, and which goods are substitutes and which complements, independently of driving prices by their demand behavior (see Schmidtz 2016).

An example illustrates the striking ways in which market processes structure economic interactions so that they incorporate individual actors' dispersed knowledge. Suppose thousands of people across several towns in northeast Georgia are suddenly and unpredictably willing to pay, and do pay, for a product *r*. In this scenario, companies from the local area and beyond that become aware of consumers' willingness to pay for *r* would then respond to the opportunity to profit by selling *r*. Firms would thereby satisfy consumers' preferences without having any idea *why* the consumers are willing to pay for *r*. By looking to prices, producers can account for information germane to consumer demand while knowing only *that* it is true, not *why* it is true.

Schmidtz (2016, sect. 3) nicely summarizes Hayek's knowledge problem for central planners:

> The problem is not lack of processing power so much as a lack of access to the information in the first place. That much seems clear enough, but the problem has a deeper level. The problem is not merely lack of *access* to information; rather the information does not exist. There is no truth about what prices should be, accessible or otherwise, except to the extent that prices represent what customers are paying for a given service.

Three points stand out here. First, the economic planner cannot *access* information he or she needs to decide how to allocate economic resources efficiently. Second, planned economies cannot *create* information in the right amounts, kinds, and distributions for efficient allocation to occur. Only participants in market processes can. Third, market economies create such information in practice, via dynamic and unpredictable processes involving the mutual adjustment of economic actors' behaviors that inclines toward the equilibration of supply and demand. It's not just that central planners lack much-needed knowledge of distributed economic information; planners also face the in-principle epistemic limit that no such information exists unless created by market participants in actual practice.

JUSTICE THEORISTS AND LOCAL KNOWLEDGE

I will now argue that justice theorists are in an epistemically similar position to central planners. The agents and organizations that justice theorists aim to guide are situated in environments in which myriad complexly related cultural, religious, social, political, and economic factors converge and interact. Some information about these variables is available to justice theorists. Other information is not. In such environments, who owes what to whom, whether interpersonally or via institutions, will partly depend on the particular characteristics of the individuals involved. As I shall argue, information of this sort about agents in justice situations will often be information that theorists lack, much as central planners lack information that buyers and sellers have. (To say this is not to claim that theorists who do not consider such information are blameworthy. The importance of local information will vary with circumstances, and theorists can be entirely right not to try to track it in their theories.)

A given theorist has from her study little access to vast swathes of local data. Informationally deprived in this way, she must resort to characterizing agents abstractly, in ways that hold local information fixed or ignore it. Once a theorist represents you (or Mother Teresa, Nat King Cole, or your local bank teller) in terms of abstract categories like "human being," "rational animal," or even "citizen," the theorist simplifies greatly. Even after giving such categorical terms fairly thick descriptive meanings, the theorist still must ignore key features that make you *you* (e.g., your practical and doxastic commitments), even though some of these features will presumably be relevant to what some other agents owe you as a matter of justice. Theories that trade primarily in conceptual categories are, then, risky theories in a qualified sense. For they risk overlooking much of what makes the agents whose actions they wish to guide—beings like you and me—the *subjects* that they are.[11] At the same time, it is hard to see how a theory of justice for a diverse society with millions of persons could do better than to traffic in generic role descriptions (e.g., "citizen") of the complex individuals and institutions to which the requirements of justice apply. What does this imply? It implies that justice theorists are inherently limited in their ability to say what justice requires for real persons. Theorists can defend a place for the role of many relevant general principles in actual agents' practical deliberations. Yet, due to the knowledge limits they face, theorists will often need to hedge such action-guiding claims with heavy qualifications like "other things being equal." (Knowing their epistemic limits, the best theorists are willing to employ such claims.)

Even only in terms of what matters for justice, it is difficult, and perhaps even impossible, to represent a *single*, actual human being accurately and comprehensively in a given natural language by way of abstract, categorical statements. Exhaustively stating a given person's duties of justice qua citizen and qua person, including in regard to what having a just character and just dispositions would look like for the individual in question, is no easy task. It would thus be even more daunting, epistemically, for a theorist to try to describe from his or her desk just what a group such as you and I—or, say, *an entire citizenry* of millions of persons—owe each other as private individuals and as citizens of the same state. In response to such weighty epistemic demands, justice theorists might seek to narrow the scope of their theorizing by homing in on, say, how people ought to act under generic role descriptions such as citizen or legislator. But to do so is to raise a fair question about whether such theorizing really does describe the requirements of justice for real people, and really does develop principles that are specific and informed enough to guide action for real people leading complex, multidimensional lives. Much as centrally planned economies block vital information about supply and demand from ever being created, justice theorizing that trades mainly in generic role descriptions risks not getting to the heart of questions about the treatment that real people and organizations ought to accord to each other as a matter of justice.

To be sure, theorists can articulate the kinds of duties and obligations that individuals have in general.[12] But due to the deep and diverse complexities of many ethical situations, theorists often cannot say how actual individuals should balance such duties and obligations. Nor can theorists say what individuals' practical reasoning about them essentially should look like. As Hayek helps to show, we theorists often cannot provide the second sort of action guidance noted above—particular proposals about how we ought to change our existing institutions and actions—even if, fortunately, we can provide the first—criteria for evaluating current institutions and actions and for retrospectively evaluating whether changes to them have been valuable.

There is a further reason why theories of justice cannot readily say what meeting justice's requirements will look like in practice. Many of the truth-makers of justice theories are inarticulable, much as consumers' knowledge of their willingness to purchase some items instead of others is often inarticulable. For illustration, take a mundane example. A bike-rider arguably cannot articulate the set of truths that a non-bike-rider must rely upon in order to ride well. The prospective rider must instead learn certain inarticulable truths by *experience*. Likewise, sometimes a person knows how to treat another person justly, but just *what* the person knows he or she cannot say even in principle. Now a theorist will be unable to incorporate inarticulate knowledge of this ilk into his or her theory. The theorist may even discount knowledge of this sort. But if treating people justly is to no trivial degree an intuitive activity, and perhaps one that theorists cannot even come close to fully describing propositionally, then this implies that justice theorists will be missing important local truths about what justice requires in practice. Later on in the chapter I shall discuss the crucial role of practical wisdom—itself much like know-how—in helping agents to satisfy justice's requirements.

A theorist's inability to guide action in a way that is both reliable and comprehensive—that tends to get it right (by accurately saying what an agent or institution ought to do) and say enough (by covering ample actual and possible cases)—is, I submit, largely the result of a combinatorial problem. The problem concerns theorists' abilities to account for the right degrees and kinds of local information. To start to see the problem, think of your preferred theory of justice: Rawls's (1971) account of justice as fairness in *A Theory of Justice*, Nozick's (1974) entitlement theory of justice in holdings in *Anarchy, State, and Utopia*, or some other account. Next, suppose there are fifteen facts on the ground (e.g., the color of an agent's shirt, as discussed shortly) each of which, taken alone, is not especially relevant to what justice requires as understood in your chosen theory. Assume also that the theory has (somehow) successfully accounted for all *other* facts that, by themselves, bear importantly on what justice requires. Can such a theory reliably describe the content of justice?

Quite possibly not, I suggest, if the theory pays no heed to the fifteen local facts *in combination*. After all, the set of trivial factors may not itself be trivial. The conjunction of facts may have normative entailments that the individual conjuncts lack. To assume it does not would be to commit the fallacy of composition, to wit, thinking that what is true of X's parts (in our case, that each individual fact implies nothing important about what justice requires) must be true of X itself (in our case, that the set of such trivial facts itself is trivial in that it implies nothing important about what justice requires).

For illustration, take a case of justice in rectification. We might consider facts that individually seem irrelevant to what justice requires from Bill to rectify his injustice of having stolen a shirt from Jane. Considered by itself, the shirt's color seems irrelevant, justice-wise. Yet this local fact becomes important if Jane *really* likes dark blue shirts, and if Bill stole her only shirt with that color precisely to get under her skin. In this case, Bill's condemnable intention renders his theft *more* unjust, all else equal. The same holds in cases of political injustice, as when one group in a democracy steals or fails to count the votes of another. Information about the purpose of that act—for example, whether it was done to weaken the voting power of an oppressed minority group, or just to win the election—could well render it more unjust. Justice theorists will *sometimes* have access to such information, which might seem irrelevant (at least in the case of shirt color) while actually being material to a determination of what justice requires. Often, though, theorists will lack such access. Further, it is true of course that justice theorists don't need to consider facts about the shirt's color to claim that stealing something from someone to get under that person's skin makes a theft more unjust. Yet this claim will need to be hedged with a "ceteris paribus" clause, which hedging greatly diminishes the specificity of the claim's action guidance.

Working up a theory from a set of abstract characterizations of individuals, organizations, and institutions requires a degree of simplification whose magnitude is easy to understate. Worse still, attempts to act upon such a theory will frequently require further knowledge: knowledge of which simplifications matter, and which don't, for what justice requires. Content *omitted* by justice theorists' simplifications may partly determine the sort of treatment due to agents or organizations. And, cumulatively, there may be a massive number of simplifications across a wide range of issues. Consequently, much as central planners traffic in simplistic representations of consumers' and producers' preferences, and, in trying to rely on these, find it difficult or impossible to allocate resources efficiently, justice theorists rely on simplified representations of real individuals and organizations, and, in trying to rely on *these*, find it difficult or even impossible to make defensible claims about what justice requires of real, highly complex individuals and organizations.

How Local Defeaters Can Block a Theory's Action Guidance: An Example

Considering a recent theory of distributive justice will help us to see better how local facts not only affect what justice requires but also are hard or impossible for theorists to grasp. John Roemer's account of how a state can realize equality of opportunity furnishes an intriguing apparent case of the theorist's knowledge problem as just described. Now, theorists' accounts can have objectionable features ranging from internal incoherence and poor fit with the evidence to ambiguities, unclarities, and much else. I shall not criticize Roemer's view on these grounds. For my goal will just be to sketch what it would look like for a view like his to guide action in a reliable way. So doing, we will see, turns out to be more difficult than one might expect.

Roemer (1995) aims to suggest some ways in which members of a society can provide each other with equality of opportunity via redistributive governmental programs. Roemer begins by adopting Ronald Dworkin's distinction between option luck and brute luck (see Dworkin 2000, 73). Each kind of luck can be good or bad for a person, but Roemer focuses on brute bad luck, or bad luck that one cannot reasonably avoid.[13] He gives an example of each kind of bad luck:

> Being hit by a truck which runs a red light while you are in the pedestrian crossing is brute bad luck. Being hit by a truck while you are jay walking is not: for in that case, you took a calculated gamble and lost, a gamble you need (and perhaps should) not have taken. Brute luck is to be contrasted with option luck, which is the luck of the voluntarily taken gamble. (Roemer 1995, 3)

Roemer argues for the value and practical possibility of realizing equality of opportunity. The basic structure of his argument consists of three main steps. First, he argues that a given society should identify the uncontrolled circumstances that affect individuals' possession of a certain good. For example, the good might be income and the circumstances might be one's level of education. Whether such circumstances are obtained is largely a matter of one's parents, their education, one's natural intelligence, one's siblings and their activities, and other facts over which one has little or no control. Roemer's second step is to partition the society' members into groups according to how much control they have over a certain good (e.g., education). For instance, one group may be Irish-American adults who grew up in low-income households with two parents with high school educations. Finally, Roemer says that to help neutralize the effects of bad brute luck for the sake of realizing equality of opportunity, the society (via its government, if we allow that a society *as such* can do so in practice) should send tax transfers to members of systematically unlucky groups. The idea here is that one's bad brute luck in being, say, born into a group with fewer valuable opportunities will be neutralized, even though "within each group, those who exercised more responsibility will be given more favorable treatment" (Roemer 1995, 6).

Now, in calling for a certain scheme of taxation, a theorist might be saying that it *would* be morally valuable, or even required by justice, for a society to adopt a redistributive scheme that the theorist has suggested, *if* the society could redistribute as suggested, and *if* the facts are as the theorist has suggested. Alternatively or additionally, a theorist might be saying that the facts *are* as he or she suggests, and thus that the society *should* redistribute resources according to the compensatory scheme the theorist endorses. Roemer's contribution is surely valuable in the first sense. He gives a thought-provoking account of how a (hypothetical) society could realize equality of opportunity via a compensation scheme aimed at neutralizing the impact of so-called bad brute luck. Still, one of his argumentative goals is "to provide a procedure by which a society can *implement* equality of opportunity as a social policy" (Roemer 1995, 4; emphasis added). This is a practical, action-guiding claim. But is the claim that a given (real, not hypothetical) society, such as the United States, Belgium, or Tanzania, should now institute such a policy, a claim we can justify?

For Roemer's view to be true about what could make one of today's actual societies more just—for example, one of the modern welfare states he discusses—many background assumptions would need to hold true. These we may divide into two sets. First, there are assumptions that must hold for any theory—that, for example, our languages and concepts are sufficient to link to reality in the right ways, without radical error or slippage; that we can know enough about justice and societies to make reliable prescriptions; and so on. Second, there is a set consisting of (unargued) assumptions and (argued for) corollaries that must hold true for Roemer's account to guide real agents' actions and organizations' behaviors in a society in which his proposal is implemented. This set includes the claims, for example, that a society *can* correct for brute bad luck (it has the necessary resources, knowledge, and social actors to do so); correcting for brute bad luck is a good thing for most societies to do via political institutions; a *particular* society S ought to correct for bad brute lack; a government can sustain such programs without falling prey to corruption and standard public choice worries; and Roemer's particular examples are plausible cases in which such correction is possible. Many such concerns are rightly viewed as background assumptions of Roemer's theory. What I wish to claim, though, is that once someone proposes to guide agents' action as Roemer does, a host of local defeaters stand ready to put that claim in doubt. If my claim is right, then my account of local knowledge vis-à-vis justice preserves the particularity of some (but not necessarily all!) justice claims.[14] What justice requires, even politically, will sometimes be knowable only at the local level, *if* it is knowable at all.[15]

To evaluate whether Roemer's account faces a Hayekian knowledge problem involving local defeaters, let's consider his argument about smokers. Roemer claims that individual smokers who contract lung cancer suffer from bad brute luck and so ought to be compensated via tax transfers. Some smokers get lung cancer. Others don't. But whether one gets lung cancer from smoking is partly determined by factors beyond one's control, since whether one smokes partly owes to factors beyond one's control (e.g., the circumstances of one's childhood). If a society (or perhaps more accurately, its members) should neutralize bad luck of this form, then, says Roemer (1995, 6), it should send tax transfers to those unfortunate smokers who are victims of lung cancer. I take this to be a pro tanto claim holding that citizens have a weighty, but not necessarily conclusive, reason to support such transfers. But notice how easily such a qualified claim succumbs to countervailing considerations. If not all but *any* claim of the above kind is false—if, for instance, the proposed compensation scheme would fall prey to manipulation by local government, or locals would interpret citizens' receipt of government compensation as reflecting an unprincipled willingness to have one's vote bought—then Roemer's argument will not be able to guide action in the ways he intends. Since his normative conclusion that a society ought to realize equality of opportunity as he proposes requires the truth of such claims, Roemer's argument will not follow *for a particular society* from the premises if just one such background assumption is false.

None of this is to deny that Roemer's proposal could guide action well, in some sense, for *some* society. Perhaps the proposal is even a correct or justified action guide for *many* societies. But whether it is will depend on various local facts to which theorists not embedded in a given society often will lack access. What we end up with in terms of Roemer's account, then, is just the (conditional) claim that states ought to neutralize bad brute luck *if* they can (a feasibility constraint), not Roemer's intended claim that modern welfare states (in fact) ought to take steps to neutralize bad brute luck for the sake of securing equality of opportunity. The issue here is reminiscent of the knowledge problem that central planners face: like central planners who try to allocate resources efficiently, theorists who aim to articulate justice's demands lack crucial information that only agents on the ground can create and access.

I am neither affirming nor denying that Roemer's proposal could work in some societies. If it would, I am saying that this would be for reasons outside the scope of his proposal and beyond a theorist's capacity reasonably to predict. Hayekian thinking helps to explain why.

THE STRENGTH OF THE EPISTEMIC LIMITATION

Now, there are two weighty reasons to take seriously the possibility that political theorists may be in a *worse* epistemic position than central planners. First, justice concerns both the allocation of economic resources (as the distribution-centered literature of recent decades insists) and various other issues such as desert, luck, equality, autonomy, freedom, need, reciprocity, legal adjudication and representation, and deep disagreement about justice itself. Since questions about appropriate economic distribution are only a subset of the questions that issues of justice implicate, identifying just actions and institutions may at times be *more* epistemically demanding than allocating economic resources efficiently. This claim could well be true even though the epistemology of resource allocation—including how markets work—is extraordinarily complex. Second, even if realizing justice were somehow only a matter of allocating resources well, theorists aiming to understand in proper depth what truly just societies would look like would still have no epistemic shortcut like a price mechanism for determining what economic justice requires. They can make general claims about, say, the need for a social minimum (e.g., a basic income guarantee). But specific further claims will be hard to make defensibly. Although socialist planners could, and did, aim to approximate efficient market allocations by looking to prices on international markets, no analogous, elegant conveyer of information can make clear who owes what to whom.[16] Notice that, while the cogency of my account does not require a verdict on the relative epistemological demandingness of central planning and justice theorizing, comparing the two helps one glimpse the massive complexity that theorists face.[17]

Now, an objector might say, "The claimed knowledge problem really is no problem at all! For if it were," the objector might continue, "then it would yield an absurd result: Hayek's knowledge problem showed that central planning is a bad idea, so we should not have central planners. If justice theorizing is similarly epistemically fraught, then this would imply that we should not have justice theorists!" Now *that* would be an untoward result in our field, if ever there were one.

The argument I have advanced does not so much imply that action guidance on a grand scale is a bad idea as that it is a surprisingly daunting epistemic enterprise. In fact, if Hayek is right about the social evolution of moral rules, then philosophers have reason to think "we are seldom if ever fully aware of the functions of any specific rule, and so we are never in a position to make a full evaluation of all of its pros and cons" (Gaus 2015, 821). This epistemic limitation justifies cautiousness when approaching theories that call for major, untested changes in our social practices.[18] But it does not mean that the epistemic difficulties of justice theorizing render the enterprise pointless.

Practical Wisdom: A Crucial Bridge Between Theory and Practice

Adam Smith (1759) complained about the *man of system*: a political leader who treats human actors as chess pieces rather than agents with their own, internal principles. Smith observes, "in the great chess-board of human society every single piece has its own private source of motion, quite different from anything that the legislature might choose to impress on it" (124).[19] Sovereigns that simply carry out their own will pay ill heed to the logic of such private motion (124–25). The statesman who "hold[s] up his judgment as the supreme standard of right and wrong" against the logic of other members of the polity and their ways of life will frequently be guilty, not merely of poor judgment, but of having "the highest degree of arrogance" (124). Now I have pointed out the risk of philosophers' treating persons whose societies they want to make more just as mere members of conceptual or real categories, since theorists often must ignore the particular features that make these "members" real, flesh-and-blood *subjects*. And, as we have seen, to guide real agents, institutions, and organizations, theorists cannot simply "guide" the members of real or conceptual sets by dealing with abstract representations of citizens, states, and so on. Real people lead lives marked by complexity that is theoretically unignorable and irreducible. The magnificent tool that is abstraction can capture much of this complexity, but not nearly all of it—especially when we multiply this degree of complexity many times on account of the large, diverse populations of modern democracies. Hence, political theorists cannot access a massive amount of data relevant to justice's demands, data in the form of facts about particular individuals that cannot be gleaned from generic descriptions of them as citizens, rational animals, and so forth.

This point about the dangers of highly abstract theorizing pushes back against a form of *ethical rationalism*. Rasmussen and Den Uyl (2005) describe this view, which they resist as well. It holds "(1) that abstract ethical principles *alone* can determine the proper course of conduct for any particular individual; and (2) that particular and contingent facts are not *morally* relevant when it comes to determining the proper course of conduct for an individual" (144, emphasis in original). By contrast, I have argued that particular facts *are* not only morally relevant to action guidance—a claim that seems to me widely embraced by many ethicists[20]—but that such facts are, indeed, highly relevant. Consider Hayek's point, noted by Theodore Burczak (2006), that "individuals can agree on . . . a fair set of rules that increases the range and domain of activities that individuals can pursue without interfering in the affairs of others" (85).[21] Achieving such agreement *requires* individuals to draw upon their own, specific knowledge of their particular lives, and of how proposed social or political rules would affect their lives, before endorsing or rejecting such rules. But since theorists cannot know what these members of society know, theorists will often be epistemically unjustified in arguing that justice requires, for a given group of individuals, some specific rules rather than others. Accordingly, epistemically cautious theorists ought to leave room for deliberators to decide on such rules on the ground, as guided by their own practical wisdom. For if, as I have suggested, practical wisdom cannot be fully captured in a set of principles of political morality, then no set of such principles advanced by theorists can by itself fully capture what justice requires.

Now, on a standard Aristotelian account, practical wisdom (or prudence[22]) is the master or directive virtue in a *eudaimon* (flourishing) life. It has two main aspects: good moral will and practical skill. As Barry Schwartz and

Kenneth Sharpe (2010) observe, practical wisdom is valuable as a guide to human action that is an alternative to rules and incentives. Might practical wisdom be a vital complement to justice theorizing? To see why it is, start by considering the fact that justice theorists ordinarily do not view their principles as ready-to-implement regardless of local circumstances. They admit that the principles need further specification. Further, it is fairly easy to ignore the important epistemic role that local actors play in discerning whether and how to implement proposed rules or principles of justice. If this "implementing" moves from very abstract principles to practical decision making, it must require a fair amount of justice theorizing by individuals or organizations on the ground during that transition.

It seems to follow that in the name of justice itself, agents will sometimes need to *modify* proposed principles of justice. Suppose, for example, that by ensuring that socioeconomic inequalities redound to the benefit of the least well off, Rawlsian members of a certain polity would incur unacceptable psychological or other costs. Suppose also that a modified version of Rawls's difference principle would not impose such costs. Practically wise citizens and leaders would not only choose the modified version for the sake of justice (and not as a mere practical concession); they would also be epistemically better positioned than theorists to know *that* they should choose it. In this way, theorists' principles of justice may need to be substantially *modified*, and not just rendered more specific or determinate, by local actors, because these actors are uniquely well-equipped to understand local facts relevant to justice's actual demands.

Many theorists propose to specify just actions or institutional arrangements in accordance with a commitment, say, to multiculturalism (e.g., Kymlicka 1995), the capabilities approach (e.g., Nussbaum 1993),[23] or social democracy (e.g., Berman 2006).[24] I submit that in response to the knowledge problem that justice theorists face, such theorists should try, when possible, to *specify in their theories* how and at what points agents and organizations would likely need to exercise practical wisdom to account for local knowledge. Justice theorists not only ought to defend their preferred substantive views of justice; to the extent reasonably possible, they also ought to build into their theories *roadmaps* of how agents can account for relevant local information when implementing and modifying those views.[25] To be sure, this is, or at least can be, a demanding requirement itself. So, to clarify: All I mean to imply here is that theorists (i) should not say that their theory of justice *will* realize justice, but just that it plausibly might (where so doing differs from adopting an attitude of fallibilism without *displaying* that attitude); and (ii) should try to indicate ways in which the truth of their claims about justice will depend upon local facts unknowable to them qua theorists. Offering such a "roadmap" could involve discussing the type and degree of work that social scientists and agents on the ground can do to generate, or draw upon, local knowledge necessary for the theory's successful realization.[26] Relatedly, theorists should also carve out space for agents' practical wisdom by doing two complementary things: (i) leaving room for agents' and institutions' own practical know-how or wisdom to guide their action (this knowledge often being somewhat inarticulate); and (ii) saying, as far as is reasonably possible, how and why such room is left. Discharging these two tasks will help theorists to complete their work as members of a dynamic, multiparty inquiry into justice's requirements that not only includes non-theorists but also ensures that justice is provided for these agents rather than the agents (merely) abstractly modeled or imagined by theorists.

Importantly, (i) involves more than simply filling in the blanks. Agents, including members of political organizations, must reflectively confirm a theory's applicability and, further, consider whether a theory's principles themselves might require alteration given diverse facts on the ground, some of which a theorist cannot antecedently account for in the formulation of his or her principles. A fact pattern that a theorist cannot account for ex ante might yield reasons that shift the balance of reasons within his or her theory. The result can be a different set of action-guiding prescriptions. Overall, much as prices embody vast amounts and many kinds of economic information, some of it inarticulate, that enable efficient resource allocation, agents' practical wisdom embodies vast amounts and kinds of information, some of *it* inarticulate, that enable agents to act, at least much of the time, with a duly informed sense of what justice requires.

THINKING ABOUT JUSTICE: A COMMUNAL ENDEAVOR

Fortunately, our Hayekian worry about justice theorizing need not leave one with an entirely bleak picture of how well theorists can guide action. Justice theorists are key articulators of some of justice's demands, no doubt, but not the only such articulators. The search for principles of justice is not a project that can be left solely to theorists. Citizens and members of organizations must participate as well. They can and must be substantive contributors to, rather than just appliers of, principles of justice, helping to fill out the content of realistic principles by relying on their cultivated practical wisdom along with their special awareness of local circumstances. For this reason, Hayek's discussion of the epistemic limits that central planners face is surprisingly apt: applying his basic knowledge problem to the enterprise of justice theorizing helps to explain why justice theorists themselves cannot articulate all of justice's demands.

In closing, I suggest that the work of justice theorists occurs between two temporal extremes: (i) a backward-looking consideration of which past theories and practices seem to have advanced the cause of justice, and (ii) a forward-looking consideration of how a theory's practically wise implementers could rely upon their particular epistemic capacities to implement wisely and, when warranted, modify a proposed theory of justice. In this way, the present work of justice theorists can be seen as bridging the past and the future. When pursuing such bridgework, justice theorists ought to see themselves as the *initiators* of a process of social inquiry into what justice requires of agents and institutions—not the last word on justice's (actual) requirements. An appreciation of Hayek's seminal epistemological contributions to political economy reveals why, when it comes to articulating actionable principles of justice, theorists themselves cannot, and fortunately need not, say all there is to say.

NOTES

1. For helpful discussion and comments, I thank participants at Mercatus Center colloquia in 2016 and 2017 and Jacob Barrett, Thomas Christiano, Adam Gjesdal, Guido Pincione, John Proios, Karina Robson, David Schmidtz, Danny Shahar, and Steven Wall.

2. The tombstone lacks the punctuation I include.

3. Justice theorists who aim to alter political practice typically try to do one or more of three things. They formulate general principles of justice, propose institutions for a just society, or defend specific institutional or non-institutional directives aimed at securing justice. For instance, Rawls (1971) formulates principles of justice for society's basic institutions that call for maximizing the position of society's worst-off members after individuals' basic liberties and fair equality of opportunity have been secured.

4. Even if philosophers could get local knowledge by living in the society about which they are theorizing, they would only then have access to a subset of relevant knowledge therein. The information they took in, and the implications they drew from it, would likely also be colored by the theorists' particular cognitive biases, desires, and so on.

5. Fischer and Ravizza (1992, 25) observe: "[I]t is not sufficient simply to formulate and defend general principles; one also must be able to apply these principles to morally complex situations, such as abortion, euthanasia, famine relief, preferential treatment, etc. An applied ethicist, for instance, might use a general principle like the Doctrine of Double Effect in order to clarify what a doctor is permitted to do to relieve the suffering of a terminally ill patient."

6. Justice theorists try to say which principles apply when agents are in a justice situation, but usually agents themselves must judge whether they are in such a context (Schmidtz 2006, 23).

7. For simplicity, I shall leave aside action guidance with respect to the development of moral character or attitudes, as well as guidance in other normative domains such as epistemology.

8. On an Aristotelian classificatory scheme, "rational animal" is the intension of "human being," and "featherless biped" the extension.

9. These preferences can concern one's needs, desires, interests, and much else.

10. Hayek describes industrial societies as based upon a very subtle system of communication. This system, which we call the market, "turns out to be a more efficient mechanism for digesting dispersed information than any that man has deliberately designed" (2014, 371).

11. This is not to deny that there are sometimes theoretical advantages to doing so. As Linda Zagzebski (2017, 5–6) observes, moral theorists leave out particular features such as "who is who"—viz., individuals' particular identities—in order to model impartiality.

12. On a standard view, obligations but not duties are voluntarily incurred.

13. I add "reasonably." In Roemer's example, the pedestrian who walks on a cross walk *could* have avoided being hit by a truck on the street. The pedestrian could have reduced risk of being hit by a truck on the street to zero by never crossing a street. But a voluntary risk reduction of this sort would be unreasonable.

14. I have not questioned in this chapter, nor do I doubt, that theorists can condemn with epistemic justification categorically evil practices such as exploitation and involuntary servitude. Less obvious cases of injustice, though, often require for their defense judgments about justice that local agents are better positioned to render than distant theorists.

15. Roemer (1995, 6) seems sympathetic to this claim when he says that it should be up to particular liberal societies to determine whether their members have made decisions autonomously. But when I say "local" above, I refer to particular communities far smaller than today's liberal democracies.

16. The point here is about the ability of planned markets to allocate resources efficiently. The defender of market distributions must also say why those distributions themselves are just rather than simply efficient (see Buchanan 1985), or deny that justice can be predicated of distributions (see Hayek 1976).

17. As we will see, agents' practical wisdom substantially mitigates the problem for theorists. Further, justice theorists seem to be under a less demanding epistemic burden than central planners insofar as theorists can stick to defending more general claims than, say, claims about the specific quantities of countless economic goods that a large, planned economy should produce.

18. A related reason to think twice: as theorists such as Michael Huemer (2016) have observed, certain political theories ("ideal" rather than "nonideal" ones) can be implemented in ways deeply detrimental to a polity, as in cases of oppressive Marxism.

19. See also Schmidtz 2016, sect. 3.

20. Wall (2016) considers perhaps an equivalent view to what Rasmussen and Den Uyl dub "ethical rationalism," to wit *determinate universalism*. On this view, "there is a universal political morality consisting of a single principle or a set of principles that are determinately ordered" (143). Further, the principle or set of principles includes

a set of hypothetical imperatives of the form "if in situation X, do Z," where this set exhausts all possible practical cases. Like Wall, I suspect that perhaps no contemporary ethicist holds such a strong view.

21. Here Burczak is discussing Hayek (1973).

22. These closely related terms are both translated from the Greek *phronesis*. But I use "practical wisdom" since, in modern times, "prudence" has become identified with a different meaning, i.e., the rational pursuit of self-interest. See Yuengart (2012).

23. Nussbaum takes up and extends Amartya Sen's project.

24. Berman provides an historical account of the rise of social democracy.

25. This point applies whether one is trying to address the age-old question of what a just society looks like or one is focusing, with theorists like Sen, on how to make societies more just. Sen (2006) calls the traditional theory "transcendental" and his theory "comparative."

26. Here I am sympathetic to Adam Swift's (2006, 364) suggestion that "social science should tell us which states of affairs are feasible and how to achieve them, but philosophers should evaluate and rank options . . . within the feasible set."

REFERENCES

Aristotle. 1962. *Nicomachean Ethics*. New York: Bobbs-Merrill.

Berman, Sheri. 2006. *The Primacy of Politics: Social Democracy and the Making of Europe's Twentieth Century*. Cambridge: Cambridge University Press.

Buchanan, Allen. 1985. *Ethics, Efficiency, and the Market*. Totowa, NJ: Rowman & Allanheld.

Burczak, Theodore A. 2006. *Socialism After Hayek*. Ann Arbor: University of Michigan Press.

Dunn, John. 1990. *Interpreting Political Responsibility*. Cambridge: Polity Press.

Dworkin, Ronald. 2000. *Sovereign Virtue*. Cambridge, MA: Harvard University Press.

Fischer, John Martin, and Mark Ravizza. 1992. *Ethics: Problems & Principles*. Fort Worth: Harcourt Brace.

Gaus, Gerald. 2015. "On F. A. Hayek, 'Freedom, Reason, and Tradition.'" *Ethics* 125 (3): 820–22.

Hayek, F. A. 1973. *Law, Legislation, and Liberty*. Vol. 1: *Rules and Order*. Chicago: University of Chicago Press.

_______. 1976. *Law, Legislation, and Liberty*. Vol. 2: *The Mirage of Social Justice*. Chicago: University of Chicago Press.

_______. 2014. *The Collected Works of F. A. Hayek*. Vol. 15: *The Market and Other Orders*. Chicago: University of Chicago Press.

Huemer, Michael. 2016. "Against Ideal Theory: Confessions of a Utopophobe." *Social Philosophy and Policy* 33 (1–2): 214–34.

Kymlicka, Will. 1995. *Multicultural Citizenship*. Oxford: Oxford University Press.

Marx, Karl. 2000. *Karl Marx: Selected Writings*. Edited by David McLellan. 2nd ed. Oxford: Oxford University Press.
Nozick, Robert. 1974. *Anarchy, State, and Utopia*. New York: Basic Books.
Nussbaum, Martha. 1993. "Social Justice and Universalism: In Defense of an Aristotelian Account of Human Functioning." *Modern Philology* 90 (S1): S46–S73.
Rasmussen, Douglas B., and Douglas J. Den Uyl. 2005. *Norms of Liberty: A Perfectionist Basis for Non-Perfectionist Politics*. University Park: Pennsylvania State University Press.
Rawls, John. 1971. *A Theory of Justice*. Cambridge, MA: Harvard University Press.
Roemer, John. 1995. "Equality and Responsibility." *Boston Review* 20 (2): 3–16.
Schmidtz, David. 2006. *Elements of Justice*. Cambridge: Cambridge University Press.
_______. 2016. "Friedrich Hayek." (Revised). *Stanford Encyclopedia of Philosophy*, December 14. http://plato.stanford.edu/entries/friedrich-hayek/.
Schwartz, Barry, and Kenneth Sharpe. 2010. *Practical Wisdom: The Right Way to Do the Right Thing*. New York: Riverhead Books.
Sen, Amartya. 2006. "What Do We Want from a Theory of Justice?" *Journal of Philosophy* 103 (5): 215–38.
Smith, Adam. 1759. *Theory of Moral Sentiments*. http://www.earlymoderntexts.com/assets/pdfs/smith1759.pdf.
Swift, Adam. July 2008. "The Value of Philosophy in Nonideal Circumstances." *Social Theory and Practice* 34 (3): 363–87.
Wall, Steven. 2016. "Political Morality and the Authority of Tradition." *The Journal of Political Philosophy* 24 (2): 137–61.
Yuengart, Andrew. 2012. *Approximating Prudence: Aristotelian Practical Wisdom and Economic Models of Choice*. New York: Palgrave Macmillan.
Zagzebski, Linda. 2017. *Exemplarist Moral Theory*. Oxford: Oxford University Press.

Chapter 3

The Silent Role of Emotions in Hayekian Political Economy

Brianne Wolf

Friedrich Hayek's thought is recognized as covering much ground.[1] He has seriously engaged with the fields of psychology, philosophy, social science, sociology, and economics, to name a few. However, there is one area related to all of these endeavors about which Hayek has had little to say—emotion. Contemporary scholars have recognized this. Grouping Hayek with all economists, they argue that the study and promotion of the market is incompatible with a recognition of the importance of morality, emotion, and community.[2] And this accusation seems to fit with Hayek's own characterization of emotion. In the few times he mentions it specifically, he refers to emotion as problematic for social coordination. Consider Hayek's statement:

> The commitment to "social justice" has in fact become the chief outlet for moral emotion. . . . What we have to deal with in the case of "social justice" is simply a quasi-religious superstition of the kind which we should respectfully leave in peace so long as it merely makes those happy who hold it, but which we must fight when it becomes the pretext of coercing other men. And the prevailing belief in "social justice" is at present probably the gravest threat to most other values of a free civilization. (Hayek 1978b, 66–67)

For Hayek, emotion, insofar as it leads to a commitment to social justice, is a threat to freedom and akin to a "superstition" rather than an integral part of society.

At the same time, charging Hayek with a dismissal of emotion does not seem to capture the whole story. After all, Hayek is highly critical of what we might think of as the opposite of emotional thinking, the exclusively rational. Hayek argues that no one mind can know enough to organize human society. Further, he has doubts about how much human beings can consciously know.

He does not suffer from the hubris of rationalism, and criticizing this position is the beginning point of much of his work, especially in arguments for the value of the price system in "The Use of Knowledge in Society," the possibility of human creativity in "The Creative Powers of a Free Civilization," and the problems with socialist regimes in *The Road to Serfdom*, *The Fatal Conceit*, and his essays on socialist calculation.

The critique of the rationalist position is also important to Hayek's understanding of freedom. He argues that without giving everyone freedom to pursue their own goals, society would lose out on many benefits from individuals' efforts. As he puts it, "What is important is not what freedom I personally would like to exercise but what freedom some person may need in order to do things beneficial to society. This freedom we can assure to the unknown person only by giving it to all" (Hayek 2011, 84). If we protect individual freedom through general rules, we will all be able to coordinate through the market and achieve more than we could have if we planned outcomes in advance. In this way, Hayek argues that freedom is the absence of coercion. The individual is coerced when "he is forced to act not according to a coherent plan of his own but to serve the ends of another" (Hayek 2011, 71).

In addition to the openness to emotion that is suggested by his critique of rationality, there are other ways in which emotion plays an implicit role in Hayek's work. He relies on thinkers such as David Hume and Adam Smith, whose work is known for the primacy of emotion, to explain and defend spontaneous orders. He also acknowledges the importance of things like custom and habit that seem to arise from something like emotional attachment to others. For example, Hayek argues that general rules are only effective if customs and habits develop around them.

So, if Hayek is relatively silent on emotion, yet also acknowledges scholarship and relationships in society that depend on emotion, what exactly is the role of emotion in the Hayekian system? Is there space for emotion? If not, is this a fatal flaw?

I have two goals in this chapter. First, I want to consider emotion in Hayek's thought. Second, I want to explore the place of emotion in political economy. I argue that while Hayek seems to mostly ignore emotions or, when he does acknowledge them, note their problematic potential, emotion lurks in the background of his thinking. We see the underlying role of emotion in his reference to and reliance on the work of eighteenth-century Scottish Enlightenment thinkers. Their work acts as pieces of Hayek's political economy puzzle and demonstrates that emotion matters for him in some capacity. Beyond the sources he makes extensive use of, I argue that Hayek needs emotion because it is essential for interactions in the market process and is the basis for forming bonds that help maintain social cohesion. However, Hayek's critique of emotion is also important and clarifies the limits of emotion in political economy. Emotion is bad, for example, when it drives us to limit the freedom of others to satisfy our own feelings and goals. Finally, I argue that by locating and clarifying the place of emotion in Hayek, we can see that the characterization of his thought as devoid of emotion is unfair. Emotion exists in Hayek's thought and is necessary for a robust definition of the freedom afforded by the market order.

In what follows, I first describe emotions as they have been conceived in the history of political thought and in disciplines beyond political science. I especially focus on the definitions of emotion given by Hume and Smith because of their role in Hayek's thought. Second, I discuss the limits to reason in Hayek's account to demonstrate that Hayek is not necessarily anti-emotion. In section three, I focus on Hayek's limited and sometimes dismissive treatment of emotion. In section four, I suggest that emotion actually does play a role in Hayek's thought and is necessary for his vision of freedom and the functioning of a healthy political economy more generally. In the conclusion, I suggest that paying attention to emotion's role in Hayek's thought and the market process could help those interested in political economy speak to others who might be skeptical of the role of the market in social life.

WHAT ARE EMOTIONS?

Emotions are almost always discussed in opposition to rational thinking. Emotions are nonrational experiences of the mind in response to external circumstances. They are not pre-planned or conscious efforts, in the same way that rational thoughts are. They are reactions to external stimuli in the world. Susan James explains that the passions are always tied to the physical in some way. First, as she puts it: "Passions, it is agreed, have intrinsic physical manifestations which bridge emotion and action and are written on the body in facial expressions, blushings, tremblings, and postures" (James 1997, 4). She also discusses passions as unmediated responses to the outside world, which has driven many to argue that they must be controlled by reason. The simplest characterization of emotion is pleasure or displeasure in response to an external stimulus. We also discuss emotions as feelings, sentiments, and passions, though scholars have recognized that they are each distinct.[3] Lord Kames, who greatly influenced Hume and Smith, referred to passions and emotions synonymously as "all the feelings raised in us by external objects, those only of the eye and the ear are honored with the name passion or emotion" (Kames [1762] 2005, 32). He distinguishes sentiments, however, as "every thought prompted by a passion" (Kames [1762] 2005, 311).

Political scientists have recently been engaged in a debate about the relevance of emotions in political life. In response to the movement toward quantitative approaches to political science beginning with the behavioral revolution of the 1920–1930s,[4] and arguments for deliberative democracy today,[5] scholars argue that we ought to "bring the emotions back in" to the political discussion (Kingston and Ferry 2008). They argue that the separation of reason and emotion in political life is harmful because it eliminates the potential for emotion to be a motivating force for justice and building community.[6] This is precisely the kind of emotion that Hayek warns against because it leads societies to direct themselves toward specific ends and in doing so impedes individual liberty. Political scientists often think of Hayek as a proponent of the rational over the affective. His theory of spontaneous order, in particular, is seen as placing order and rationality above the affective, which is ironic because through his theory of spontaneous order Hayek means to reject theories that place rational systems above individual desires and pursuits.[7]

Cognitive and neuroscientists, however, are demonstrating that perhaps political scientists have created a false dichotomy between reason and emotion. Cognitive science has shown that emotions and rational thinking are the result of similar processes in the brain.[8] Similarly, neuroscience has shown that there is no real biological difference between these kinds of thinking.[9] Yet, in the history of political thought, emotion and reason have often been treated as opposed. The tension between emotion and reason is resolved with the argument that reason should control the passions.[10] This separation began with the ancients. For example, Plato's *Republic* argues for the need for reason to rule appetite and *thumos*, or spirit in the soul, in the same way that the philosopher kings should rule over the artisans and auxiliaries in the ideal city. Likewise the Roman philosophers, specifically the Stoics, argue for self-control by using the mind, or reason, to control the passions.

Eighteenth-century philosophers, however, argued for the importance of emotion in social and political interactions. For both David Hume and Adam Smith, emotions are the central basis for interactions among individuals in society, interactions that often result in some kind of social order. Emotions are defined as a prerational process by which we experience the world around us. For Hume, our emotions are based on our sensory impressions in society, while Smith focuses more on our emotions as facilitators for both conveying our experiences to others and understanding their experiences in turn through the mechanism of sympathy. In this chapter, I follow the Scots in defining emotion in terms of the passions or those impressions formed based on our experiences interacting with the world around us and other human beings.

Emotion in the Scottish Enlightenment Tradition

Hayek does not place much weight on the emotions that might inspire the system of coordination that he celebrates. He worries, as I have suggested, about emotions that motivate concerns for social justice because they interfere with our ability to coordinate with others based on our individual ends. However, the Scottish Enlightenment thinkers whose work forms part of the basis for his notion of spontaneous order argue that emotions are at the center of these kinds of orders. While Hayek argues that emotion can serve to undermine freedom and the coordination possible through the market process, Hume and Smith argue that emotion is essential for forming the human relationships that make political economy possible.

In his *A Treatise on Human Nature*, David Hume separates the kinds of thoughts that human beings have into impressions and ideas. Ideas, or our rational thoughts, are assessments of the impressions we have of the world. But ideas only occur in response to our impressions of the world. He defines impressions in terms of our emotional response to sensory experiences:

> Original impressions or impressions of sensation are such as without any antecedent perception arise in the soul, from the constitution of the body, from the animal spirits, or from the application of objects to the external organs. Secondary, or reflective impressions are such as proceed from some of these original ones, either immediately or by the interposition of its idea. Of the first kind are all the impressions of the senses, and all bodily pains and pleasures: Of the second are the passions, and other emotions resembling them. (Hume [1738] 2001, 2.1.1.1)

The passions come from our sensory experience with the external world, and Hume characterizes them as a kind of emotion. Our reasoning about the world comes from these affective judgments, rather than from *a priori* knowledge. He emphasizes throughout the *Treatise* that any reasoning about these passions can only occur after we have experienced them:

> Our ideas upon their appearance produce not their correspondent impressions, nor do we perceive any colour, or feel any sensation merely upon thinking of them. On the other hand we find, that any impression either of the mind or body is constantly follow'd by an idea, which resembles it, and is only different in the degrees of force and liveliness. The constant conjunction of our resembling perceptions, is a convincing proof, that the one are the causes of the other; and this priority of the impressions is an equal proof, that our impressions are the causes of our ideas, not our ideas of our impressions. (Hume [1738] 2001, 1.1.1.8)

For Hume, our passions are based on our reactions to the world around us as perceived through our senses. We then ascribe praise or blame to the things we experience. Reasoning, or ideas about impressions, only occurs after the initial experience of a sensation.

In fact, Hume's notion of justice as artifice and convention also begins with emotion. Rules of property and of justice arise from our interpersonal relationships with others and the things we agree on in families and small communities. Hume explains that justice is not an abstract idea, then, but based on emotions:

> 'Twas therefore a concern for our own, and the public interest, which made us establish the laws of justice; and nothing can be more certain, than that it is not any relation of ideas, which gives us this concern, but our impressions and sentiments, without which every thing in nature is perfectly indifferent to us, and can never in the least affect us. The sense of justice, therefore, is not founded on our ideas, but on our impressions. (Hume [1738] 2001, 3.2.2.20)

Justice is an artifice agreed on by people—a convention—in Hume's view. It is not based on universal concepts, but the particular experiences in any community. Rules of justice do not come from our reason, but from our reaction to the realities of our self-interest and scarce resources.

Adam Smith, however, focuses on how emotions are at the source of our experiencing sympathy, or fellow-feeling with those around us. The "principles in his [man's] nature, which interest him in the fortune of others," that famous first line in *Theory of Moral Sentiments*, are "pity or compassion, the emotion which we feel for the misery of others, when we either see it, or are made to conceive it in a very lively manner" (Smith [1759] 1982, I.i.1.1). He continues to describe these principles as "sentiments" and "original passions of human nature" (Smith [1759] 1982, I.i.1.1). For Smith, sympathy is a mechanism that allows us to put ourselves in another person's shoes. It is through our imagination that we conceive of what it would be like for our senses to experience what another is experiencing: "Though our brother is upon the rack, as long as we ourselves are at our ease, our senses will never inform us of what he suffers. They never did, and never can, carry us beyond our own person, and it is by the imagination only that we can form any conception of what are his sensations" (Smith [1759] 1982, I.i.1.2). In a similar manner to Hume's conception of the passions, for Smith, the senses still form the basis for our emotions, but are mediated through the imagination when we are experiencing fellow-feeling with another human being rather than experiencing what we might think of as a direct emotion based on our own experience of the world.

The kind of emotions Smith is most interested in, then, are those that are inspired in someone who is trying to sympathize with another, or the spectator who is experiencing sympathy with another person. He explains, "Whatever is the passion which arises from any object in the person principally concerned, an analogous emotion springs up, at the thought of his situation, in the breast of the attentive spectator" (Smith [1759] 1982, I.i.I.3). He is also interested in how this sympathetic process affects the emotions of the person principally concerned, that is how the person attempts to bring his or her emotions into harmony, or as Smith puts it "lowering his passion to that pitch" which those around the person can understand (Smith [1759] 1982, I.i.4.7). Our emotions are, through this process, the basis for our agreement or disagreement with others: "When the original passions of the person principally concerned are in perfect concord with the sympathetic emotions of the spectator, they necessarily appear to this last just and proper, and suitable to their objects; and, on the contrary, when, upon bringing the case home to himself, he finds that they do not coincide with what he feels, they necessarily appear to him unjust and improper" (Smith [1759] 1982, I.i.3.1). The judgments we make of virtue and vice depend on this emotional, sympathetic interaction between individuals. Smith summarizes this well when he says: "I judge of your sight by my sight, of your ear by my ear, of your reason by my reason, of your resentment by my resentment, of your love by my love. I neither have, nor can have, any other way of judging about them" (Smith [1759] 1982, I.i.3.10). For Smith, we connect to others through our emotions, and subsequently judge their behavior and our own. Sympathy is the basis for social coordination and connection to others in his account.

For Smith, freedom is usually thought of as independence. Interactions in the market through sympathy and self-interest allow individuals to coordinate with one another. Ryan Hanley puts it:

> His second defense [of commercial society] shares two fundamental similarities with the first defense . . . it rests on the resolution of a second paradox—in this case, the demonstration of how social interdependence promotes individual independence by severing direct dependence. Put differently, the mechanisms of commercial society promote not only universal opulence but also a universal freedom of which the weak are the principal beneficiaries. (Hanley 2009, 19)

Smith argues that our sympathetic and market interactions with one another allow us to coordinate so that we do not have to depend on one person in power who can exercise arbitrary authority over us. In other words, we no longer depend on a feudal lord for our daily sustenance.[11] But Smith also refers to a different kind of independence that comes from our emotional interaction with others through sympathy. When we continue to sympathize with others, we refine our notion of moral and immoral behavior. We learn to reflect on our own behavior through the approval or disapproval of others. Through these repeated interactions we develop what Smith calls the "impartial spectator," which allows us to judge the behavior of others and our own as an independent and objective observer would. Samuel Fleischacker describes this second kind of independence in Smith saying, "Independence is an ability to stand apart from both the material pressures and the moral attitudes of others: to shape one's own individual life despite the fact that one's very ability to think has itself been shaped by immersion in society" (Fleischacker 1999, 153). For Smith, emotional interactions with others are the basis for achieving political independence and personal autonomy.

For Hume and Smith, emotions are initial or natural reactions to things in the world that are then mediated by reason. In this way, emotions act as the basis for political and economic ties to others. Freedom is tied to emotion for both thinkers. For Hume, just rules that ensure individual liberty only arise from emotional interaction with others. Similarly for Smith, freedom can only be realized through sympathetic interaction with others that relies on fellow-feeling. For each thinker, freedom comes from social coordination. Political economy is unrealizable in either thinker's system without the role of emotions.

THE PRETENSE OF REASON

Hayek is very concerned about the rationality of the order that results from human action, not human design, and he situates this order in the eighteenth-century debates over rationality that began with Descartes.[12] Still, though Hayek is critical of emotion, he does not exactly fit into the dichotomy of reason versus emotion because he is also critical of the rational tradition. He argues against rational constructivism in favor of an evolutionary approach to the organization of society that he will sometimes defend based on theories of the Scottish Enlightenment. He emphasizes that the main difference between these two views is that "the rationalist tradition assumes that man was originally endowed with both the intellectual and the moral attributes that enabled him to fashion civilization deliberately, the evolutionists made it clear that civilization was the accumulated hard-earned result of trial and error" (Hayek 2011, 118). Hayek argues that the belief in reason sometimes leads individuals to think that they can organize society to meet certain ends, the same ends that are motivated by the emotional pull of justice. Hayek explains:

> The illusion that leads constructivist rationalists regularly to an enthronement of the will consists in the belief that reason can transcend the realm of the abstract and by itself is able to determine the desirability of particular actions. Yet it is always only in combination with the particular, non-rational impulses that reason can determine what to do, and its function is essentially to act as a restraint on emotion, or to steer action impelled by other factors. The illusion that reason alone can tell us what we ought to do, and that therefore all reasonable men ought to be able to join in the endeavor to pursue common ends as members

> of an organization, is quickly dispelled when we attempt to put it into practice. But the desire to use our reason to turn the whole of society into one rationally directed engine persists, and in order to realize it common ends are imposed upon all that can be justified by reason and cannot be more than the decisions of particular wills. (Hayek 1978a, 32)

The problem with rational constructivism is a belief in reason, especially the reason of one person, the planner, to solve all problems. Hayek argues for a limit to reason here because no one can possibly organize society such that every need of every individual will be met. He says this is particularly the case in large societies that are no longer "face-to-face" (Hayek 1978b, 12). Large societies are too diverse for everyone to agree on one set of ends. Therefore, he argues for a combination of the rational and nonrational to create rules in society. As he puts it, "If emotion or impulse tells them what they want, the conventional rules tell them how they will be able and be allowed to achieve it" (Hayek 1978b, 12). Interestingly, we see that Hayek allows for a supporting role for emotion here.

Hayek also describes the limits to reason in his argument for a price system in "The Use of Knowledge in Society." He argues, "the economic problem of society is thus not merely a problem of how to allocate 'given' resources . . . it is a problem of the utilization of knowledge which is not given to anyone in its totality" (Hayek 2014, 93–94). Society cannot be centrally planned because no one mind possesses all of the relevant information. In other words, no single mind possesses sufficient reason to know all of the information necessary to convey the prices of goods. This is why the price system is necessary: "Fundamentally, in a system in which the knowledge of the relevant facts is dispersed among many people, prices can act to coordinate the separate actions of different people in the same way as subjective values help the individual to coordinate the parts of his plan" (Hayek 2014, 99). The price system coordinates all of the information that is dispersed among members of society.

The critique of positivism in both his philosophy and psychology presents another form of Hayek's argument about the limits to reason. The positivists think that we can only study what can be observed and seen. Hayek disrupts this notion by presenting the mind as a spontaneous order itself. The mind constantly perceives and organizes information that is not specifically known to the individual's consciousness. In doing so, his description of the mind also emphasizes the limits to human reason. He critiques positivism, namely behavioral psychology, in this instance because it is focused on analyzing human beings' external responses to stimuli. The natural sciences are especially guilty of focusing only on what can be empirically studied in this manner. Hayek explains that facts in biology and facts in social science are different:

> I mention this because this historical relativism is a typical product of so-called "historicism" which is, in fact, a product of the misapplication of the scientistic prejudice to historical phenomena—of the belief that social phenomena are ever given to us as the facts of nature are given to us. They are accessible to us only because we can understand what other people tell us and can be understood only by interpreting other people's intentions and plans. (Hayek 2014, 92)

The natural sciences only are interested in facts that can be tested through observing external responses. Facts in the social sciences, however, must be interpreted through the researcher's own experience as a human being. Hayek explains the larger problem of what the behavioral approach misses about human consciousness:

> This reformulation of the central problem of psychology has thus been made necessary by the fact that the physical sciences, even in their ideal perfect development, give us only a partial explanation of the world as we know it through our senses and must always leave an unexplained residue. After we have learnt to distinguish events in the external world according to the different effects they have upon each other, and irrespective of whether they appear to us as alike or different, the question of what makes them appear alike or different to us still remains to be solved. . . . We want to know the kind of process by which a given physical situation is transformed into a certain phenomenal picture. (Hayek [1952] 2014, 7)

Hayek is interested in uncovering why certain things appear to the senses as similar or different. He wants to demonstrate what is possible for human beings to know and what is not. By acknowledging the existence of another order beyond the physical, the phenomenal order, he hopes to show that human beings cannot predict everything in the world based on external responses. The social sciences cannot limit themselves to this reality or they will miss part of the human experience.

Likewise, Hayek acknowledges that though all senses come from our experiences or external environment, they are not all controlled by these experiences: "There is, therefore, on every level, or in every universe of discourse, a part of our knowledge which, although it is the result of experience, cannot be controlled by experience, because it constitutes the ordering principle of that universe by which we distinguish the different kinds of objects of which it consists and to which our statements refer" (Hayek [1952] 2014, 169–70). This suggests that there must be some role for nonrational thought, be it senses or emotion that lies outside of the construction of society.

Still, Hayek argues that even in this alternative approach, considering human beings' sensory responses to external stimuli in the mind, that the mind cannot know everything about itself because the mind is doing the analysis. In his words, trying to complete the task of this kind of science is a "contradiction in terms" (Hayek [1952] 2014, 194). He makes a similar point in his "The Facts of the Social Sciences" about the limitation of human reason and the mind. He notes that though we process social phenomena via our own experiences because this is all we can do, this does not mean that all social facts are contained within the human mind.[13] It would be hubris to assume that one could know all the relevant facts. In other words, there is a limit to what we can know about the world through our rational capacity alone.

HAYEK'S SILENT EMOTIONS?

While Hayek emphasizes the importance of the nonrational, there is not an obvious role for emotion in his social theorizing. He is often silent on the role of emotion. For instance, even though Hayek relies on their work as the basis for his argument about spontaneous order and the market process, he does not emphasize the emotions underlying both Hume and Smith's theories. Further, Hayek does not distinguish between emotion-based theories that move us toward order in society. In fact, he groups together Mandeville, Smith, and Hume on this score. Hayek says of Mandeville:

> His main contention became simply that in the complex order of society the results of men's actions were very different from what they had intended, and that the individuals, in pursuing their own ends, whether selfish or altruistic, produced useful results for others which they did not anticipate or perhaps even know; and, finally, that the whole order of society, and even all that we call culture, was the result of individual strivings which had no such end in view, but which were channelled to serve such ends by institutions, practices, and rules which also had never been deliberately invented but had grown up by the survival of what proved successful. (Hayek 1978c, 253)

Hayek focuses on the way that Mandeville arrives at the notion of a kind of order—the hive—from the strivings of individuals, but passes over the selfish motivation behind these strivings. He similarly argues that the story is often read as "their 'selfish' aims which led the different persons to render services to each other" but argues that "This is much too narrow a view of the matter. Division of labour is extensively practiced also within organizations; and the advantages of the spontaneous order do not depend on people being selfish in the ordinary sense of this word" (Hayek 1978b, 110). In both cases, for the Scots and for Mandeville, Hayek focuses on the resulting order, not the emotional impetus that advances their theories in the direction of order.

Yet Smith feels that he and Mandeville are very far apart on whether we coordinate with one another based on selfish principles or our natural disposition to sympathize with another. For Smith, the basis of sympathy is an emotional interest in connecting to the experiences of other human beings. We desire the approbation of others. Further, we are naturally interested "in the fortune of others" and seek to imagine the situation of others and experience fellow-feeling with them (Smith [1759] 1982, I.i.1.1–4). But for Mandeville, Smith says, we only do things out of self-love: "Dr. Mandeville considers whatever is done from a sense of propriety, from a regard to what is commendable and praise-worthy, as being done from a love of praise and commendation, or as he calls it from vanity. Man, he observes, is naturally much more interested in his own happiness than in that of others, and it is impossible that in his heart he can ever really prefer their prosperity to his own" (Smith [1759] 1982, VII.ii.4.7). Smith sees his project as conflicting with Mandeville's because they see different emotional bases for human interaction.

Hayek sometimes acknowledges the role of something like Smithean sympathy that drives the ordering of society, but he also will critique Smith's overreliance on emotion. For example, in "The Creative Powers of a Free Civilization" Hayek asserts, "The successful combination of knowledge and aptitude is not selected by common deliberation, by people seeking a solution to their problems through a joint effort; it is the product of individuals imitating those who have been more successful and from their being guided by signs or symbols, such as prices offered for their products or expressions of moral or aesthetic esteem for their having observed standards of conduct—in short, of their using the results of the experiences of others" (Hayek 2011, 79–80). Here, Hayek sounds like Smith. He acknowledges the role of moral or aesthetic esteem in conveying information that allows individuals to pursue their ends and coordinate with others. Yet he also critiques Smith for elision between economic principles and emotions: "It was somewhat misleading, and did his cause harm, when Adam Smith gave the impression as if the significant difference were that between the egoistic striving for gain and the altruistic endeavor to meet known needs" (Hayek 1978b, 145). Hayek argues that people are better served when they seek their own ends without concern for others, in accordance with general rules. He uses the invisible hand metaphor to argue that social justice is best achieved when people are not actively seeking it. Here Hayek seems to resist the separation that Smith wanted to create between himself and Mandeville.

For Hayek, spontaneous orders are affectively neutral: "The important point about the catallaxy is that is reconciles different knowledge and different purposes which, whether the individuals be selfish or not, will greatly differ from one person to another" (Hayek 1978b, 110). Again, the motivation for action matters little. It does not matter whether emotion is present in an individuals' motivation for action, so long as the structure of the society allows individuals to coordinate this behavior resulting in an order that does not seek specific ends.

Hayek further passes over the importance of emotion in Smith's vision of commercial society in an essay titled "Adam Smith's Message in Today's Language." He argues that Smith has moved beyond a theory of society where emotions matter for the structure of society:

> It is an error that Adam Smith preached egoism: his central thesis said nothing about how the individual should use his increased product; and his sympathies were all with the benevolent use of his increased income. He was concerned with how to make it possible for people to make their contribution to the social product as large as possible; and this he thought required that they were paid what their services were worth to those to whom they rendered them. But his teaching nevertheless offended a deeply ingrained instinct that man had inherited from the earlier face-to-face society, the horde or the tribe, in which through hundreds of thousands of years the emotions were formed which still govern him after he has entered the open society. These inherited instincts demand that man should aim at doing a visible good to his known fellows, the "neighbor" of the Bible. (Hayek 1978c, 268)

Hayek is right that Smith does not argue that people often seek to achieve a visible good for another, but he does argue that there are general rules of morality and principles of justice that play a role when sympathetic interactions fail, namely when we practice self-deceit.[14] In short, the market mechanism is not the whole story in Smith's work. Emotions facilitate, coordinate, and also help provide limits to problematic passions, such as when we overvalue ourselves and do not see ourselves as an impartial spectator would. There is an important role for emotion in Smith's account of political economy that Hayek dismisses.

The few times that Hayek specifically refers to emotion are critical. His main critique of emotion is its role in motivating social justice. It is not that Hayek thinks helping the least advantaged is a problem, but he thinks that directing the economy toward a specific end—however well-meaning—disrupts the potential of the market to provide wealth and freedom. He argues that in this sense, emotions problematically lead individuals to a kind of hubris that makes them believe they can plan the economy and direct it toward specific ends. He explains:

> The commitment to "social justice" has in fact become the chief outlet for moral emotion, the distinguishing attribute of the good man, and the recognized sign of the possession of a moral conscience. Though people may occasionally be perplexed to say which of the conflicting claims advanced it its name are valid,

> scarcely anyone doubts that the expression has a definite meaning, describes a high ideal, and points to grave defects of the existing social order which urgently call for correction. (Hayek 1978b, 66)

Hayek thinks that the passion for social justice has become a form of coercion where people are expected to ascribe to it, though its meaning is unclear. Second, the commitment to social justice is ill-defined and non-scientific. Third, he argues that these emotions do not actually bring about social justice, but harm individuals more by preventing the spontaneous order that could have otherwise originated without planning: "I believe that 'social justice' will ultimately be recognized as a will-o'-the-wisp which has lured men to abandon many of the values which in the past have inspired the development of civilization—an attempt to satisfy a craving inherited from the traditions of the small group but which is meaningless in the Great Society of free men" (Hayek 1978b, 67). Hayek worries that this commitment to social justice has replaced other commitments, such as that to freedom that he argues inspired constitutional order in the first place.

He also critiques emotions when they interfere with our ability to coordinate with one another. He calls appeals to this part of our mind "tribal and primordial." For Hayek, society has expanded beyond the small tribe where this kind of communal, affective reasoning made sense. He argues that while some thinkers in the history of political philosophy, namely Rousseau, argue that emotion is natural, it is actually a product of our various experiences and the context of the society in which we live:

> The Rousseauesque nostalgia for a society guided, not by learnt moral rules which can be justified only by a rational insight into the principles on which this order is based, but by the unreflected "natural" emotions deeply grounded on millennia of life in the small horde, leads thus directly to the demand for a socialist society in which authority ensures that visible "social justice" is done in a manner which gratifies natural emotions. (Hayek 1978b, 147)

Hayek questions the idea that emotions are natural. This wrong-headed thinking is what leads people to direct society toward specific ends, such as Rousseau's society in the *Social Contract* where the legislator directs and educates the general will. He also questions whether "natural" emotions are the only way of fostering morality in society.

FREEDOM, EMOTION, AND POLITICAL ECONOMY

For Hayek, the critique of rational constructivism and the subsequent defense of the evolutionary development of society result in his argument for spontaneous order. These orders are the result of human action, not human design. He calls the particular kind of spontaneous order that arises in a market society a catallaxy (Hayek 1978b, 109). Hayek draws on the Scots to describe how this catallactic order arises without the deliberative intention of people to pursue specific ends: "The results of a catallaxy can never be judged just or unjust, only the actions of the individuals who participate, according to the rules of the order" (Hayek 1978b, 70). In a catallaxy, all individuals pursue their own ends. This idea further supports his critique of the rational constructivist mindset that plans society to meet specific ends, even those associated with achieving social justice. Hayek connects this insight to Adam Smith, arguing that he knew that the motivations of those who participate do not matter in the end, but they do need feedback about their actions in the process in order for everyone participating to get the relevant information.

Hayek will also use the Scots to describe how such an order arises without anyone seeking it. He argues that this order arises without any concern for emotion, conceived as directing society toward specific values or ends. Hayek explains how such an order arises: "In the Great Society we all in fact contribute not only to the satisfaction of needs of which we do not know, but sometimes even to the achievement of ends of which we would disapprove if we knew about them" (Hayek 1978b, 109–10). It is this idea of spontaneous order arising from the market process that Hayek adopts from Smith's metaphor of the invisible hand. However, Smith talks about the invisible hand first in his essay "The History of Astronomy," in reference to the hand of Jupiter, which human beings believe in to create order from a disordered universe.[15] The desire to seek order arises from a sentiment—wonder.

Hayek acknowledges this sentiment himself. For example, in "The Theory of Complex Phenomena," Hayek says, "Man has been impelled to scientific inquiry by wonder and by need" (Hayek 2014, 257). Hayek also footnotes this statement with a reference to Adam Smith's essay "History of Astronomy" where Smith discusses wonder as an important sentiment that motivates us to seek order in the world (Smith [1795] 1980, Intro.1). Smith explains why and how the sentiment of wonder motivates human beings to seek order, using his invisible hand metaphor for the first time:

> For it may be observed, that in all Polytheistic religions, among savages, as well as in the early ages of Heathen antiquity, it is the irregular events of nature only that are ascribed to the agency and power of their gods. Fire burns, and water refreshes; heavy bodies descend, and lighter substances fly upwards by the necessity of their own nature; nor was the invisible hand of Jupiter ever apprehended to be employed in those matters. But thunder and lightening, storms and sunshine, those more irregular events, were ascribed to his favour, or his anger. Man, the only designing power with which they were acquainted, never acts but either to stop, or to alter the course, which natural events would

> take if left to themselves. . . . And thus, in the first ages of the world, the lowest and must pusillanimous superstition supplied the place of philosophy. (Smith [1795] 1980, III.2)[16]

Smith argues that we used to attribute order and disorder in nature to the gods, but now human beings seek order in the world through their study of philosophy. But without the sentiment of wonder, we would never pursue such studies, in Smith's view. Wonder acts as a motivator for philosophy:

> Wonder, therefore, and not any expectation of advantage from its discoveries, is the first principle which prompts mankind to the study of Philosophy, of that science which pretends to lay open the concealed connections that unite the various appearances of nature; and they pursue this study for its own sake, as an original pleasure or good in itself, without regarding its tendency to procure them the means of many other pleasures. (Smith [1795] 1980, III.3)

Still, Smith is clear that those who study philosophy do so for its own sake, and not as a means to an end. And yet, there was an emotional impulse for this pursuit. Hayek appears to understand the importance of this sentiment, acknowledging it as motivation that compels human beings to study the world around them, just like Smith. However, though Smith discusses this within the context of the invisible hand, for Hayek, the notion of sentiment involved in the invisible hand metaphor disappears in his discussion of order.

Though Hayek is not explicit about its role, emotion seems to be part of the subtext of his argument for spontaneous orders that rely on culture for the institutional arrangements that support them. His emphasis on relationships demonstrates a concern for the emotion at the core of his work. Catallaxy is characterized by the ability of individuals to coordinate with one another without first having to agree on a set of outcomes. Catallaxy relies on relationships between individuals that are not enforced by a higher power. This is also the difference between the evolutionary and rationalist accounts. No one pre-plans the relationship between individuals in a catallaxy whereas they are predetermined in a centrally planned economy (Hayek 1978b, 114).

Nonrational bonds between human beings such as custom and tradition are important for Hayek because of their role in supporting institutional orders. Because they have grown up around and with institutions, customs become "both a product and a condition of freedom" (Hayek 2011, 123). These customs include "moral rules," "unconscious patterns of conduct," and "established habits and traditions" (Hayek 2011, 123). They are important for freedom because they are part of the framework that allows human beings to realize their plans. Understanding the customs and habits of others allows us to interact with them, and even to study them through the social sciences.[17] They form part of the spontaneous order.[18] Further, quoting Hume, Hayek acknowledges that morality does not come from our reason, but instead argues that it is part of the rules we decide on to coordinate our actions (Hayek 2011, 124). He mocks the hubris of the rationalists who think that the human mind is capable of constructing a framework that includes all of these aspects (Hayek 2011, 124). Recall also that Hayek suggests that emotion helps clarify what rules would best serve society: "If emotion or impulse tells them what they want, the conventional rules tell them how they will be able and be allowed to achieve it" (Hayek 1978b, 12). Yet he emphasizes that ultimately reason is a restraint on emotion.

Hayek's argument for political economy emphasizes a specific type of liberty that results from the kind of order he envisions. In "Liberty and Liberties," Hayek describes the kind of freedom he is interested in as individual or personal freedom, which he defines as reducing coercion "as much as is possible in society" (Hayek 2011, 57). The key distinction he makes is from freedom conceived only in terms of the community—what we typically call positive freedom, as discussed by Isaiah Berlin ([1958] 1969). But Hayek acknowledges that freedom always "refers solely to a relation of men to other men" (Hayek 2011, 60). Freedom is about relationships for Hayek and these relationships require leaving others free to choose their own actions and shape their lives as they wish, rather than coercing them to pursue ends that someone else has decided for them. Hayek distinguishes this freedom from many other kinds, but one important distinction he makes is between "inner freedom," which we think of as strength of will to pursue one's intentions and not being "slave to the passions" (Hayek 2011, 64). However, Hayek argues that this kind of freedom is not as important as ensuring that people are free from coercion.

Hayek's understanding of freedom relies on the notion of spontaneous order. They are co-constitutive. When individuals are free from pursuing the will of another, they are able to coordinate in many ever-changing, diverse ways that could never have been predicted by a single, rational mind. This allows for infinite creativity in human society, eventually improving the situation of everyone.

This conception of freedom is important for Hayek's seeming omission of emotion, because without emotion, Hayek's vision of freedom could not be realized. His notion of individuals being free from coercion relies on their coordination with one another through the market process without the direction of the state. The key distinction for Hayek is where and when the emotion is conceived. As we have seen, emotion should not be the motivating force for organizing society toward a specific goal. If this is the case, his condition of freedom as being free from coercion could never be realized because individuals would then lose the ability to develop relationships with one another as they seek unspecified ends. His system requires interaction and relationship between individuals to form spontaneous orders. How does this interaction happen without emotion? As the Scots teach us, emotion both drives our participation in the market, fueled by our desire to acquire, but also encourages us to moderate our passions so we can get what we need from others in society. As Smith puts it, "in the middling and inferior stations of life, the road to virtue and that to fortune . . . are happily in most cases, very nearly the same" ([1759] 1982, I.iii.3.5). Because market interactions incentivize us to care about others, we behave more morally toward them than we otherwise might (Storr forthcoming). Our sympathetic connection to others helps us achieve our individual goals but also helps us better relate to those around us. Our interaction with others helps us refine our behavior and consequently makes us more virtuous overall.

Hayek also repeatedly emphasizes the cultural interactions that must accompany spontaneous orders for them to persist. In one example Hayek gives of how the rules for such institutional arrangements are formed, he refers to Hume's theory of justice as artifice. Reflecting on the example, Hayek argues, "though these rules ultimately serve particular (though mostly unknown ends), they will do so only if they are treated not as means but as ultimate values, indeed as the only values common to all and distinct from the particular ends of the individuals. . . . Those rules which are common values serve the maintenance of an order of whose existence those who apply them are often not even aware" (Hayek 1978b, 17). Even though these rules are created, according to Hume because of the particular ends of individuals, including their emotional impressions of the world around them, Hayek has very little to say about the role of institutions in fostering or channeling emotions. Yet Hayek is clearly interested in the shared values that support the rules that allow the order to function.

Hayek thinks what I would call "productive emotions" come about from having a society governed by rules, though he does not specifically refer to emotions as such. He argues that all the connections we feel in the context of a society are only the result of the rules of that particular society:

> What we call the tradition or the national character of a people, and even the characteristic man-made features of the landscape of a country, are not particulars but manifestations of rules governing both the actions and perceptions of the people. Even where such traditions come to be represented by concrete symbols—a historical site, a national flag, a symbolic shrine, or the person of a monarch, or leader—these symbols "stand for" general conceptions which can be stated only as abstract rules defining what is and what is not done in that society. (Hayek 1978b, 12)

The important point here is that these emotions do not precede society, but are developed out of the order that human beings create together in society.

However, as we have seen in his discussion of Hume's theory of justice and Smith's discussion of wonder, Hayek also recognizes how emotions can contribute to our ability to form rules of conduct and coordinate with one another. Further, these rules help maintain a moral society because they teach individuals how to refine their behavior. The rules keep individuals responsible for their actions. Hayek explains, saying,

> If we allow men freedom because we presume them to be reasonable beings, we also must make it worth their while to act as reasonable beings by letting them bear the consequences of their decisions. This does not mean that a man will always be assumed to be the best judge of his interests; it means merely that we can never be sure who knows them better than he and that we wish to make full use of the capacities of all those who may have something to contribute to the common effort of making our environment serve human purposes. (Hayek 2011, 139)

Freedom requires trusting individuals to make their own decisions given an agreed upon set of rules. They will adjust their behavior in response to the rules. Hayek also dismisses the pretense of reason here. Individuals are not totally rational beings, but they understand themselves better than any outside person could.

Hayek resists that idea that emotions are the precursors to living together in society, and instead argues that we develop affection for others in society after we have spontaneously agreed upon rules that allow everyone to pursue their own ends. He argues commitments to social justice are "primordial" (Hayek 1981, 165). Hayek also resists these primordial emotions because they are opposed to individual freedom. He explains that emotions are the result of tribal society and opposed to the abstract order because they encourage individuals to seek specific ends and therefore obstruct freedom: "Yet it was the very restriction of coercion to the observance of the negative rules of just conduct that made possible the integration into a peaceful order of individuals and groups which pursued different ends; and it is the absence of prescribed common ends which makes a society of free men all that it has come to mean to us" (Hayek 1978b, 110–11). In tribal communities, emotion used to restrict behavior; however, in a market society "just conduct" is enforced by rules. For instance, Hayek cites Smith's belief in a natural justice as an example of property rights (Hayek 1978b, 109, f. 6). Still, it seems that Hayek cannot envision emotion on a scale other than the totality of society—"solidarity" (Hayek 1978b, 111)—which is ironic because Smith and Hume meet precisely this qualification.[19]

For Hayek, emotion is problematic when it interferes with the formation of spontaneous orders, as in the case of tribal or primordial emotions. Emotion is also problematic when it interferes with freedom in the market process because people are not allowed to determine and seek their own ends. In both of these cases, emotion problematically interferes with the rationality of the resulting order. However, these are specific limits on emotion. Hayek, however, also implicitly acknowledges the role of emotion in forming bonds between individuals in society, whether through a temporary market interaction, or through customs that reinforce the rules governing a catallaxy.

CONCLUSION

This chapter has shown that though Hayek wants to bracket emotion from his notion of political economy because of the danger of emotion leading to central planning, it is a necessary part of his theory and for our understanding of the market process more generally. I have shown where Hayek discusses emotion and have argued that he does not fall clearly on either side of the emotion versus reason debate. However, Hayek did himself no favors by writing as though emotion served no part of his project. By dismissing emotion and concerns for social justice, Hayek contributes to visions of the market as devoid of moral concerns. Hayekian scholars have done much to change this perception of the market as morally reprehensible (e.g., Boettke 2004; Lavoie and Chamlee-Wright 2000; Storr 2008), showing how Hayek's argument brings about morally desirable outcomes in society that satisfy our emotional desires for justice and bettering the situation of the least advantaged; but they have not interrogated the concept of emotion in Hayek's corpus.

This chapter opens the possibility for thinking about emotion playing an important role in Hayek's theory and in political economy more generally. It is an attempt to show that there is room for the affective in Hayek's project and that it is, in fact, necessary for a robust definition of freedom in his work. Further, this chapter also corrects misconceptions of Hayek's work as treating individuals as automatons who operate only on rational bases. Emotion plays a specific role in Hayek's conception of the market process. Emotion is key for the interactions and eventual relationships that make spontaneous orders possible. But it is important for his conception of political economy that emotion not direct orders toward specific ends. Though Hayek appears to be almost silent on emotion, it is there in the background of his theory, doing the important work of allowing individuals to coordinate with one another.

NOTES

I would like to thank Peter Boettke, Jayme Lemke, Virgil Storr, and the members of the Adam Smith Fellowship Research Sequence 2016–2017—Mikołaj

Barczentewicz, Crystal Dozier, Adam Frost, Dan Gibbs, Samantha Godwin, Caleb Harrison, Liz Hemsley, Brian Kogelmann, Matthew Martinez, and Greg Robson—for their difficult questions and excellent insights on earlier versions of this chapter which helped to bring it to completion. All remaining errors are my own.

1. See, for example, Peter J. Boettke, Christopher J. Coyne, and Peter T. Leeson (2008, 7).

2. Sandel argues that the market cannot adequately account for all moral considerations, though he does not specifically mention Hayek (Sandel, 2012). Galeotti argues that Hayek's theory should include a communitarian aspect because no account of social coordination can exclude this aspect of human life or there will be conflict in the society (Galeotti 1987).

3. Michael Frazer (2013), for example, argues that sentiments are moral judgments that contain emotions and passions, but are not relativistic.

4. For an account of behavioralism in political science, see Robert A. Dahl (1961). See also Thomas S. Engeman (1995). Engeman discusses specifically the tension between the history of political thought and scientific approaches to political science.

5. For a summary of deliberative democracy and its role in promoting rational political conversation, see A. Gutmann and D. Thompson (1996).

6. See, for example, Sharon R. Krause (2008); Martha Craven Nussbaum (2013).

7. See, for example, Michelle Schwarze and John T. Scott (2015). Schwarze and Scott argue that Hayek reads only spontaneous order into Smith's theory, missing his emphasis on the role of disorder and sympathy, especially in promoting justice.

8. See, for example, Gerd Gigerenzer (2007). Gigerenzer shows that decision making is not strictly a rational endeavor, but also relies on unconscious processes.

9. See, for example, Antonio R. Damasio (1995). Damasio argues that our rational capacity relies on both the high- and low-level brain regions and that emotions are also regulated by these same low-level brain regions (1995, xiii). Also note that Hayek blames the emphasis on rational constructivism in Europe on Descartes (Hayek 2014, 293; McDermott 2004).

10. Albert Hirschman has famously traced the development of the idea that interests should control the passions (Hirschman 2013).

11. See for example, "Such a proprietor, as he feeds his servants and retainers at his own house, so he feeds his tenants at their houses. The subsistence of both is derived from his bounty, and its continuance depends upon his good pleasure" (Smith [1776] 1981, 414–15).

12. See "The Results of Human Action but Not of Human Design," in *The Market and Other Orders* (Hayek [1967] 2014).

13. "If we can understand only what is similar to our own mind, it necessarily follows that we must be able to find all that we can understand in our own mind" (Hayek 2014, 82).

14. See Samuel Fleischacker (2011).

15. This is a key piece of evidence marshaled by Schwarze and Scott in their argument that Smith was a theorist of disorder in addition to order. See Schwarze and Scott (2015).

16. For more on Smith's first use of the term "invisible hand," see Alec Macfie (1971).

17. See *The Market and Other Orders* (Hayek 2014, 249). "The problem which arises here is known in the discussion of the methodology of the social sciences as that of Verstehen (understanding). We have seen that this understanding of the meaning of actions is of the same kind as the understanding of communications (i.e. of action intended to be understood). It includes what the eighteenth-century authors described as sympathy and what has more recently been discussed under the heading of 'empathy.' Since we shall be concerned chiefly with the use of these perceptions as data for the theoretical social sciences, we shall concentrate on what is sometimes called rational understanding (or rational construction), that is, on the instances where we recognize that the persons in whose actions we are interested base their decisions on the meaning of what they perceive."

18. For more on how culture helps form spontaneous order by facilitating social cooperation, see Peter Boettke (1990).

19. Consider, for example, Smith's argument about the limits to our ability to sympathize with distant others: "Men, though naturally sympathetic, feel so little for another, with whom they have no particular connexion, in comparison of what they feel for themselves; the misery of one, who is merely their fellow-creature, is of so little importance to them in comparison even of a small conveniency of their own" ([1759] 1982, II.ii.3.4). For a helpful argument on the implications of this part of Smith's theory, see Fonna Forman-Barzilai (2005).

REFERENCES

Berlin, Isaiah. [1958] 1969. "Two Concepts of Libery." In *Four Essays on Liberty*. Oxford: Oxford University Press.

Boettke, Peter. 1990. "The Theory of Spontaneous Order and Cultural Evolution in the Social Theory of F. A. Hayek." *Cultural Dynamics* 3 (1): 61–83.

_______. 2004. "Morality as Cooperation." In *Morality of Markets*, edited by P. J. Shah, 43–50. New Delhi: Academic Foundation.

Boettke, Peter J., Christopher J. Coyne, and Peter T. Leeson. 2008. "The Continuing Relevance of F. A. Hayek's Political Economy." *Explorations in Austrian Economics* 11: 79–98.

Dahl, Robert A. 1961. "The Behavioral Approach in Political Science: Epitaph for a Monument to a Successful Protest." *American Political Science Review* 55 (4): 763–72.

Damasio, Antonio R. 1995. *Descartes' Error: Emotion, Reason, and the Human Brain*. New York: Avon Books.

Engeman, Thomas S. 1995. "Behavioralism, Postbehavioralism, and the Reemergence of Political Philosophy." *Perspectives on Political Science* 24 (4): 214–17.

Fleischacker, Samuel. 1999. *Third Concept of Liberty: Judgment & Freedom in Kant & Adam Smith*. Princeton, NJ: Princeton University Press.

_______. 2011. "True to Ourselves? Adam Smith on Self-Deceit." *Adam Smith Review* 6: 75–92.

Forman-Barzilai, Fonna. 2005. "Sympathy in Space(s): Adam Smith on Proximity." *Political Theory* 33 (2): 189–217.

Frazer, Michael. 2013. "Sentimentalism without Relativism." *Nomos* 53: 19–37.

Galeotti, Anna Elisabetta. 1987. "Individualism, Social Rules, Tradition: The Case of Friedrich A. Hayek." *Political Theory* 15 (2): 163–81.

Gigerenzer, Gerd. 2007. *Gut Feelings: The Intelligence of the Unconscious*. New York: Viking.

Gutmann, A., and D. Thompson. 1996. *Democracy and Disagreement*. Cambridge, MA: Harvard University Press.

Hanley, Ryan Patrick. 2009. *Adam Smith and the Character of Virtue*. Cambridge: Cambridge University Press.

Hayek, Friedrich A. [1952] 2014. *The Sensory Order: An Inquiry into the Foundations of Theoretical Psychology*. Mansfield Centre, CT: Martino Fine Books.

_______. [1967] 2014. "The Results of Human Action but Not of Human Design." In *The Collected Works of F. A. Hayek*. Vol. 15: *The Market and Other Orders*. Chicago: University of Chicago Press.

_______. 1978a. *Law, Legislation and Liberty*. Vol. 1: *Rules and Order*. Chicago: University of Chicago Press.

_______. 1978b. *Law, Legislation and Liberty*. Vol. 2: *The Mirage of Social Justice*. Chicago: University of Chicago Press.

_______. 1978c. *New Studies in Philosophy, Politics, and Economics and the History of Ideas*. London: Routledge.

_______. 1981. *Law, Legislation and Liberty*. Vol. 3: *The Political Order of a Free People*. Chicago: University of Chicago Press.

_______. 2011. *The Constitution of Liberty: The Definitive Edition*. Chicago: University of Chicago Press.

_______. 2014. *The Collected Works of F. A. Hayek*. Vol. 15: *The Market and Other Orders*. Chicago: University of Chicago Press.

Hirschman, Albert O. 2013. *The Passions and the Interests Political Arguments for Capitalism before Its Triumph*. Princeton, NJ: Princeton University Press.

Hume, David. [1738] 2001. *A Treatise of Human Nature*. Edited by David Fate Norton and Mary J. Norton. Oxford: Oxford University Press.

James, Susan. 1997. *Passion and Action: The Emotions in Seventeenth-Century Philosophy*. Oxford: Oxford University Press.

Kames, Lord, Henry Home. [1762] 2005. *Elements of Criticism*. Vols. 1 and 2. Indianapolis: Liberty Fund.

Kingston, Rebecca, and Leonard Ferry. 2008. *Bringing the Passions Back In: The Emotions in Political Philosophy*. Vancouver: UBC Press.

Krause, Sharon R. 2008. *Civil Passions: Moral Sentiment and Democratic Deliberation*. Princeton, NJ: Princeton University Press.

Lavoie, Don, and Emily Chamlee-Wright. 2000. "The Market Order and the Moral Order." In *Culture and Enterprise: The Development, Representation, and Morality of Business*, 104–27. London: Routledge.

Macfie, Alec. 1971. "The Invisible Hand of Jupiter." *Journal of the History of Ideas* 32 (4): 595–99.

McDermott, Rose. 2004. "The Feeling of Rationality: The Meaning of Neuroscientific Advances for Political Science." *Perspectives on Politics* 2 (4): 691–706.

Nussbaum, Martha Craven. 2013. *Political Emotions: Why Love Matters for Justice*. Cambridge, MA: Belknap Press of Harvard University Press.

Sandel, Michael J. 2012. *What Money Can't Buy: The Moral Limits of Markets*. New York: Farrar, Straus and Giroux.

Schwarze, Michelle, and John T. Scott. 2015. "Spontaneous Disorder in Adam Smith's Theory of Moral Sentiments: Resentment, Injustice, and the Appeal to Providence." *Journal of Politics* 77 (2): 463–76.

Smith, Adam. [1759] 1982. *The Theory of Moral Sentiments*. Edited by D. D. Raphael and A. L. Macfie. Indianapolis: Liberty Fund.

_______. [1776] 1981. *An Inquiry into the Nature and Causes of the Wealth of Nations, Vols. 1 and 2*. Edited by R. H. Campbell, A. S. Skinner, and W. B. Todd. Indianapolis: Liberty Fund.

_______. [1795] 1980. "The History of Astronomy." In *Essays on Philosophical Subjects*, edited by W. L. D. Wightman. Indianapolis: Liberty Fund.

Storr, Virgil Henry. 2008. "The Market as a Social Space: On the Meaningful Extra-economic Conversations That Can Occur in Markets." *Review of Austrian Economics* 21 (2–3): 135–50.

_______. Forthcoming. "The Impartial Spectator and the Moral Teachings of Markets." In *Oxford Handbook of Freedom*, edited by D. Schmidtz. New York: Oxford University Press.

Chapter 4

Justificatory Failures and Moral Entrepreneurs

A Hayekian Theory of Public Reason

Brian Kogelmann

> Reason can only help us to *see what are the alternatives before us*, which are the values which are in conflict, or which of them are true ultimate values and which are, as is often the case, only mediate values which derive their importance from serving others values. Once this task is accomplished, however, *reason cannot help us further*.
>
> —F. A. Hayek, "Kinds of Rationalism" (1967 [2014]; emphasis added)

Ever since John Locke asserted in the *Second Treatise of Government* that all men naturally exist in "a state of perfect freedom to order their actions" as well as "a state also of equality, wherein all the power and jurisdiction is reciprocal," the ideas of freedom and equality have been at the normative bedrock of liberalism (Locke [1690] 1980, 8). The most sophisticated contemporary articulation of these twin ideals is done by a school of political theories that all fall under the broad heading *public reason liberalism*. Beginning with John Rawls's *Political Liberalism* and reaching its current (though certainly not final) zenith in Gerald Gaus's *The Order of Public Reason*, public reason liberalism holds—very roughly—that coercive rules implemented and enforced by the state must be justified to all persons in society. When such is the case we treat persons *freely*, because it is each person's own reason that is sovereign in terms of deciding which sorts of commands must be obeyed; and we treat persons *equally*, because no person's reason claims authority over the reason of any other.

There is a trite yet forceful criticism of public reason liberalism in the current literature: that the set of coercive rules that is indeed justified to *everyone* happens to be the *empty set*. That is, given the diversity in terms of evaluative standards we find characterizing contemporary liberal orders, the prospect of actually finding a set of rules to live by justified to all is slim indeed. Call this the *justificatory failure critique* (JFC). The JFC is usually cashed out in terms of illiberal dissenters: the presence of those holding illiberal values will effectively veto liberal institutions as justified (Abbey 2007; Okin 2005; Quong 2012, 2014; Raz 1998; Sleat 2013; Taylor 2011).The JFC need not rely on such individuals, though. Even when all hold liberal values, it is by no means obvious we can find a set of rules to live by that meet the public reason liberal's justificatory demands—witness here the sharp policy divides between Democrats and Republicans (both typically in the broadly liberal camp) over questions such as abortion, welfare entitlements, and so on. Though many rejoinders have been offered by public reason liberals in response to the JFC, I believe that all such attempts fail (§2). In response, this chapter uses the tools and insights from F. A. Hayek's social philosophy to rescue public reason liberalism from this powerful criticism.

In our rescue of public reason, we begin by noting an assumption the JFC makes: that all possible institutional arrangements that could serve to help us live better together are currently known to us as theorists (§3). But once we take seriously Hayek's insights concerning the limits of human knowledge then such an assumption is obviously untenable: knowledge of such a kind is either dispersed in a decentralized manner or, quite possibly, not yet known by anyone at all. But, as Hayek further notes, though individuals always face incurable ignorance, structuring institutions properly can allow for society to grapple with this knowledge problem by both allowing and incentivizing individuals to reveal the private information they have that no one else does, as well as discover new information currently known by none.

This suggests a novel solution for the public reason liberal in the face of justificatory failures: the public reason liberal should endorse institutions that allow for and incentivize the discovery of institutional arrangements that can meet public reason liberalism's justificatory demands. Such a response prompts an investigation into which institutions best perform this function. We begin by turning to the emerging literature on epistemic democracy, which holds that democratic institutions possess desirable epistemic properties, perhaps allowing persons to find arrangements satisfying the public reason liberal's justificatory requirements (§4).

But there is a problem with such proposals: though epistemic democrats highlight mechanisms detailing how such rules can be found, such mechanisms do not *incentivize* the discovery of such rules. This spurs an investigation into a quite different mechanism with desirable epistemic properties that is *also* incentive-compatible: namely, Hayek's emphasis on the use of competition as a discovery procedure (§5). It is here argued that the public reason liberal should endorse a system of competition in governance—or, in other words, a polycentric governance system—that allows and incentivizes persons to find rules justified to all (§6). That is, the public reason liberal should endorse a system where moral entrepreneurs remedy our justificatory failures, just as entrepreneurs remedy market failures. This, I think, is the best hope we have of living in a just and stable liberal society that lives up to the ideals of freedom and equality lying at the very heart of the liberal ideal. There is a concluding section.

PUBLIC REASON AND JUSTIFICATORY FAILURES

Public reason liberalism says that coercive rules and institutions must be justified to all. We shall call this normative requirement the *public justification principle*. If a society satisfies the public justification principle, then it treats all as free and equal moral persons—all coercive restrictions on behavior are grounded in each person's own reason, which means that people are free in the sense that it is their own standards governing their life, and equal in the sense that no one person's reason is sovereign over any other's. If a society fails to satisfy the public justification principle, then it does not treat all persons as free and equal—some people are forced to obey the reason of others, meaning they are not free. And, since some are subjects and others sovereigns, persons are also not equal.

The JFC says that the public justification principle likely will not be satisfied. To see why, we need to flesh out more details of the public reason framework; in doing so we follow Gaus's most recent articulation of the public reason project (Gaus 2011). We can think of all citizens as having preferences over possible rules available for them to implement when it comes to some certain domain of social interaction—say, what restrictions on rights of transfer should be. Suppose we have three persons in society: Althea, Bertha, and Cassidy. Further suppose that there are five rules up for debate (r_1–r_5), and that our three parties rank the rules as shown in Table 4.1.

Notice in Table 4.1 the option of "blameless liberty." When blameless liberty obtains there is no rule regulating the particular area of social interaction we are theorizing about—something like anarchy obtains, though the exact

Table 4.1 Ranking of Proposals

Althea	*Bertha*	*Cassidy*
r_1	r_1	r_2
r_2	r_2	r_1
r_3	r_3	r_3
r_4	r_4	r_5
Blameless Liberty	Blameless Liberty	Blameless Liberty
r_5	r_5	r_4

way of specifying what the absence of any regulation looks like is a difficult question that we push to the side (Gaus 2011, 310–21). In placing a particular way of regulating social interaction (say, r_5) below blameless liberty Althea is saying that she would rather have *no* rule regulating this area of social life than *that* rule because, according to her evaluative standards, the rule placed below blameless liberty is *so objectionable* that she would rather run the risk of no regulation at all than be subject to the authority of the particular rule in question.

Clearly, implementing a rule that Althea places below blameless liberty fails to treat her as free and equal. On the standard public reason picture, treating Althea as a free and equal moral person entails only claiming authority over Althea that Althea herself could endorse. But if Althea, after careful consideration, finds a way of regulating social life to be so objectionable that she prefers blameless liberty to it, then clearly she does not reflectively endorse that particular rule, making implementation of that rule inconsistent with treating her as free and equal. The JFC thus holds that it is likely that *every* candidate rule will be placed below blameless liberty by at least *some* citizen—every rule will be considered by some citizen as worse than a state of no rule regulating the relevant area of conduct at all. Thus, the purveyor of the JFC says that situations, like those shown in Table 4.2 below, are the rule, not the exception. In this case there is no possible rule to implement that satisfies the public justification principle—there is no possible way we can treat all persons as free and equal.

There are three broad strategies public reason liberals employ in response to the JFC. The first strategy appeals to *idealization*. Now, when public reason liberals hold that coercive rules must be justified to all persons, they are not seeking actual consent, what Gaus calls *justificatory populism* (Gaus 1996, 130–31). Rather, they want to ensure that all persons have reason to endorse a society's system of coercive rules. Here is an example of this distinction. Suppose a man is about to walk across a broken bridge, yet he does not know it is broken. Further suppose that if the man knew it was

Table 4.2 Justificatory Failure

Althea	*Bertha*	*Cassidy*	*Dupree*	*Esau*
r_1	r_2	r_3	r_5	r_4
r_5	r_5	r_1	r_2	r_5
r_4	r_1	r_4	r_4	r_3
r_2	r_3	r_2	r_3	r_1
Blameless Liberty	Blameless Liberty	Blameless Liberty	Blameless Liberty	Blameless Liberty
r_3	r_4	r_5	r_1	r_2

broken then he would not try to cross it. A worried onlooker wrestles the mistaken man down, only to have the would-be bridge-crosser resist. Here, the man trying to cross the bridge does not actually consent to the coercive interference imposed by the onlooker—but, by assumption of the case, such interference is justified by the man's own reason.

One response to the JFC holds that if we idealize enough—if we make sure persons reason perfectly and never error—then they will all endorse a non-empty set of coercive restrictions. This response thus holds that the reason so many rules are placed below blameless liberty by so many actual citizens is because they are not reasoning well; they are not fully considering what their own evaluative commitments say is actually justified. There are two problems with this response to the JFC. First, it could be that idealizing persons too much ends up defeating the initial purpose of the public reason project. On Gaus's account of moderate idealization, idealization of an individual's reasons "must be accessible" to persons in a world "in which cognitive activity has significant costs" (Gaus 2011, 253). But suppose we idealize even further beyond this moderate account in hopes of finding the agreement we seek. If we do idealize to the point that our idealized model of individuals is no longer accessible to their actual counterpart, then it is hard to see how we treat them freely and as equals—or, at the very least, it is hard to see how *they themselves* could see that they are being treated freely and equally. Note: This is very different from the case of the man about to cross the bridge where we moderately idealize; it should not take too much thought for him to realize that he did indeed have reason not to cross that bridge. But if we idealize too greatly in search of agreement, then justifications of coercion may not be accessible to the actual persons we are supposedly trying to justify the coercion to.

A second worry is that *even if* there was no problem with radically idealizing persons in our search for agreement, it is still by no means obvious that modeling persons as perfect reasoners would actually rid us of justificatory failures. For the idealization rejoinder to the JFC to be compelling some kind of proof must be provided—it must be shown that flawless reasoning will indeed lead all individuals to endorse the same sorts of coercive rules and institutions. Since no uncontroversial proof of this exists, the idealization strategy fails to effectively counter the JFC.

Another response to the JFC is to narrow the scope of persons to whom we owe justification to. This is the approach taken by Jonathan Quong in his recent articulation of the public reason project (Quong 2011). According to Quong, public reason liberalism is not about justifying *actual* rules to *actual* persons in *actual* societies—because this is true, we do not have to worry about the evaluative diversity characterizing contemporary liberal orders as leading to justificatory failures. Rather, public reason liberalism is about modeling ideally just liberal orders populated by a specific type of individuals. As such, the public justification principle only requires we justify coercive rules to those kinds of persons that inhabit such a model society. Such an understanding of the public reason project "does not see the fact of reasonable pluralism as something external to liberal theory. It is not simply a fact about the world, like scarce resources, to which liberal theory must accommodate itself. It is, instead, a fact about liberalism" (Quong 2011, 142).

Now, I do not think there is anything particularly wrong with Quong's version of the public reason project—it is an interesting intellectual exercise to model ideal liberal societies, determine the kinds of conditions that would characterize them, and then check to see if these conditions are consistent with our normative ideals of freedom and equality. I do not, however, see why this is the only way the public reason project must succeed. There are many motivations for inquiring into the normative status of our shared social world, and some of these motivations require we take seriously the actual levels of evaluative diversity we confront, rather than circumscribe our attention to idealized models. One such motivation, in the words of Gaus, is to see, when we demand that others obey the rules and regulations we place on them, whether we actually have authority to make such claims or whether we are just "pushing people around" (Gaus 2011, 16). To make sure we take seriously the possibility that we are just pushing people around we cannot assume away the actual diversity that surrounds us. But if this is so then Quong's response to the JFC is off-limits: we cannot address the problem of nothing being publicly justified by circumscribing our attention to idealized models while remaining faithful to the original goals of the theoretical exercise.

A final response to the JFC is to change what it is that public reason is about. This is the approach taken in a recent article by Chad Van Schoelandt (2015). Van Schoelandt argues that though public justification is not necessary for justifying coercion, it *is* necessary for forming a *bona fide* moral community—a community where persons hold each other responsible for their actions via the reactive attitudes of blame and resentment. Thus, it is important to make sure all have reason to endorse the rules we place on them *not* to justify the coercion these rules inflict, but rather to form the right kind of community with our fellow citizens. Here I do not want to disagree with Van Schoelandt's claim concerning the relationship between moral communities and the public justification principle. Still, there must be *something* that justifies the state's use of coercive force, lest we inhabit a world that is unjust to its core. And, if it is liberal values that are to do this job, then there must be some relationship between the ideas of freedom and equality that tell us when the state's use of force is justified or not. Arguing that there exists an important relationship between public justification and moral community leaves this puzzle unsolved—the puzzle we are primarily concerned with, and the puzzle the JFC doubts can indeed be solved at all.

THE JFC'S FATAL CONCEIT

The JFC says that given the evaluative diversity we find characterizing contemporary liberal orders, there is no set of rules that all persons deem justified; since this is true nothing is justified, meaning the public reason project fails. In making this charge the purveyor of the JFC must reason as follows: first, we begin by looking at the set of all possible rules $R = \{r_1, r_2,\ldots, r_n\}$. From there we look at the set of evaluative standards we find in contemporary liberal societies $E = \{e_1, e_2,\ldots, e_n\}$. Then, we see that for every r_m in our set R there will be at least one e_m in our set E that judges r_m to be unjustified, in that e_m places r_m below blameless liberty. This means that every r_m fails to satisfy the public justification principle.

Note, though, that purveyors of the JFC have made two key assumptions here: that they can enumerate in detail both sets R and E. Now enumeration of set E depends on empirical observation of the kinds of diversity we find in liberal societies and thus does not seem terribly implausible. Let us then focus attention on the first assumption, that the purveyors of the JFC can offer a precise characterization of all those elements in R. To show that there is always some member of R that has a corresponding member of E that could reasonably reject it, one must be able to enumerate all the members making up R. That is, for any given domain of social interaction one must be able to say what *all* the different possible rules for regulating that domain of interaction are. Then, and only then, can one plausibly argue that each member of R could be rejected by some member of E.

The assumption that the theorist propagating the JFC possesses such knowledge lines up with what Hayek in many places calls the *rational constructivist* approach to social order. In the *The Constitution of Liberty*, Hayek draws a distinction between two different schools of historical thought that are broadly understood as being defenders of the liberal order, even though they differ greatly in their underlying theoretical commitments (Hayek [1960] 2011, chap. 4). One school of thought is associated with the Scottish Enlightenment and thinkers such as Adam Smith, David Hume, and Bernard Mandeville. We can label this broad school of thought as *anti-rationalist*. The other school of thought is associated with the French Enlightenment and thinkers such as René Descartes, Jean-Jacques Rousseau, and Marquis de Condorcet. We can label this broad school of thought as *rational constructivist*—the school of thought that the purveyor of the JFC implicitly lines him- or herself up with.

Broadly speaking, those associated with the Scottish Enlightenment understood all social order and hence the development of liberal institutions as the result of a slow, spontaneous, evolutionary process. These thinkers "find the origin of institutions, not in contrivance or design, but in the survival of the successful . . . [They stress] what we call the political order is much less the product of our ordering intelligence than is commonly imagined" (Hayek [1960] 2011, 112). Those associated with the French Enlightenment, however, understood all social order as the result of deliberate human planning and engineering—a sort of literal social contract where parties to this contract design society from scratch. With this cluster of theories, the "idea of intelligent men coming together for deliberation about how to make the world anew" is the characteristic feature all such theories share in common (Hayek [1960] 2011, 113).

A large body of Hayek's work highlights the impossibility of rational constructivism along with the dangers of attempting to carry out a rationally constructivist project and, inevitably, failing. There are, I believe, two key premises to Hayek's argument concerning the impossibility of rational constructivism: (1) Hayek lists all the information required in order for one to successfully carry out such a project; and (2) Hayek points out that no single person or group of people actually possesses the requisite knowledge enumerated in (1). Thus, one cannot successfully carry out a rational constructivist project, making rational constructivism an empirically as well as normatively flawed social theory.

These two premises are succinctly captured in the following passage:

> Complete rationality of action in the Cartesian sense demands complete knowledge of all the relevant facts. A designer or engineer needs all the data and full power to control or manipulate them if he is to organize the material objects to produce the intended result. But the success of action in society depends on more particular facts than anyone can possibly know. And our whole civilization in consequence rests, and must rest, on our believing much that we cannot know to be true in the Cartesian sense. (Hayek [1973] 1998, 13)

It is important to note just how strong a claim Hayek makes with premise (2). He is not merely saying that acquiring this knowledge would be difficult or is currently infeasible. Rather, Hayek says that our ignorance is "necessary," "irremediable," and "incurable" (Hayek [1973] 1998, 14). It is a part of the human condition—something we must learn to live with.

Now the claim I want to make in this section is *not* that the purveyor of the JFC is a rational constructivist—given that those who make this critique only necessarily have in the common the fact that they criticize public reason in a similar way, it would be a stretch to claim that they endorse the constructing and designing of social orders *de novo*. What I do want to emphasize, though, is that the defender of the JFC is committed to rational constructivist assumptions, assumptions that Hayek forcefully argues against. More specifically, purveyors of the JFC—when they tell the public reason liberal that for every member in *R* there exists a defeater in *E*—*assume that they know the full content of R*. That is, they assume they can list out all possible ways of organizing social order and then, from there, are able to show how no such possible arrangement will actually satisfy the public justification principle. Contrast this with Hayek's anti-rationalist claim that the true "inventors" of liberal institutions did not design nor could they foresee the benefits such institutions would bring—rather, through a slow evolutionary process such institutions developed, and it was only *after* they developed that their desirable properties could be appreciated by those theorists of the Scottish Enlightenment (Hayek [1960] 2011, 107–8).

It should be noted that the public reason liberal is not committed to these constructivist assumptions. Public reason liberals do not assert that it will necessarily be the case that there will in fact be at least one member of *R* that every member of *E* deems justified—if they did do this, then they too would be committed to being able to fully enumerate *R*. Though Gaus does offer some considerations for why he thinks the set of justified rules will not be the empty set, it is not a foregone conclusion of the public reason project that things will work out so smoothly (Gaus 2011, 323). Indeed, in Rawls's initial attempt at the public reason project he often says that the existence of an overlapping consensus on a shared system of rules is a mere hope, not something to be taken for granted (Rawls [1993] 2005, 40, 65, 172, 246, 252, 392).

Purveyors of the JFC might have a response to our Hayekian critique: they are not claiming that there is *no* member of *R* that could pass the public justification test. For—they might grant after a quick study of Hayek—such a set could not fully be enumerated. Rather, the critic of public reason may simply say that there is no member of a *particular subset* of *R* that could pass the public justification test, where such a subset is determined by the theorist. Compare here to how Rawls specifies those menu options deliberators confront in the original position. Though "ideally of course one would like to say that they are to choose among all possible conceptions of justice," Rawls notes that "an obvious difficulty is how these conceptions are to be characterized so that those in the original position can be presented with them" (Rawls 1971, 122). Because one cannot possibly list all possible conceptions of justice, Rawls presents a limited menu of options and argues that justice as fairness is best among that menu. Similarly, those putting forth the JFC might take a limited subset of *R* and merely say that no member of that subset can satisfy the public justification principle. Call this the *modified JFC*.

Now whether the modified JFC is a successful criticism of public reason depends on just how extensive the subset of *R* is. If the subset is very limited then the modified JFC looks like a strawman; it looks as though the subset was constructed just to get the result the critic of public reason intended. (Imagine here the reactions to Rawls's theory of justice if utilitarianism was not included on the menu presented to deliberators.) But the modified JFC need not be so weak. To see why, let *R** be the set of all rules that we currently see implemented in liberal societies, or could plausibly imagine being implemented in liberal societies in the near future. It could very well be—as some convincingly argue—that for every member of *R** there exists a member of *E* capable of justifiably rejecting it. Now *this* is certainly a worrying criticism the public reason liberal must address. Though Hayek's insights suggest there may be rules not in *R** yet still in *R* that we have not yet discovered that could satisfy the public justification principle, this is surely not a resounding response in the face of our modified JFC.

IN SEARCH OF JUSTIFICATION: THE EPISTEMIC TURN

At first glance Hayek's thesis concerning the necessary limits of our knowledge may lead one to despair: after all, such knowledge seems both helpful and desirable for an optimally functioning social order. Yet, if Hayek is right, then no one person or group of persons can ever achieve such knowledge—it is something that simply cannot be done. But though *individuals and groups* cannot possess and thus make use of the knowledge presumed by the rational constructivist in social theory, *society* can still make use of dispersed knowledge and currently undiscovered knowledge to facilitate harmonious social life.

In fact, Hayek tells us that *the* economic problem every society faces is how to organize itself to make use of our dispersed knowledge and the currently unknown: "To put it briefly, it is a problem of the utilization of knowledge which is not given to anyone in its totality" (Hayek [1945] 2014, 94). Societies can do better or worse jobs of discovering and utilizing this knowledge through different institutional arrangements: different institutions will vary in terms of how well they discover what is unknown, incentivize persons to reveal what it is they and only they know, and aggregate dispersed knowns to yield information essential for cooperative social life.

For Hayek, then, the fact that we as individuals face incurable ignorance is thus more a call to arms than cause for despair: it "raises for a competitive society the question, not how we can 'find' the people who know best, but rather *what institutional arrangements* are necessary in order that the unknown persons who have knowledge specially suited to a particular task are most likely to be attracted to that task" (Hayek [1948] 2014, 108; emphasis added). This is essentially the point Hayek makes in his papers spanning the socialist calculation debate. If we grant ourselves the assumption of omniscience (as most equilibrium models did at the time, and as most defenders of socialist calculation did), then institutions matter little. But, if we admit our incurable ignorance, then we need to select those institutions that best discover and make use of the dispersed and currently unknown.

Inspired by Hayek's call to arms, one possible response the public reason liberal can offer to the modified JFC is as follows: though it may be that there exists no rule in *R** justified to all, there may be a rule in the complement of *R** (that is, a rule in *R* but not in *R**) that *is* justified to all that we have simply not yet discovered. To make this a compelling response, however, the public reason liberal must give some account of how we do indeed find such a rule. Public reason liberals cannot merely assert that there may indeed exist a rule in the complement of *R** satisfying their justificatory demands. To be convincing, they must identify some kind of mechanism by which such a rule can be discovered.

Relevant here is the growing literature on epistemic approaches to democracy (Anderson 2006; Estlund 2008; Knight and Johnson 2011; Landemore 2013; Ober 2008, 2013). Epistemic approaches to democracy hold that, when compared to other methods of social choice, democratic institutions are more likely to select the "best" or "correct" choice from the set of available options. As Hélène Landemore notes in her important work on epistemic democracy, epistemic democrats are committed to *political cognitivism*, which says that (i) there exists a procedure-independent standard of correctness for evaluating social choices and that (ii) we can know, or at least get some grasp of, this standard (Landemore 2013, 208). Now the assumption of political cognitivism might seem at odds with the idea of public reason, for political cognitivism seems to imply some kind of robust moral realism, whereas the public reason liberal holds that standards of right ultimately lie in the commitments of individuals—in short, what these individuals have reason to endorse. Yet we need not interpret political cognitivism's procedure-independent standard as being determined by some kind of controversial notion of moral truth. Rather, such a standard can "take for granted a given set of values shared by a community and take this as the touchstone of 'correct' political judgments" (Landemore 2013, 217). Public reason liberals can thus endorse an epistemic account of democracy insofar as democratic institutions are more likely to find rules justified to all when compared to other methods of social choice. It is democratic institutions, the public reason liberal might insist, that will find us rules in the complement of *R** satisfying the public justification principle.

According to Melissa Schwartzberg's thorough review article, there are three broad approaches in the current epistemic democracy literature detailing mechanisms for finding such rules (Schwartzberg 2015, 196). First, some epistemic democrats appeal to the *Condorcet jury theorem*, which holds that if certain conditions obtain, then as the size of a collectivity increases the likelihood of the collectivity selecting the correct answer to some binary proposition approaches one (Condorcet 1785). Or, the *miracle of aggregation* holds that when we average a collectivity's estimates of some scalar value then—again, so long as certain conditions obtain—as the size of the collectivity increases the likelihood of the collectivity selecting the correct value approaches one (Galton 1907). Finally, many appeal to Lu Hong and Scott Page's *diversity trumps ability theorem*, which says that groups of diverse yet less-capable problem solvers can outperform homogenous yet more-capable problem solvers so long as certain conditions are met (Hong and Page 2001, 2004; Page 2007). The Condorcet jury theorem and miracle of aggregation are both voting-based epistemic mechanisms: it is the simple casting of a vote or estimation of a value that leads to the collectivity finding rules justified to all. The Hong-Page theorem, however, models the epistemic properties of deliberation. Here, it is democratic discourse that finds rules satisfying the public justification principle. Most epistemic democrats argue in defense of the epistemic properties of democracy by appealing to some combination of voting and deliberation. It is thus an overall democratic structure, then, that the public reason liberal might appeal to in the face of the modified JFC.

Though the epistemic democracy literature is optimistic that democratic institutions can produce better outcomes—in our terms, find rules in the complement of R^* that satisfy the public justification principle—there are many who doubt this. Indeed, some think the exact opposite is true: that democratic institutions are quite bad at producing good outcomes. The main claim that such detractors make is that we should expect widespread ignorance to be the norm in a democracy: the costs of acquiring information and becoming informed radically outweigh the benefits of being an informed voter and participant in democratic discourse (Brennan 2016; Caplan 2007; DeCanio 2014; Downs 1957; Pincione and Tèson 2006; Somin 2016). Because of this widespread ignorance, it is hard to see how mere discourse and aggregation will produce desirable results; we have a simple case of garbage in, garbage out. Since this is so we should expect democracies to make quite bad decisions, casting doubt on the supposed desirable epistemic properties epistemic democrats claim such institutions possess.

These two literatures are, I think, talking past one another. The epistemic democrats do indeed highlight mechanisms by which democratic institutions can make good decisions—the Condorcet jury theorem, the miracle of aggregation, and the Hong-Page theorem are all mathematical results whose logical verity are beyond doubt. The detractors, however, essentially point out that (i) the mechanisms cited rely on specific behavioral assumptions—that voters and participations in deliberation possess some minimal threshold of epistemic competence—but (ii) democratic institutions do not *incentivize* persons to actually satisfy these competency requirements. As an example, the classical model of the Condorcet jury theorem says that if voters have a better than equal chance of being right and, if they vote independently, then as the size of the group increases the chances of a simple majority voting procedure selecting the correct answer approaches one. To which the detractor responds: persons in the democratic process are not incentivized to have a better than equal chance of being right, nor are they incentivized to vote independently.

It is not enough, then, that the public reason liberal highlight a mechanism by which rules satisfying the public justification principle in the complement of R^* be found. The public reason liberal must also show that this mechanism is *incentive-compatible*. This, again, is a lesson Hayek teaches us. He notes that we seek "a social system which does not depend for its functioning on our finding good men for running it, or on all men becoming better than they now are, but which makes use of men in all their given variety and complexity, sometimes good and sometimes bad, sometimes intelligent and more often stupid" (Hayek [1946] 1996, 12). The epistemic democracy literature gives us proposed mechanisms for finding publicly justified rules, but one that requires persons behave very differently than they currently do. In other words: we have not yet adequately addressed the modified JFC.

COMPETITION AND MORAL ENTREPRENEURS

Here is where things currently stand. The modified JFC says that there is no rule in the set R^* that is publicly justified. To adequately respond, the public reason liberal can identify a mechanism by which rules satisfying the public justification principle in the complement of R^* can be found. Yet not only must they identify such a mechanism, but in the last section we saw that they must also show that this mechanism is incentive-compatible—that people will actually be motivated to participate in the proposed method of finding justified rules that respect the freedom and equality of all. Epistemic accounts of democracy fail to satisfy this latter requirement.

One critical tool for discovering the unknown is competition within a market system. By competition I mean those activities engaged in by individuals and firms in hopes of capturing profits. Referencing again the knowledge that no one individual or group of individuals can attain, Hayek argues we should view competition "as a procedure for the discovery of such facts as, without resort to it, would not be known to anyone, or at least would not be utilized" (Hayek [1968] 2014, 304). Noting that competition is an integral component of the market system, we can link up these remarks concerning the relationship between competition and discovery with what Hayek says more generally about the market's ability to extricate ourselves of our incurable ignorance: "We must look at the price system as such a mechanism for communicating information if we want to understand its real function. . . . The most significant fact about this system is the economy of knowledge with which it operates, or how little the individual participants need to know in order to be able to take the right action" (Hayek [1945] 2014, 100).

But how exactly does competition within a market act as a discovery procedure? Here, it is important to distinguish between three different beneficial things the market might do for a society, two of which involve discovering the unknown (Kirzner 1988, 4). First, the market allocates resources to their most efficient uses in a world of scarcity. Here, there is no way in which the market acts as a discovery procedure. Second, the market communicates information from one part of the economy to another. To borrow an example from Hayek, if there is a shortage of tin for some reason—and Hayek emphasizes that it does not matter what the cause of this shortage is—then the market conveys information of this shortage by raising the price of tin (Hayek [1945] 2014, 99). Consumers of tin respond by economizing their use of this resource. Here, the market is acting as a discovery procedure in that it discovers decentralized information concerning the supply and demand of various goods in the economy.

Third, "the price system promotes alertness to and the discovery of as yet unknown information (both in regard to existing opportunities for potential gains from trade with existing techniques and in regard to possibilities for innovative processes of production)" (Kirzner 1988, 4). As an example, disequilibrium prices across a market for a specific good signals a market failure—the fact that gains from trade that could have been captured have been passed by, and that the market has not cleared (Kirzner 1992, 144–46). But more so than merely discovering market failures, the market system—and this is what is most important for our purposes—through its "heady scent of profits" also *incentivizes* the entrepreneur to remedy these failures by using existing technologies or *introducing new technologies* to capture these forgone opportunities (Kirzner [1973] 2013, 178). *This* is the sense of discovery we are most interested in: the ability of the competitive market process to signal failures and the ability of the market system to incentivize the discovery of novel solutions to help remedy these failures through the reward of profits.

Using Hayek's insights concerning the relationship between ignorance and the competitive market process, we now see clearly how the public reason liberal can respond to the modified JFC in the face of the failures of epistemic democratic approaches. The modified JFC says that though there *may* be rules satisfying the public justification principle, those rules we currently know of do not. The public reason liberal can respond by endorsing those institutions that best allow society to discover unknown forms of social organization capable of solving these justificatory failures; and, moreover, those institutions that incentivize persons to actually go out and find such forms of social organization. Following Hayek, the answer lies in setting up a system of governance that relies on competition to achieve these ends: if there is competition in governance, then we incentivize persons to find arrangements justified to all, thereby adequately addressing the modified JFC. Just like entrepreneurs remedying market failures through discovering new technologies, moral entrepreneurs remedy justificatory failures through discovering new rules satisfying the public reason liberal's justificatory demands.

POLYCENTRIC PUBLIC REASON

Now we all know how market competition works when it comes to normal consumer goods—things like bicycles, books, and batteries. It is less clear, though, how we can have market competition in the choice of rules and institutions, which is essentially what the current proposal requires if we are to have competition act as a discovery procedure in the manner described above. Relevant here is the literature on polycentric or decentralized forms of governance. Polycentricity perhaps received its clearest exposition in a piece by Vincent Ostrom, Charles M. Tiebout, and Robert Warren examining metropolitan governance. The authors begin by noting that metropolitan governance usually consists of "overlapping jurisdictions" of authority, "duplication of functions" concerning the provision of public goods and services, and "many centers of decision making that are formally independent of each other" (Ostrom et al. 1961, 831). This is opposed to monocentric or "gargantuan" approaches to governance, where authority, decision making, and the provision of public goods and services are limited to one single governance unit, such that this one single unit's jurisdiction does not overlap with any other unit's jurisdiction. Importantly, when governance jurisdictions and functions are broken up and dispersed in a polycentric as opposed to a monocentric order, a market mechanism is induced over the provision of these public goods and services: "Patterns of competition among producers of public services in a metropolitan area, just as among firms in the market, may produce substantial benefits by inducing self-regulating tendencies with pressure for the more efficient solution in the operation of the whole system" (Ostrom et al. 1961, 838). Because of this, "much of the flexibility and responsiveness of market organization can be realized in the public service economy" (Ostrom et al. 1961, 839).

Let us try to make this notion of polycentricity more precise. Following Paul Dragos Aligica and Vlad Tarko, we can say that polycentric orders consist of the following three basic features (Aligica 2014; Aligica and Tarko 2013):

> *Multiplicity of Decision Centers*, where there are distinct units of governance that compete with one another.
>
> *Overarching System of Rules*, which defines the limits of a polycentric governance system and specifies how separated governance units relate to and interact with one another.
>
> and
>
> *Spontaneous Order*, which is the result of the polycentric order, generated by competition among competing governance units.

The multiplicity of decision centers is the defining feature of polycentric governance structures: instead of a single set of rules coming from a single centralized authority, there are multiple sets of rules coming from multiple authorities. Competition among such sources of authority is what induces the discovery procedure that, we saw in the section above, Hayek emphasizes in his analysis of markets. The overarching system of rules not only serves to define what is and is not part of a polycentric order, but also how different units of governance within the order must relate to and interact with one another—think here of how property rights in traditional markets define what persons in such a market may or may not do. And finally, the spontaneous order element characterizes the resulting states of affairs produced by polycentric orders: they are the result of human action, but not of human design.

Competition among different jurisdictions of authority in polycentric orders helps to resolve our justificatory failures through the use of experimentation and learning: novel ways of organizing our social and political lives can be tried out (which persons may or may not decide to sort themselves into), and the results of these experiments can inform other communities how they ought to organize their social and political institutions. This is something Aligica notes in his work on polycentricity. He writes:

> If experimentalism is a central issue . . . then one can hardly think of a better arena of experimentation than polycentricity. It is a system of reciprocal monitoring and assessment in dynamic interdependence. The various units and decision-making centers depend on each other or compete with each other or both. They must stay informed about (and be prepared to adjust to) the evolutions of other units. (Aligica 2014, 66)

As an example, if governance unit g_2 thinks that many are unhappy with the current rules in governance unit g_1—many residing in g_1 live according to rules they deem unjustified—then governance unit g_2 can implement a set of rules that has never been tried out before to get some of those residing in g_1 to switch over to g_2. This is where the desirable effects of experimentation come in. Suppose g_2 actually does this and is successful: many dissatisfied in g_1 move to g_2 which has rules they deem to be justified. Then, other governance units in a similar position to g_1—those who, like g_1, harbor many citizens who think the current set of rules fails to be justified—might then take a similar approach to g_2 to keep their citizens from emigrating over to g_2. This is where the desirable effects of learning come in.

The idea of polycentricity and competition in governance might initially seem a bit foreign to many political philosophers, but upon a second glance it should not. Robert Nozick's framework for utopia, I think, mirrors closely what an ideal polycentric order looks like, though there are certainly some deviations. According to Nozick's vision, "There will not be one kind of community existing, and one kind of life led in utopia. Utopia will consist of utopias, of many different kinds of divergent communities in which people lead different kinds of lives under different institutions" (Nozick 1974, 311–12). Chandran Kukathas's vision of a liberal order given in *The Liberal Archipelago* also resembles closely polycentricism. Kukathas offers a vision of "a society of societies which is neither the creation nor the object of control of any single authority; though it is a form of order in which authorities function under laws which are themselves beyond the reach of any singular power" (Kukathas 2003, 3).

Not only are polycentric forms of governance held as ideals in political philosophy, but the idea is being employed more frequently in the public reason literature as well. Gaus, for instance—quite independent of the current claim that polycentric orders have discovery mechanisms important for the public reason project—argues that given the sheer diversity we confront in contemporary societies, the only way for rules to be justified to all is to fracture ourselves into different communities that can be tailored to suit our heterogeneous preferences (Gaus 2016, 184–87). As another example, I have recently argued that once we admit that reasonable people disagree about not only the good but also the right, the only way of satisfying all the normative criteria Rawls employs when appraising different models of social order is by endorsing a polycentric model of governance, *contra* most the current literature (Kogelmann 2017).

To end we consider two objections to our proposed polycentric solution to public reason liberalism's justificatory failures problem. First, it might be argued that (i) though polycentricity is perhaps our best hope of uncovering rules that are justified to all through a competitive process, (ii) there is no guarantee that persons will actually sort themselves into those communities regulated by the rules they deem to be justified. As an example, Althea may live in governance unit g_1 regulated by rules she deems unjustified *even though* governance unit g_2 is a regulated by rules she does deem to be justified. It is easy to see how this might occur: though my optimal rules are in Texas, I have compelling work-related reasons to live in Washington, DC. There are two responses to this objection. First, it should be noted that if the current proposal can help at least find rules justified to all, *even if* persons do not end up living under such rules, then the current proposal will have taken us further than any other proposal has. This is certainly desirable progress. And second, the suspect nature of living under rules one does not deem justified intuitively seems reduced when one *does* have the option of living under rules one does deem justified. Consider an example. If one is a celiac then being forced to eat gluten is intuitively bad. Yet if one is a celiac who eats gluten when a gluten-free option is available then, though this is still undesirable, it seems less bad than the first case we considered, where no such option is available.

As a second objection, it might be argued that (i) in order for public reason liberals to endorse polycentricism to solve their problems it must be the case that (ii) polycentrism itself is justified to all, yet (iii) it is unlikely that (ii) is true. Now there is something important to this objection, but as it currently stands it seems mistaken. The public reason liberal holds that the demands of freedom and equality require that persons live according to rules they deem justified. In a polycentric order, though, there will be many communities composed of many sets of rules that persons do not live under: if Althea lives in governance unit g_1 she will not be subject to governance unit g_2's rules. So it is wrong to think that the public reason liberal must show that polycentricism *itself* is justified to all: why think that g_2's rules must be justified to Althea when she is not subject to the demands of such rules? But the public reason liberal must still show that the rules persons do in fact live under—in the jurisdictions they reside in and are thus subject to—are indeed justified to them. Now the very point of polycentricism is to introduce market-like competition so jurisdictions can experiment with rules that persons may find justified. So polycentricity increases the likelihood of this happening when compared to current proposals in the literature. But recall one of the defining features of polycentricity we noted above when discussing Aligica and Tarko's definition of polycentricism: there is an overarching system of rules specifying how different governance units interact with and relate to one another. The major hurdle for the public reason liberal on the current proposal, then, is to show that *these* rules are justified. For *regardless* the jurisdiction one resides in, one is subject to such rules. A fuller defense of the current proposal must offer a resounding response to this worry.

CONCLUSION

This chapter began with a challenge to public reason liberalism, the dominant conception of liberalism in current liberal political theory: it is unlikely that there exist rules capable of satisfying public reason liberalism's justificatory demands. We saw first that the strong version of this criticism rests on untenable knowledge assumptions concerning the theorist's ability to know all possible forms of social organization, something Hayek's work on rational constructivism helped illustrate. A modified version of the criticism, though, suggests it is merely those rules we know of that cannot meet the public reason liberal's justificatory demands.

In response, the public reason liberal can grasp on to Hayek's insights concerning competition and discovery: competition within a market system can help us discover new ways of remedying our current justificatory failures by signaling where and when such failures occur and incentivizing the entrepreneur to find new remedies to these existing problems. We ended by examining just how this might work: in a system where there is competition among governance units, moral entrepreneurs are incentivized to find arrangements justified to all. Endorsing such a system is the public reason liberal's greatest hope of finding a set of rules that help us live better together while also treating persons according to those ideals that are the cornerstone of the liberal order: as persons born both naturally free and naturally equal.

REFERENCES

Abbey, Ruth. 2007. "Back Toward a Comprehensive Liberalism? Justice as Fairness, Gender, and Families." *Political Theory* 35 (1): 5–28.

Aligica, Paul Dragos. 2014. *Institutional Diversity and Political Economy: The Ostroms and Beyond*. Oxford: Oxford University Press.

Aligica, Paul Dragos, and Vlad Tarko. 2013. "Co-Production, Polycentricity, and Value Heterogeneity: The Ostroms' Public Choice Institutionalism Revisited." *American Political Science Review* 107 (4): 726–41.

Anderson, Elizabeth. 2006. "The Epistemology of Democracy." *Episteme* 3 (1–2): 9–22.

Brennan, Jason. 2016. *Against Democracy*. Princeton, NJ: Princeton University Press.

Caplan, Bryan. 2007. *The Myth of the Rational Voter: Why Democracies Choose Bad Policies*. Princeton, NJ: Princeton University Press.

Condorcet, Marie Jean Antoine Nicolas de. 1785. *Essai sur l'application de l'analyse `a la probabilit´e des d´ecisions rendus `a la pluralit´e des voix*. Paris: De l'Imprimerie Royale.

DeCanio, Samuel. 2014. "Democracy, the Market, and the Logic of Social Choice." *American Journal of Political Science* 58 (3): 637–52.

Downs, Anthony. 1957. *An Economic Theory of Democracy*. New York: Harper and Row.
Estlund, David. 2008. *Democratic Authority: A Philosophical Framework*. Princeton, NJ: Princeton University Press.
Galton, Francis. 1907. "Vox Populi." *Nature* 75 (5): 450–51.
Gaus, Gerald. 1996. *Justificatory Liberalism: An Essay on Epistemology and Political Theory*. Oxford: Oxford University Press.
_______. 2011. *The Order of Public Reason: A Theory of Freedom in a Diverse and Bounded World.* Cambridge: Cambridge University Press.
_______. 2016. *The Tyranny of the Ideal: Justice in a Diverse Society*. Princeton, NJ: Princeton University Press.
Hayek, F. A. [1945] 2014. "The Use of Knowledge in Society." In *The Collected Works of F. A. Hayek.* Vol. 15: *The Market and Other Orders*, edited by Bruce Caldwell, 93–104. Chicago: University of Chicago Press.
_______. [1946] 1996. "Individualism: True and False." In *Individualism and Economic Order,* 1–32. Chicago: University of Chicago Press.
_______. [1948] 2014. "The Meaning of Competition." In *The Collected Works of F. A. Hayek.* Vol. 15: *The Market and Other Orders*, edited by Bruce Caldwell, 105–16. Chicago: University of Chicago Press.
_______. [1960] 2011. *The Constitution of Liberty*. Chicago: University of Chicago Press.
_______. [1967] 2014. "Kinds of Rationalism." In *The Collected Works of F. A. Hayek.* Vol. 15: *The Market and Other Orders*, edited by Bruce Caldwell, 39–53. Chicago: University of Chicago Press.
_______. [1968] 2014. "Competition as a Discovery Procedure." In *The Collected Works of F. A. Hayek.* Vol. 15: *The Market and Other Orders*, edited by Bruce Caldwell, 304–13. Chicago: University of Chicago Press.
_______. [1973] 1998. *Law, Legislation, and Liberty, Vol. 1: Rules and Order*. New York: Routledge.
Hong, Lu, and Scott E. Page. 2001. "Problem Solving by Heterogeneous Agents." *Journal of Economic Theory* 97 (1): 123–63.
_______. 2004. "Groups of Diverse Problem Solvers Can Outperform Groups of High-Ability Problem-Solvers." *Proceedings of the National Academy of Sciences* 101 (46): 16385–89.
Kirzner, Israel M. [1973] 2013. *Competition and Entrepreneurship*. Indianapolis: Liberty Fund.
_______. 1988. "The Economic Calculation Debate: Lessons for Austrians." *Review of Austrian Economics* 2 (1): 1–18.
_______. 1992. *The Meaning of the Market Process: Essays in the Development of Modern Austrian Economics*. New York: Routledge.
Knight, Jack, and James Johnson. 2011. *The Priority of Democracy: Political Consequences of Pragmatism*. Princeton, NJ: Princeton University Press.
Kogelmann, Brian. 2017. "Justice, Diversity, and the Well-Ordered Society." *Philosophical Quarterly* 67 (269): 663–84.
Kukathas, Chandran. 2003. *The Liberal Archipelago*. Oxford: Oxford University Press.

Landemore, Hélène. 2013. *Democratic Reason: Politics, Collective Intelligence, and the Rule of the Many*. Princeton, NJ: Princeton University Press.

Locke, John. [1690] 1980. *Second Treatise of Government*. Indianapolis: Hackett.

Nozick, Robert. 1974. *Anarchy, State, and Utopia*. New York: Basic Books.

Ober, Josiah. 2008. *Democracy and Knowledge: Innovation and Learning in Classical Athens*. Princeton, NJ: Princeton University Press.

_______. 2013. "Democracy's Wisdom: An Aristotelian Middle Way for Collective Judgment." *American Political Science Review* 107 (1): 104–22.

Okin, Susan Moller. 2005. "'Forty Acres and a Mule' for Women: Rawls and Feminism." *Politics, Philosophy, & Economics* 4 (2): 233–48.

Ostrom, Vincent, Charles M. Tiebout, and Robert Warren. 1961. "The Organization of Government in Metropolitan Areas: A Theoretical Inquiry." *American Political Science Review* 55 (4): 831–42.

Page, Scott. 2007. *The Difference: How the Power of Diversity Creates Better Groups, Firms, Schools, and Societies*. Princeton, NJ: Princeton University Press.

Pincione, Guido, and Fernando R. Téson. 2006. *Rational Choice and Democratic Deliberation: A Theory of Discourse Failure*. Cambridge: Cambridge University Press.

Quong, Jonathan. 2011. *Liberalism without Perfection*. Oxford: Oxford University Press.

_______. 2012. "Liberalism without Perfection: Replies to Gaus, Colburn, Chan, and Bocchiola." *Philosophy & Public Issues* 2: 51–79.

_______. 2014. "What is the Point of Public Reason?" *Philosophical Studies* 170: 545–53.

Rawls, John. 1971. *A Theory of Justice*. Cambridge, MA: Harvard University Press.

_______. [1993] 2005. *Political Liberalism*. New York: Columbia University Press.

Raz, Joseph. 1998. "Disagreement in Politics." *American Journal of Jurisprudence* 43: 25–52.

Schwartzberg, Melissa. 2015. "Epistemic Democracy and Its Challenges." *Annual Review of Political Science* 18: 187–203.

Sleat, Matt. 2013. "Coercing Non-Liberal Persons: Considerations on a More Realistic Liberalism." *European Journal of Political Theory* 12 (4): 347–67.

Somin, Ilya. 2016. *Democracy and Political Ignorance: Why Smaller Government Is Smarter*. Palo Alto, CA: Stanford University Press.

Taylor, Robert S. 2011. *Reconstructing Rawls: The Kantian Foundations of Justice as Fairness*. University Park: Pennsylvania State University Press.

Van Schoelandt, Chad. 2015. "Justification, Coercion, and the Place of Public Reason." *Philosophical Studies* 172 (4): 1031–50.

Part II

POLITICAL AND LEGAL RIGHTS

Chapter 5

The Case for Opening Borders

A Hayekian Critique of Discretionary Immigration Controls

Liz Hemsley

Immigration controls are the measures states use to control the types of people who may enter and reside in their territory, for how long they may remain, and what activities they may engage in once inside. In this sense, as Chandran Kukathas (2012) points out, simply being permitted *entry* to a state is not sufficient to understand the borders of that state as "open" to you. Rather, the openness of a border depends upon the level of access aliens are permitted to the host *society*. As Kukathas observes, "a border is more open if people are free not only to *enter* for brief visits but also to *reside,* to *work,* to *settle,* and perhaps even to *join* the political community that borders help to define" (Kukathas 2012, 652). For the purposes of this chapter then, immigration controls refer to the types of controls designed by states to regulate the participation of aliens in the society the state represents.

In today's world, all functioning states have some form of immigration policy, and these policies are generally designed to ensure that where immigration takes place, it is to the benefit of the receiving nation. Depending on their priorities and interests then, states will favor some categories of immigrants over others, and these preferences will be represented in their immigration policies. The policies that states adopt and how they are designed are therefore *discretionary*, meaning that each state—represented by its government—can determine the design of its own immigration policy according to its current priorities. Governments can typically alter immigration policy as their perception of the national interest changes, and in democratic nations, immigration policy can be revised and overhauled with changes of government. This has seen immigration policy become something of a "political football," particularly in western democracies, with different political parties proposing different approaches to controlling and managing immigration as a means to winning votes.

We might contrast discretionary immigration controls with border controls directed at enforcing a far more general entry policy, an example of which might be: those with infectious diseases, or traveling from places where such diseases are rife, can be stopped at the border and denied entry. This policy is general because it does not aim at bringing about any specific end—for example, a desired distribution of a certain type of immigrant within the native population. Rather, it seeks simply to prevent the arrival of infectious diseases into the country. For the majority of states in the world today, the immigration controls they exercise are discretionary, rather than general. This chapter argues that discretionary immigration controls represent unjustifiable exercises of arbitrary coercion that are uniquely harmful to the freedom of individuals and society. On the basis of this argument, this chapter concludes that borders should be made far more open than they currently are.

In advancing this defense of open borders, I draw upon Hayek's account of freedom and the free society to elucidate a distinction between general coercion—understood simply as coercion employed to enforce general, or "abstract" rules—and coercion that is *arbitrary* in nature. In doing so I seek to demonstrate that—while some forms of general state coercion *may* be permissible, that is to prevent certain harms or to protect certain social goods—coercion that is *arbitrary* is uniquely harmful from a liberal perspective. I then argue that discretionary immigration controls are paradigmatic cases of arbitrary coercion and are thus entirely unacceptable from a liberal perspective, even where we might be willing to accept instances of state coercion that are non-arbitrary, or "general." I finally examine a defense of the right of states to implement and enforce discretionary immigration controls that sees this as not only permissible, but as an essential feature of the moral rights of states. This is the argument from national self-determination. I again employ a Hayekian framework to demonstrate that this argument is grounded on a false account of the nature of the state and the "national interest," and therefore fails as a defense of discretionary immigration controls. On the basis of these arguments, I conclude that we have good reason to reject discretionary immigration controls and seek far more general immigration policies than are currently employed in the world today.

THE COERCIVE NATURE OF DISCRETIONARY IMMIGRATION CONTROLS

What's Wrong with Coercion, Anyway?

Immigration controls limit the scope of individual freedoms, both for the immigrants who are subjected to these controls and for members of the host society who find their desired interactions with these immigrants precluded by state regulations (Carens 1987; Kukathas 2012; Lomasky and Teson 2015). What is more, the restrictions immigration controls place on individual liberties are enforced by the state through practices like the policing of borders, the deportation of illegal immigrants, and the sanctioning of citizens who employ or otherwise engage with immigrants in ways the state has ruled impermissible. On this basis, immigration controls can be understood as a form of state coercion (Abizadeh 2010; Huemer 2010). The state relies on the threat, and sometimes the actual use of force to direct people—both citizens and outsiders—to behave in compliance with its immigration policies. Given this, liberal nations would seem to require a strong justification for their exercise of immigration controls. It is after all an established liberal principle that coercive restrictions to individual freedoms require robust justification if they are to be morally permissible. However, a straightforward acknowledgement of the coercive nature of immigration controls is not, by itself, sufficient to ground the claim that they should be removed. This is because it is also a generally accepted principle in liberal societies that some individual freedoms may be permissibly limited via the coercive instruments of the state, where this is necessary to reduce harms or produce social benefits. Indeed, this is precisely what happens when the state enforces traffic regulations or prohibitions on driving under the influence, for example. These regulations limit the scope of individual freedoms by restricting certain actions, and back these restrictions with the threat of sanctions where individuals fail to comply. In these instances, and many others, the state restricts the scope of individual negative liberties to protect something of value to the society as a whole—safe and efficient roads and highways, in the examples offered here. If we are seeking to elucidate the specific harm of immigration controls then, as a means to defending a system of far more open borders, we need to explain why the coercive nature of immigration controls can ground an argument for their removal, even where we accept many other forms of state coercion.

Michael Huemer has argued against immigration controls on the basis that they represent a form of *seriously harmful* coercion (Huemer 2010). According to Huemer, immigration restrictions applied by developed economies (he refers specifically to the United States) seriously harm the global poor by denying them access to the jobs and opportunities that would enable them to drastically improve their lives. He argues that many of those excluded by coercive immigration restrictions "suffer from oppression or poverty that could and would be remedied if only they were able to enter the country of their choice" (Huemer 2010, 434). The central claim of his article then, is that the governments of developed nations—specifically the US government—violate a negative duty to not subject others to seriously harmful coercion when they forcibly impose immigration restrictions. Huemer bases his claim around an analogy in which a starving man, Marvin, is forcibly prevented from accessing a marketplace where he would be able to trade goods for the food he desperately needs. In the scenario Huemer describes, the person preventing Marvin from accessing the marketplace is guilty of coercing him in a seriously harmful way, which culminates in Marvin's death from starvation. If only Marvin had not been prevented from accessing the marketplace, he could have reduced the severity of his situation and would have survived. Huemer understands Marvin's coercer as analogous with the US government, and Marvin as analogous with the global poor, who are coercively prevented from improving their situations through taking up employment opportunities in the United States by its restrictive immigration policy.

If Huemer is correct, his argument could provide a strong, rights-based reason for us to reject immigration controls as an *especially harmful* form of coercion. It is certainly true that immigration restrictions that preclude the global poor from participating in beneficial associations appear to subject them to avoidable harms. This claim is supported by Michael Clemens, whose analysis of the potential efficiency gains of relaxing immigration controls suggests that "the emigration of less than 5 percent of the population of poor regions would bring global gains exceeding the gains from total elimination of all policy barriers to merchandise trade and all barriers to capital flows" (Clemens 2011, 84). Where the opening of borders permits more of those in poor nations to benefit from participation in the workforce of advanced economies, then, it seems that relaxing immigration controls has the potential to greatly improve overall well-being. On this basis it seems we do have a strong prima facie reason to reject immigration controls that prevent the global poor from being able to take up opportunities in wealthy nations, where this would enable them to avoid desperate poverty. However, not all instances of immigration control cause the kinds of material harms that Huemer refers to, and Huemer's account has little to say about immigration restrictions that do not cause the serious, material harms he describes. If we are concerned with the restrictions immigration controls place on our general freedoms, Huemer's account has little to tell us. Insofar as we want to be able to say that immigration restrictions are generally objectionable because of the limitations they place on our freedoms, we need a wider explanation than the one Huemer provides. For the remainder of this section, I will provide such an explanation. I will do this by invoking Hayek's account of the ills of arbitrary coercion, and in doing so I will seek to elucidate the undesirable nature of discretionary immigration controls as compared with more general forms of coercion.

Hayek and the Ills of "Arbitrary Coercion"

In much of his work—and perhaps most prominently in *The Road to Serfdom* and *The Constitution of Liberty*—Hayek is concerned to explain the nature and value of the condition of freedom and the free society. Central to this concern is his attempt to provide an account of the necessary limitations that must be placed on state action if societies are to avoid a slide into authoritarianism. Hayek's main prescription for the preservation of freedom in society is for state coercion to be limited to the enforcement of *formal* or *abstract* rules. These are rules governing human conduct that are entirely general in their application; they "tell people in advance what action the state will take in certain types of situation, defined in general terms, without reference to time and place or particular people" (Hayek 1944, 114). These rules do not seek advantages or protections for any specific group, but apply to all people in precisely the same way. Insofar as they are not intended to bring about any specific distribution in resources or opportunities, these abstract rules are non-arbitrary. For Hayek, state coercion enforcing abstract rules—hereafter "general coercion"—is far less objectionable than state coercion enforcing arbitrary rules—hereafter "arbitrary coercion." So, what precisely is "arbitrary coercion," and why does Hayek find it so objectionable?

Perhaps the best way to understand the problem with arbitrary coercion is via a brief elucidation of Hayek's objection to central planning. In the instance of a planned economy, the individual members of the society to which it applies must be induced to comply with the plan, even where doing so is not in accordance with their own interests or preferences. Where this entails obliging people to act in ways not directly preferred by them, ensuring compliance with the plan will require some form of coercion by the state, for example, via sanctions for non-compliance. It is on this basis that Hayek asserts, "Most planners who have seriously considered the practical aspects of their task have little doubt that a directed economy must be run on more or less dictatorial lines" (Hayek 1944, 124). For Hayek, the enforcement of rules in a planned economy is paradigmatic of arbitrary coercion, since within a planned economy rules are directed at bringing about specific distributions of economic goods. In this way, the rules are not general but are arbitrary or ad hoc—they exist to advance specific ends rather than general ones.

One of the problems with a planned economy for Hayek is that the goal toward which a planned economy aims will always be one that favors the interests of some members of society above those of others. This is because there exists no single, shared interest toward which all individuals in a society will be equally happy to direct their efforts. Instead, as Hayek observes, "the welfare of a people, like the happiness of a man, depends on a great many things that can be provided in an infinite variety of combinations"

(Hayek 1944, 101). What this means, then, is that in choosing *how* to plan the economy, and what type of end-state distribution to favor, the state must choose among any number of possibilities, each of which will advance the interests and welfare of some individuals above those of others. The implication is that in a planned economy, all individual interests must be ranked such that the planner can determine *this* end-state distribution as preferable to any of the possible alternatives. As Hayek points out, the process of directing the economy toward the achievement of a specific goal "presupposes . . . the existence of a complete ethical code in which all different human values are allotted their due place" (Hayek 1944, 101). In reality of course, there exists no "complete ethical code" of the kind that would allow us to definitively assert that the overall utility gained from raising the salary of nurses is greater than that gained from subsidizing the production of agricultural products, for example. Instead, in a planned economy the state must base these decisions on subjective value judgments. In this sense, economic planning necessarily entails the state trading off the interests of some for the interests of others based on subjective, often obscure value judgments or, perhaps more concerningly, based on the varying degrees of political capital held by different interest groups. In this way, Hayek asserts, a planned economy "necessarily involves deliberate discrimination between particular needs of different people, and allowing one man to do what another must be prevented from doing" (Hayek 1944, 116). In a planned economy, then, some people are always directed—via the coercive mechanisms of the state—away from the actions that best reflect their own intentions, and toward the actions that best serve the intentions of the state, themselves a proxy for the intentions of some specific sub-group of individuals. In this way, the mechanisms of the state are used to bring about specific outcomes *not* preferred by many of those directed toward their achievement. This is one of Hayek's major objections to arbitrary coercion—that by advancing the interests of some above those of others, it violates the liberal principle of equality (Hayek 1944).

Hayek's other major objection to arbitrary coercion expresses an epistemological concern, namely that arbitrary coercion prevents individuals from making effective use of their local knowledge, and thereby reduces the efficiency and prosperity of society as a whole. To understand this claim, consider what is meant by "local knowledge." Local knowledge is what Hayek has referred to as "the knowledge of the particular circumstances of time and place" (Hayek 1945, 521). This knowledge is the type that individuals use all the time in their day-to-day lives to achieve small advantages for themselves. My knowledge that my neighbor plans to take a cab to the railway station just half an hour before I plan to, for example, allows me to coordinate sharing a single trip and splitting the fare. It is with respect to this type of knowledge that Hayek asserts "practically every individual has some advantage over all others because he possesses unique information of which beneficial use may be made" (Hayek 1945, 521). However, the benefit gained from employing local knowledge does not pertain only to the individual making use of it, but also spreads to society at large. Consider again the taxi example. In this instance, my very specific knowledge of my neighbor's travel plans enables me to act so as to reduce the fare I would have paid to get to the railway station. However, the benefit does not end there. My neighbor also saves some fare, which she will perhaps spend on a coffee at the train station, passing the benefit on to the coffee seller also. What is more, by taking just one taxi, we have also freed up the additional journey for someone else who may otherwise have had to find another means of transport. In these ways, then, my local knowledge creates wider efficiencies than simply my reduced cab fare.

Arbitrary coercion precludes the effective use of local knowledge. In subjecting individuals to rules aimed at specific ends it prevents them from freely directing their actions in accordance with their own knowledge and preferences, and in this way subverts a process via which individuals are able to continually respond to local information to most effectively bring their specific plans to fruition. Instead, subjection to arbitrary coercion forces them to follow plans devised by a centralized body that will not be fully aware of or responsive to local information. Indeed, the local knowledge individuals possess is far too complex and dispersed to ever be effectively collected and collated such that the efficiencies this knowledge is naturally able to produce could be made effective use of. As Hayek observes: "The sum of the knowledge of all the individuals exists nowhere as an integrated whole" (Hayek 1960, 75). Instead, everyone in society possesses knowledge relevant to themselves and their own circumstances. What is more, this knowledge is not "rational" or "scientific" knowledge of the type that could—even theoretically—be possessed by any single person or group. Rather, it is simple knowledge of local events and circumstances. It is, therefore, knowledge that is created almost simultaneously with being used. If it is not acted on with swiftness, the opportunities presented by the possession of this type of knowledge are lost. It is Hayek's contention that the efficiency gains generated by the use of local knowledge in a free society cannot be replicated by a central planner. In the absence of relevant local knowledge, central planners cannot capitalize on all opportunities for making these efficiency gains. What is more, without relevant local knowledge, any central planner will be ignorant of many of the important variables that may affect how their rational plan unfolds in practice, and the full range of impacts it will have. In this way, not only are central planners unable to replicate the efficiency gains available in a free society, they are also unable to accurately predict all the effects the implementation of their plan will have. This is at least in part because much of the knowledge and information a planner would need to anticipate all possible outcomes of a plan do not exist until the point at which the plan is put into effect. Rather, much of the information is created as different individuals respond—on the basis of their relevant local knowledge—to the change in circumstances that the implementation of the plan brings about. It is because no centralized body could ever possess sufficient local knowledge to fully predict the impacts of their plan, or to take full advantage of the potential efficiency gains available from cooperation between free individuals, that Hayek eschews central planning and the arbitrary coercion it entails.

For Hayek, arbitrary coercion has the undesirable implications described precisely because of its arbitrary nature. General coercion—even where it limits the full scope of individual negative liberties—does not have the objectionable characteristics that arbitrary coercion does. In the case of respect for formal equality it is easy to see that this is the case, since coercion undertaken to enforce compliance with general rules applies to all people in the same ways. Take for example the enforcement of national speed limits on motorways and highways. While some may deeply resent being made to comply with this rule, it is clear that this rule is designed to affect all motorists in the same way. An arbitrary version of this rule might be one stating that certain categories of driver be permitted to drive in accordance with different speed limits, based perhaps on their levels of experience, or the age and reliability of the car they are driving. This version of the rule entails treating some people differently under the law, based on some favored characteristics. So, arbitrary coercion is discriminatory in a way that general coercion is not.

When it comes to Hayek's epistemological concern, it is not so immediately obvious that general coercion is any better than arbitrary coercion. After all, insofar as we are coerced by the state to comply with certain centrally designed rules, rather than to act freely in accordance with our own knowledge and preferences, our ability to capitalize on our local knowledge will be diminished. Taking again the example of a general rule enforcing compliance with a national speed limit, imagine that I make the same journey to work along the same stretch of road each day and happen to know that the road is always empty at the time I am driving on it. In the absence of general coercion vis-à-vis the speed limit I could save fifteen minutes each day by driving a little faster, without endangering myself or anyone else. However, the general rule against driving above a certain speed prevents me from doing so. The important point from Hayek's perspective, though, is that general rules are easier to predict and plan around than arbitrary ones. Indeed, general rules make it easier for individuals to plan their lives according to their own interests and preferences, because they make the behaviors of others more predictable and reliable. Applying the speed limit example again, my knowledge of this rule and its general application mean that I can accurately predict how long I have to perform a maneuver in the road before an approaching vehicle reaches me, for instance. Compare this with the arbitrary version of this rule, according to which different "categories" of drivers must observe different limits. This rule does not assist me in predicting the behavior of other drivers unless and until I know what category of driver they are. In this way, then, general rules become part of the local knowledge that individuals use to plan their lives, in a way that arbitrary rules cannot. Of general or "formal" rules, Hayek states that "they could almost be described as a kind of instrument of production, helping people to predict the behavior of those with whom they must collaborate, rather than as efforts toward the satisfaction of particular needs" (Hayek 1944, 113).

A further point to note here is that because Hayek understands freedom in a very specific way, as "the possibility of a person's acting according to his own decisions and plans" (Hayek 1960, 59), he interprets arbitrary coercion as precisely the antithesis of freedom in a way that general coercion is not. This explains why Hayek suggests that the freest societies will be those in which there is only general coercion. However, an objection which may be leveled against Hayek's account here is that the "formal rules" and general coercion he advocates could still limit the sphere of individual, negative liberty in highly undesirable ways. Take for example general rules stating that all citizens must undertake military service. Surely these types of rules, in forcing individuals to undertake actions they would not otherwise have chosen, and which seriously affect their lives, amount to a violation of individual liberty and freedom of action, at least as these concepts are commonly understood. It might be objected, therefore, that Hayek's prescription that state action be limited to the enforcement of general rules is entirely insufficient to protect individuals from violations of their freedom. The first point to note here, however, is that from Hayek's own perspective, and given his understanding of freedom, this objection does not make direct contact with his argument. For Hayek, freedom is not interpreted as a metaphysical right. Rather, he understands it more as a social condition. On this basis, it is perfectly possible for Hayek to accept, and indeed he does appear to accept, that some coercive restrictions on individual freedom of action may be unavoidable in civil society. He simply does not see this as the most pressing problem for contemporary societies to grapple with. At the very least, it is not the problem his account of freedom and coercion in society seeks to solve. The more pressing problem of freedom in society, as far as Hayek is concerned, is how to limit the kinds of coercion that prevent individuals from being able to direct their lives according to their own plans. Indeed, considering the example of forced military service he expressly states:

> though compulsory military service, while it lasts, undoubtedly involved severe coercion, and though a life-long conscript could not be said ever to be free, a predictable limited period of military service certainly restricts the possibility of shaping one's own life less than would, for instance, a constant threat of arrest resorted to by an arbitrary power to ensure what it regards as good behavior. (Hayek 1960, 210)

So, it is not part of Hayek's aim to develop an account of the state that fully elucidates the morally permissible scope of individual liberty, taken as a natural right. Hayek's main concern in contemplating how the state ought to act is the prevention of arbitrary coercion, rather than the protection of bald individual liberty. As such, the complaint that his account insufficiently protects bald individual liberty will be of little direct concern.

If we approach Hayek's argument from outside, however, we may still feel some concern that it appears to permit limitations to the sphere of individual liberty that, from the perspective of much liberal theory, look intolerable. Indeed, for those who wish to see a much wider scope of individual liberty protected than simply the freedom to direct one's life according to one's own plans, Hayek's account will look inadequate to the task of explaining how this liberty may be preserved. This may be reason enough for some to reject his account out of hand. The point to make here though is that neither Hayek's specific objection to arbitrary coercion, nor his prescription that state's limit themselves to the enforcement of general rules, actually *precludes* the preservation of wider spheres of liberty than they expressly provide for. The pertinent point is that, regardless of whether we understand freedom as consisting in freedom from arbitrary coercion or freedom from coercion per se, the enforcement of arbitrary rules aimed at bringing about specific ends will *always* violate freedom. The limitation of state action to the enforcement of general rules can therefore be taken as a *minimally* necessary condition for the protection of individual freedom. Even if we possess doubts about whether it is also sufficient to fully guarantee all the liberties we would like to see protected, this does not mean that these more minimal protections *threaten* freedom, or that we need to reject Hayek's account. Indeed, Hayek can defend his position vis-à-vis arbitrary coercion without ever declaring that the removal of this from society is sufficient to provide the perfectly desired level of individual liberty. He can eschew arbitrary coercion while remaining ambivalent about the further measures that may be needed to preserve a yet wider sphere of liberty. In this sense then, I suggest that we take Hayek as providing a *negative* account of the types of action that absolutely cannot coexist with freedom, rather than an exhaustive, positive list of the social conditions that must obtain if individual liberty is to be fully and maximally preserved.

Having elucidated the Hayekian account of the specific ills of arbitrary coercion, I will conclude the first section of this chapter by arguing that discretionary immigration controls can be understood as a precise example of arbitrary coercion in action. If this is the case, we will have a reason for rejecting these controls that can explain what is objectionable about them from the perspective of liberty without relying on an outright rejection of all forms of state coercion as a matter of principle.

Discretionary Immigration Controls as Arbitrary Coercion

We have seen that coercion is arbitrary when it aims at bringing about specific, subjectively preferred ends that advance the interests of one particular group or body over those of everyone else. Discretionary immigration controls fulfill precisely this role, and indeed are designed to do so. Consider for example an immigration policy that prevents low-skilled, low-paid workers from outside the host nation from participating in its labor market. The intention behind this type of policy is to protect the wages and jobs of native workers employed in the same low-skilled industries as the would-be immigrants. The complaint of these native workers may be something like: "If immigrants are allowed to enter and compete with me for work, there will be too many people competing for the same kinds of jobs, they will put downward pressure on my wages, and may even replace me." For these reasons, they see the restriction of low-skilled immigrants into the native economy as being beneficial, even essential, to their interests. In reality, the interests of these workers will likely be better served if they are enabled and encouraged to move into different sectors of the economy. Much low-skilled work is at risk from automation anyway, besides the fact that it is often dangerous, low paid, and unpleasant. In many cases, the arrival of a low-skilled immigrant workforce into these industries can actually expedite the process of native workers transitioning into different sectors of the economy. This is because, in their willingness to accept worse conditions and lower pay, immigrants can bring about a general worsening of conditions in a sector, which then encourages a fall-off in native workers who no longer regard these jobs as worthy of their time. Alongside this, the entry of immigrant workers willing to accept low wages can increase the productivity of an industry, allowing for the creation of additional jobs in different sectors that may be more appealing to native workers. Up-skilling programs might need to be implemented to facilitate such transitions, although, where permitted to, they will likely occur naturally over a gradual period. However, where low-skilled workers are permitted to apply pressure on the state to protect their jobs and wages from outside competition, for example through unionization, this process does not occur.

Instead, discretionary immigration policies are used to advance the declared interests of this specific group.

Note that, as is commonplace with arbitrary coercion, in advancing the interests of this particular group through its discretionary immigration policy, the state elevates their interests above not only those of would-be immigrants, but also over those of other citizens. Observing precisely this point, Chandran Kukathas points out that "keeping out foreign labour may keep local wages higher and benefit domestic labour; but the costs will be borne by other citizens, who will have to endure the higher prices that are the consequence of higher wage costs" (Kukathas 2012, 657). As well as the economic effects discretionary immigration controls may have on the domestic population, it is clear that these controls also limit the freedoms of those members of the domestic population who wish to associate with would-be immigrants. In particular the right of freedom of association is restricted. Observing this point, Joseph Carens offers the following summary:

> Suppose a farmer from the United States wanted to hire workers from Mexico. The government would have no right to prohibit him from doing this. To prevent the Mexicans from coming would violate the rights of both the American farmer and the Mexican workers to engage in voluntary transactions. (Carens 1987, 253)

In agreement with Carens, Lomasky and Teson point out: "Association is a two-way (or more) relationship. . . . If Bennet is desirous of hiring Dashwood to tend his garden and clean his swimming pool then Bennet's liberty, every bit as much as Dashwood's is impugned by her exclusion" (Lomasky and Teson 2015, 95). Just as in the instance of a planned economy, in the case of discretionary immigration controls individual freedoms are restricted in ways that favor the interests of some over those of others and which are ultimately economically inefficient.

The inefficiency of discretionary immigration controls arises in precisely the ways it does in the example of central planning of the economy; as a result of individuals being prevented from acting on local knowledge. Consider, for example, the owner of a small business who wants to hire a certain number of individuals with a specific skill set. Imagine that, for whatever reason, the skills this employer needs are not prevalent among the native population, but she receives applications for the jobs from highly qualified candidates from abroad. In the absence of discretionary immigration controls, this employer can freely direct her specific knowledge of her own business needs to recruit those candidates best equipped to meet them. This is obviously good for her business, allowing it to flourish, take on more workers, and produce more goods. However, in a world in which immigration is heavily controlled by the state, the state acts as a block to this process. Now our employer can only bring in those candidates who meet the criteria set out by the state, rather than those set out by her own direct business needs. Because the state is far less effective than she is at interpreting her needs, it is very unlikely it will be able to reflect these in its policy in time for our employer to benefit, if it can interpret and incorporate them at all. In this way, the restriction discretionary immigration controls place on the freedom of our would-be employer has a negative impact on the overall efficiency and prosperity of society. That this situation is also ethically objectionable from the perspective of liberal equality is clear if we consider that the state has likely introduced discretionary immigration policies to satisfy some specific interest that it has arbitrarily elevated above the interests of our business owner. Perhaps a majority of the voting public objects to employers being allowed to bring in whom they please from abroad because they dislike the impact immigration has on the homogeneity of their local communities. However, in prioritizing the satisfaction of the interests of this group, the state, possibly inadvertently, elevates its wants above those of the business owner and anyone else with an interest in associating with immigrants. The two distinct interests are not given equal status, and instead the recruitment practices of the business owner are coercively directed toward the satisfaction of the ends of a distinct group in the population.

In this section I have argued that because discretionary immigration controls represent a form of arbitrary coercion, this provides us with a reason to seek their replacement with more general rules of admission. However, this reason may yet be overridden if there are strong countervailing reasons to permit these discretionary controls. The following section will examine precisely such a claim, which seeks to ground a *right* of discretionary border controls in the moral status of the communities that states represent. This is the argument from national self-determination. I will first examine this argument and then, invoking a Hayekian analysis of the nature of society and the modern state, will argue that the argument from national self-determination fails as a defense of discretionary immigration controls.

DISCRETIONARY IMMIGRATION CONTROLS AND THE RIGHT OF NATIONAL SELF-DETERMINATION

The Argument from National Self-Determination

The previous section sought to demonstrate that if we find arbitrary coercion at all concerning, then we have a reason to eschew discretionary immigration controls and to demand they be replaced with general rules of admission.

On this Hayekian account, the eschewal of discretionary immigration controls is not grounded in any specific rights claim, but simply in an exposition of the threats arbitrary coercion poses to the freedom of individuals and wider society. If the state can be understood as an entity in possession of a *right* to employ discretionary immigration controls, this will provide at the very least a countervailing reason to defend the continued use of these controls. Given the stringency of rights-claims, the existence of such a right may even "trump" our concerns about the use of arbitrary coercion. If this is the case, it might be that we are morally required to accept the arbitrary coercion that discretionary immigration controls represent to preserve a more important, moral right. The vital question, then, is: *Do* states possess a right to exercise discretionary immigration controls? One argument that defends the existence of such a right is the argument from national self-determination, according to which states possess rights of self-determination that include the right to direct policy—including immigration policy—in line with their national interests. This claim has been defended by David Miller (2005, 2016) and Christopher Wellman (Wellman and Cole 2011), who both advance a version of the claim that the ability to control immigration at their discretion is a moral right held by states and exercised on behalf of the national communities they represent.

Defending the right of states to exercise discretionary immigration controls based on the right to national self-determination entails demonstrating firstly that states are the kinds of entities that possess rights of self-determination, and secondly that this right necessarily includes a right to exercise discretionary immigration controls. The claim that states possess rights of national self-determination relies upon an understanding of states as representing political or cultural communities, which have shared histories and common interests and aims. Defending this position, Miller asserts, "People who form a national community in a particular territory have a good claim to political self-determination; there ought to be put in place an institutional structure that enables them to decide collectively matters that concern primarily their own community" (Miller 2000, 27).

Miller's assertion is demonstrative of the view that states possess the right of self-determination in virtue of the rights of the community they represent. On the basis of this understanding, both Miller (2016) and Wellman (Wellman and Cole 2011) interpret the right of national self-determination as conditional upon the representative and "legitimate" nature of the state. For Miller, states with democratically elected governments are ideal candidates for self-determination, on the basis that they are "representative of the population in a strong sense" (Miller 2016, 60). However, he adds that "democracy is not always necessary" and suggests additional ways that legitimacy may be conferred, for example "by inherited allegiance to a ruling family, or by recognizing the supreme authority of religious leaders" (Miller 2016, 60). Along similar lines, Wellman understands legitimate states as those that protect the basic human rights of their citizens (while also respecting the human rights of outsiders) (Wellman and Cole 2011). Insofar as the government of a state adequately serves the interests of the national community, it is understood as acquiring the right to determine national policy according to priorities it determines for itself (in line with basic human rights). This is on the strength of the presumption that these priorities will also be the priorities of the national community, or will at the very least derive from the general interests of this community. States that oppress rights and fail to represent the collective interests of their citizens are not candidates for the right of self-determination.

Both Miller and Wellman argue that preventing states from determining their own policy agendas would violate the rights of the citizens they represent to determine their collective destiny via their own institutions. They each see immigration as a policy area over which national communities have a right of control, and understand the state as exercising this right on behalf of these communities. For Wellman, the right of national communities to control immigration is grounded in their right of freedom of association, which he understands as a necessary condition for self-determination. If the right to freedom of association is to be fully respected, he argues, then it must include the right to refuse associations. Where the citizens of a nation decide that they do not wish to associate with outsiders, or wish to associate with them on specific terms, their wishes must be respected. A failure to respect these wishes would amount to a violation of the right to self-determination, and the denial of the right of states to set immigration policy at its discretion fails to respect these wishes. On this basis then, we must recognize the right of states to exercise discretionary immigration controls (Wellman and Cole 2011).

For Miller, national self-determination consists in "the right of a democratic public to make a wide range of policy choices within the limits set by human rights" (Miller 2016, 62). Immigration policy is included in the list of areas over which national communities must be permitted to exercise their will because of the strong potential that immigration has to affect the communal life of the national group. Arguing this, Miller suggests that "the public culture of their country is something that people have an interest in controlling: they want to be able to shape the way that their nation develops, including the values that are contained in the public culture" (Miller 2005, 200). He observes that the numbers of immigrants entering a country, as well as the "personal characteristics" of the immigrants, will affect areas of communal life that are of vital importance to a nations' citizens, for example, the size of the domestic population, expenditure on public services, and the general cultural composition of the national group (Miller 2016). Insofar as citizens have a shared interest in maintaining some control over these features of their communal life, Miller argues that they must be permitted the right to control immigration at their discretion. When it comes to rules governing immigration then, Miller asserts that "a *political judgement* needs to be made about the scale and type of immigration that will enrich rather than dislocate the existing public culture" (Miller 2005, 201; emphasis added). For Miller, a self-determining national community "must have the *right* to control its borders in order to preserve a meaningful range of policy choices" (Miller 2016, 62).

In defending the rights of states to control immigration, both Miller and Wellman understand this right as precisely the right of discretionary control such as is exercised by most states today. If national communities possess the right to determine for themselves the nature of their communal life and their relation to outsiders, then they must have the right to manage who is permitted to enter their community, in what numbers, and on what terms. Losing control of these matters would preclude national communities from being able to effectively manage vital features of their communal life and would therefore undermine national self-determination. On this argument then, national communities must be permitted to manage immigration in accordance with their collective interests. Neither Miller nor Wellman can accept a scenario whereby states are only permitted to control borders in line with general principles. Rather, what they seek to defend are the rights of states to choose what kinds of people can become immigrants, when and how, and to revise their judgments as they see fit. In this vein, Wellman concludes that "legitimate states are morally entitled to unilaterally design and enforce their own immigration policies, even if these policies exclude potential immigrants who desperately want to enter" (Wellman and Cole 2011, 13).

The Failure of the National Self-Determination Defense

There are two levels of objection to the national self-determination argument for discretionary border controls. At the first level is the observation that the right of states to self-determination, understood as derived from the rights of their citizens to direct their own affairs, does not obviously or necessarily include a right of states to freely introduce any policies they choose, especially where doing so causes the kinds of ill effects described in the first section. In fact, the right of national self-determination is best understood (and has traditionally been understood) as the purely *negative* right of legitimate states to non-intervention. Understood in this sense, the right of national self-determination is taken as deriving from the right of a population to be governed by the institutions it recognizes as legitimate according to its own procedural standards, be these democratic, constitutional, or otherwise.

This entails a right of non-intervention for the obvious reason that coercive impositions into the running of one state by the government of another are entirely incompatible with the rights of citizens to be governed by institutions that they recognize as procedurally legitimate. This is not to say that in the absence of outside intervention, citizens will definitely find themselves governed by procedurally legitimate institutions, but rather to state a minimal standard (the standard of non-intervention) for the achievement of this end. It is along these lines that John Stuart Mill, an early advocate of the principle of non-intervention, defined it as the right of a people to "become free by their own efforts" (Mill 1987).

In interpreting national self-determination as essentially entailing a right of arbitrary coercion, both Miller and Wellman extend the concept well beyond its original meaning to advance what Bas Van-der Vossen has called a "control of destiny" argument (Vossen 2014). Vossen summarizes this type of argument as follows:

1. States with a right to self-determination have the right to choose their political destiny;
2. Immigration affects the state's political destiny;
3. Therefore, states with a right to self-determination have the right to choose whether or not to allow immigration. (Vossen 2014, 274)

However, as Vossen points out, premise one is simply false; "self-determination does not entitle groups to have control over just anything that might affect their destiny" (Vossen 2014, 274). To demonstrate the point, he constructs an example in which Canada, having become a prosperous and desirable destination, decides to introduce a policy of fully open borders. In the example, many US citizens decide to take advantage of the opportunities offered by this situation and move to Canada. As Vossen observes, this is precisely the type of scenario in which the political destiny of the United States is affected. Many people who contribute to the US budget through taxation may be among those who leave, for instance. But this does not create a right, held by the United States, to prevent Canada from pursuing its open borders policy. Nor does it entitle the US administration to coercively prevent its citizens from leaving and taking up opportunities in Canada. In much the same way, then, the simple fact that a spontaneous phenomenon—like an inflow of immigrants—affects the "political destiny" of a state is in no way sufficient to ground a right, held by that state, to coercively restrict that phenomenon.

What Vossen's critique of the "control of destiny" argument reveals is that in their use of the national self-determination defense, both Wellman and Miller introduce an additional, unsupported claim into their understandings of the concept. This is the claim that communities of individuals possess rights to have their values and preferences actualized in public policy, and that they confer to legitimate states the right to design and direct this policy on their behalf. However, as we have seen, this presumption is not contained in the original meaning of national self-determination. It therefore requires additional justification before it can be relied upon. The justification on which the argument from national self-determination relies, however, includes a presumption about the nature and rights of national communities that is not borne out in reality; namely, that they exemplify sufficient homogeneity of interests and preferences such that a single, collective interest can be established and captured in any number of policy decisions, including those about the kinds of immigration that are desirable. It is here that we arrive at the second level of objection to the argument from national self-determination; it relies upon a false account of the nature of national communities. This account has been exposed to critique by Hayek in his second volume of *Law, Legislation and Liberty*, and an elucidation of this critique will be the focus of the remainder of this section.

The national self-determination defense of discretionary immigration controls relies on the idea that there exist within national communities, collective values, interests, and preferences such that the community as a whole can be understood as supporting and endorsing certain positive actions by the state as being genuinely representative of its collective aims. Thus, David Miller asserts, "Self-determination assumes that there exists a group—the 'self'—that is sufficiently cohesive that one can attribute to it a range of aims and values that the members recognise as part of their collective identity, even though no individual member is likely to subscribe to them all" (Miller 2016, 69).

However, the "control of destiny" presumption, when applied to collectives, only works if *either* the group in question is a voluntarily formed collective, such that members can enter and leave as they desire, *or* a sufficiently homogeneous collective, such that nontrivial sets of shared values can actually be said to exist. This is because the alleged right of the group to control its own destiny must be ultimately derived from the rights of the individual members to the same. This transfer of rights from the individual to the group can only happen, though, if either (a) all members possess the same values and preferences such that the desires and aims of each individual are simply *identical with* the desires and aims of the group or (b) the members who dissent from the collective position have given their consent to be bound by the group decision on all issues, such that they can be legitimately considered obliged to so conform. Since states are not entities with voluntary membership, the latter justification is not open to the "control of destiny" account. However, the former justification that the desires and aims of each individual citizen are identical with the desires and aims of the group, is not borne out in the modern nation state, except perhaps in respect of a very narrow range of broad and general issues. The idea that positive policy decisions on specific topics like the design of immigration controls can enjoy anything like a broad consensus or can be condensed into anything like a representative, national position is extremely far-fetched. The "control of destiny" defense of discretionary immigration controls relies upon a presumption of collective values and preferences that does not exist in reality.

Hayek makes precisely this point in his analysis of the nature and conditions of what he calls the "Great Society." By this, Hayek means the type of society contained within the modern-day nation state, in which diverse individuals coexist alongside one another and coordinate primarily through their economic interactions. This he contrasts with the "tribal society," a more primitive form of human community in which individuals coexisted in smaller groups that were bound together by familial relations and genuinely shared goals (Hayek 1976). In the modern, non-tribal societies contained within the nation state Hayek observes "there will exist no agreement on the relative importance of their respective ends" and argues that "what makes agreement and peace in such a society possible is that the individuals are not required to agree on ends but only on means which are capable of serving a great variety of purposes" (Hayek 1976, 3).

Chandran Kukathas summarizes this Hayekian position neatly when he points out that—in today's world at least—"society is not subsumed by the state" (Kukathas 2012, 664). Critiquing a version of the argument from national self-determination, he points out that societies "have a life independent of the state" (Kukathas 2012, 664), such that even where a society of individuals with genuinely shared goals exists and can be understood to possess the right of self-determination, this right will not be directly conferred to any recognized state (Kukathas 2012). Indeed, we can go further than this to argue that no contemporary state can claim to possess rights of self-determination on the basis of the rights of any community of shared interests to the same. This is because, as Hayek points out, the modern state does not exist as a community of individuals with the relevant shared goals and interests. Instead what exists in the Great Society, as exemplified by the contemporary nation state, is a collective of individuals with diverse, conflicting, and incommensurable ends, such that the state cannot possibly hope to represent them all through positive policy agendas. Any attempts to do so will result in policy that reflects the ends of only a proportion of the individuals who make up the society. The important point then is that, in the absence of a genuinely unified, collective position about the specific ends toward which the rules of a contemporary state should aim, it is not possible to claim—as the control of destiny position does—that the state can possess a right to enforce these rules. This includes discretionary immigration controls.

In enforcing these controls, the state is by definition engaged in the practice of arbitrary coercion, which has been the subject of this chapter. What is more, it can claim of no rights-based justification for this, since the alleged group right it must rely on to do so cannot exist in the contemporary states that claim these rights.

Are Non-Arbitrary Immigration Controls Possible?

This chapter has argued that discretionary immigration controls entail a form of Hayekian arbitrary coercion that subverts freedom by preventing individuals from being able to effectively plan their lives, and that violates the liberal principle of equality. For these reasons, I contend that discretionary immigration controls should be rejected in favor of more general policies that do not fall foul of the Hayekian critique outlined in this chapter. At this point, however, there are two further, related worries that should be briefly addressed. The first is that the requirement for non-arbitrary immigration controls may be too demanding, such that it is simply impossible to envisage any immigration policy besides totally open borders that does not fall foul of the objection. The second is that the requirement for non-arbitrary immigration controls is not demanding enough, and that it is entirely possible to envisage a general rule on immigration that is far more restrictive than the discretionary policies this chapter has critiqued.

Taking the first worry, it might be argued that given Hayek's point about the diversity of ends in the contemporary nation state, it is simply impossible to envisage *any* immigration policy that does not advance the interests of some over those of others. If this is the case, *all* immigration policy will be considered arbitrary and thus objectionable on this Hayekian framework. However, what this worry confuses are the effects of a policy versus its intentions. It may be the case that a general rule—for instance the rule that theft is wrong—ultimately protects the interests of those with property over the interests of those without. However, the crucial point from the Hayekian perspective is that those who gain by the rule have not been selected by the state as the essential beneficiaries. Indeed, the generality of the rule means it will not always be the same people who benefit from it. While I may own property today, you may own property tomorrow, and provided the rule affords us the same protections vis-à-vis any property we do own, it is not arbitrary. On the subject of immigration controls then, it is entirely possible to envisage general policies—for instance the policy of excluding those who have been exposed to infectious diseases—which, while benefitting those who are well at any given time at the expense of those who may be sick at any given time, do not *aim* at the advancement of any specific group as the primary policy agenda.

The second worry is related to the concerns discussed in the above section "Hayek and the Ills of 'Arbitrary Coercion'" that the Hayekian prescription for avoiding arbitrary coercion may be insufficient to protect the sphere of liberties we would ideally like to see protected in society. In relation to immigration controls, we may worry that the Hayekian account can justify extremely restrictive immigration policies, provided these are grounded in general rules. Could we, for example, given our Hayekian account, justify a maximally restrictive immigration policy that simply states that no one born outside a territory will ever be permitted to enter? This policy seems to meet the criteria of a general rule, insofar as it is not intended to favor any particular interests, and it is fixed and stable such that citizens can predict the effects (there will be no immigration) and can plan around these. However, it is also a severely restrictive policy, even more so than many of the discretionary policies this chapter has critiqued. If it is justifiable under a Hayekian account then, the account may be of little worth to us, at least insofar as we wish to avoid such restrictive policy.

There are two main points to make in response to this worry. The first is that the idea that such a policy actually does exemplify a general rule, and does not seek to advance any specific interest, does not seem entirely accurate. There seems to be no generally applicable reason, outside a situation of extreme emergency, for a state to entirely close its borders, and indeed under ordinary circumstances such a policy is almost guaranteed to do a lot more harm to the domestic economy than any good it can achieve. For this reason, it seems that any state adopting such a policy must either be acting *entirely* arbitrarily, on the total whim of the administration, or it must be responding to some pressing concern within some element of the population. The idea that any state would have a generally relevant reason to adopt such an extreme policy seems almost inconceivable. However, let's assume that such a reason exists and this policy is implemented and genuinely meets the criteria of a general rule. Does this now mean that it is justified under a Hayekian account? I maintain that it does not. In light of Hayek's arguments on the ills of arbitrary coercion, I suggest that Hayek's prescription regarding the preferability of general rules be taken as the minimal standard for avoiding the kind of coercion he is most concerned with—that which both limits our ability to plan and reduces our status as equals in society. I do not believe Hayek intends this prescription as a guarantee of how to avoid all forms of coercion and all interruptions to our freedom. As such, while it may be the case that Hayek cannot preclude the adoption of a highly restrictive immigration policy purely on the strength of his argument about the harms of arbitrary coercion, this certainly does not mean his account endorses or justifies this restrictive approach. Indeed, if Hayek can demonstrate that a policy of entirely closed borders causes an equivalent disruption to the economic efficiency of a society as do discretionary border controls (which he almost certainly can), he may still be able to condemn this policy on purely consequentialist grounds.

CONCLUSION

This chapter has argued that discretionary immigration controls of the kinds exercised by contemporary nation states are paradigmatic of the kind of arbitrary state coercion described by Hayek in his attacks on central planning. On the basis of this argument, and via an elucidation of Hayek's account of the specific harms that arbitrary coercion causes to the freedom of individuals and society, I have suggested that discretionary immigration controls should be eschewed and replaced with more general rules of admission. Having set out this argument, I have also examined a putative defense of the right of states to exercise discretionary immigration controls, grounded in the notion of the right of national self-determination. Via an elucidation of Hayek's arguments about the nature of the modern nation state, I have demonstrated that any rights of communal self-determination that do exist cannot attach to contemporary nation states in anything but a negative sense, which entails nothing more than the principle of non-intervention. The right of discretionary immigration controls is not one that can correctly be said to belong to modern states. On this basis, I have concluded this chapter with the claim that the exercise of discretionary immigration controls by states represents a serious threat to the liberty of individuals and society, and cannot be defended on the basis of the rights of states. As such, insofar as they value individual freedom and the social prosperity it gives rise to, liberal societies have strong reasons to abandon discretionary immigration controls.

REFERENCES

Abizadeh, Arash. 2010. "Democratic Legitimacy and State Coercion: A Reply to David Miller." *Political Theory* 38 (1): 121–30.

Carens, Joseph. 1987. "Aliens and Citizens: The Case for Open Borders." *Review of Politics* 49 (2): 251–73.

_______. 2013. *The Ethics of Immigration.* Oxford: Oxford University Press.

Clemens, Michael. 2011. "Economics and Emigration: Trillion Dollar Bills on the Sidewalk?" *Journal of Economic Perspectives* 25 (3): 83–106.

Hayek, F. A. 1944. *The Road to Serfdom.* Chicago: University of Chicago Press.

_______. 1945. "The Use of Knowledge in Society." *American Economic Review* 35 (4): 519–30.

_______. 1960. *The Constitution of Liberty*. Chicago: University of Chicago Press.

_______. 1976. *Law Legislation and Liberty*. Vol. 2: *The Mirage of Social Justice*. Chicago: University of Chicago Press.

Huemer, Michael. 2010. "Is There a Right to Immigrate?" *Social Theory and Practice* 36 (3): 429–61.

Kukathas, Chandran. 2012. "Why Open Borders?" *Ethical Perspectives* 19 (4): 649–75.

Lomasky, Loren E., and Fernando R. Teson. 2015. *Justice at a Distance: Extending Freedom Globally*. Cambridge: Cambridge University Press.

Mill, John Stuart. 1987. "A Few Words on Non-Intervention." *Foreign Policy Perspectives* 27 (3): 252–64.

Miller, David. 2000. *Citizenship and National Identity*. Cambridge: Polity Press.

_______. 2005. "Immigration: The Case for Limits." In *Contemporary Debates in Applied Ethics*, edited by Andrew I. Cohen and Christopher H. Wellman, 193–206. Oxford: Wiley Blackwell.

_______. 2009. *National Responsibility and Global Justice*. Oxford: Oxford University Press.

_______. 2016. *Strangers in Our Midst*. Cambridge, MA: Harvard University Press.

Nozick, Robert. 1974. *Anarchy, State, and Utopia*. Malden, MA: Blackwell.

Vossen, B.V. 2014. "Immigration and Self-Determination." *Politics, Philosophy & Economics* 14 (3): 270–90.

Wellman, Christopher Heath, and Philip Cole. 2011. *Debating the Ethics of Immigration: Is There a Right to Exclude?* Oxford: Oxford University Press.

Chapter 6

A Liberal Response to Group Rights

Samantha Godwin

Contemporary political discourse has been greatly influenced by ideological positions that center on group identity, on both the political right and the left (Lilla 2016). While the "collectivism" of twentieth-century communist, fascist, and authoritarian ideologies subordinated consideration of individual interests to the ostensible collective interests of society or the state, contemporary group identity centered politics discounts individual interests in a somewhat different way: by viewing the consideration owed to individuals as modified by the identity groups to which they belong (Foulkes 1990, 252).[1]

The politics of group identity has both analytical and normative components. The group-centered mode of social analysis holds that society cannot be accurately described by looking to the individuals who make it up and their individual choices. Instead, scholars like S. H. Foulkes argue that individuals cannot be understood except through relation to the groups they belong to, and, in turn, society can only be understood through analysis of the groups that compose it (Foulkes 1990, 252).

Current iterations of group identity politics have adopted the older group-centered mode of social analysis as a basis for a corresponding normative project. The normative position of group identity politics may be summarized as an insistence that groups have a moral value distinct from the individuals that compose them, such that *groups qua groups* may have moral rights, and that these rights may modify the moral entailments of individuals. These positions are presented in direct opposition to both methodological individualism and liberal moral individualism.

To define the stakes of the debate between the contemporary analytic and normative positions of group identity politics, and the analytic and normative positions of liberal individualism, it is instructive to look to F. A. Hayek's contributions to the debate between individualism and older versions of collectivism.

In this chapter I will first explore Hayek's contributions to the prior individualism/collectivism debate as a means of framing a critique of contemporary group-based identitarianism. Employing this liberal individualist framework, I then offer a set of criticisms of group rights claims that have emerged from the communitarian critiques of liberalism.[2] Next, I will offer a background on communitarian critiques of liberalism. I then will introduce some conceptions of group rights that follow from the communitarian or group rights critiques of liberalism. Finally, I will seek to categorize three sorts of group rights claims. Each type of claim will then in turn be critically evaluated. A commonality that runs throughout the various group rights claims is a reliance on unequal standards of moral evaluation in a manner that cannot be applied consistently and equally to everyone. This leads the group rights advocate to internally inconsistent positions. The moral failings of the more atomistic version of liberal individualism[3] that are said to motivate communitarian and group rights paradigms are correctable within liberal individualism and are not effectively addressed by group rights.

THE STAKES OF ANALYTIC AND MORAL INDIVIDUALISM

In "Individualism: True and False," Hayek offers an account of the social analysis of what he calls "true individualism":

> [True individualism] is primarily a *theory* of society, an attempt to understand the forces which determine the social life of man, and only in the second instance a set of political maxims derived from this view of society . . . its basic contention is . . . that there is no other way toward an understanding of social phenomena but through our understanding of individual actions directed toward other people and guided by their expected behavior. This argument is directed primarily against the properly collectivist theories of society which pretend to be able to directly to comprehend social wholes like society, etc., as entities *sui generis* which exist independently of the individuals which compose them. (Hayek 1948, 6)

As compared to Foulkes's group-centered analysis, Hayek's analysis of the relationship between individuals and collectives can be seen as a precisely inverse account of how individuals and society can be understood in relation to each other.

The need to analyze society in terms of the individuals who compose it rather than viewing individuals as constituted by society is in part explained by Hayek as a result of the limits of human knowledge and human action. People "cannot know more than a tiny part of the whole of society and that therefore all that can enter into his motives are the immediate effects which his actions will have in the sphere he knows" (Hayek 1948, 14). People do not experience society as a whole, they experience their own minds, desires, consciences and actions—we exist in relation to each other, but we relate to each other via individual interactions that cannot be captured by a top-down group-based analysis (Hayek 1948, 15).[4]

From Hayek's individualist social analysis follows Hayek's individualist normative positions. Hayek writes that "[f]rom the awareness of the limitations of individual knowledge and from the fact that no person or small group of persons can know all that is known to somebody, individualism also derives its main practical conclusion: its demand for a strict limitation of all coercive or exclusive power" (Hayek 1948, 16). Alternatives to these strict limits on coercion against individuals necessarily involve "coercive or arbitrary intervention of authority" (Hayek [1944] 2007, 86).

Hayek suggests that the principle moral dispute between the leftwing variants of collectivism and liberal individualism is not principally about *ends* but about *means*. In *The Road to Serfdom*, Hayek writes that socialism "may mean, and is often used to describe, merely the ideals of social justice, greater equality, and security, which are the ultimate aims of socialism. But it means also the particular method by which most socialists hope to attain these ends and which many competent people regard as the only methods by which they can be fully and quickly attained [that of a planned economy]" (Hayek [1944] 2007, 83). While liberals individualists and left collectivists aim for similar principled ideals, they differ in methods for pursuing those ideals: "[n]early all the points which are disputed between socialists and liberals concern the methods common to all forms of collectivism and not the particular ends which the socialists want to use them; and all the consequences with which we shall be concerned in this book follow from the methods of collectivism irrespective of the ends for which they are used" (Hayek [1944] 2007, 84).

One way that Hayek identifies the central moral dispute between the individualist and collectivist positions is that:

> The question is whether . . . it is better that the holder of coercive power should confine himself in general to creating conditions under which the knowledge and initiative of individuals are given the best scope so that *they* can plan most successfully; or whether a rational utilization of our resources requires *central* direction and organization of all of our activities according to some consciously constructed "blueprint." (Hayek [1944] 2007, 85)

In this way, a defense of methodological individualism hints at reasons to favor principles of non-coercion between individuals.

The core moral insight of Hayek's *Road to Serfdom* may be the identification of the individual as the proper unit of moral consideration, as opposed to a morality that considers groups *qua* groups or society distinct from the individuals who compose it to be the proper subjects of moral consideration. Hayek writes that "[t]he essential features of individualism . . . are the respect for the individual man *qua* man, that is, the recognition of his own views and tastes as supreme in his own sphere, however narrowly that may be circumscribed, and the belief that it is desirable that men should develop their own individual gifts and bents" (Hayek [1944] 2007, 68).

By framing the debate in terms of a disagreement over what are the proper subjects of moral consideration, individuals, groups, or both, the challenge to liberal egalitarian morality from the morality of group rights is brought into focus. Either moral entitlements, rights, and duties attach to individuals *qua* individuals alone, as Hayek argues, or moral entitlements, rights, and duties attach to groups *qua* groups—either alone or groups in competition with individuals. When moral entitlements attach to groups, the *mutually exclusive* moral claims of individuals are correspondingly diminished. Where a group rights claim that conflicts with an individual right is taken to be morally cognizable, the recognition of that individual right is discounted in proportion to the degree the group rights claim is recognized. When coercion deployed on behalf of group rights claims, liabilities attach to individuals in instances where they would be free from coercion absent the recognition of the group rights. In this way, extending moral and legal recognition of group rights comes at the expense of at least some individual rights when they come in direct conflict.

THE GROUP RIGHTS CRITIQUE OF LIBERAL INDIVIDUALISM

The liberal conception of morality has a number of distinguishing characteristics that have been subject to communitarian critique. First, it is individualistic in two senses. Liberal individualism first holds individuals to be the sole unit of moral consideration (Hayek [1944] 2007, 68). As such, liberal individualism analyzes the foundation of individual rights and interests, in the first instance, as bearing interests distinct and independent from other people, groups, culture, and resulting social contingencies. This can be described as a position that people are each "a subject given prior to and independent of [their] objects" (Sandel 1998, 7). According to Sandel's account, the liberal "subject is something 'back there,' antecedent to any particular experience, that unifies our diverse perceptions and holds them together in a single consciousness" (Sandel 1998, 8). People are "independent in the sense that our identity is never tied to our aims and attachments" (Sandel 1998, 179).

People are also conceived of individualistically in a second sense of having the "moral power to form, to revise, and rationally to pursue a conception of the good" (Rawls 1980, cited in Sandel 1998). Michael Sandel summarizes this position as holding that "we are not defined by the particular traditions we inhabit or the convictions we espouse; instead, we are independent of our aims and attachments, capable, at least in principle, of standing back to assess and revise them" (Sandel 1989b, 598). Charles Taylor describes an extreme version of this position as "atomism," that "everyone defines his or her purposes in individual terms" (Taylor 1989, 413).[5]

Second, liberalism insists on neutrality between competing conceptions of the good (Rawls 2005, 192). Will Kymlicka describes this as "[a] distinctive feature of contemporary liberal theory is its emphasis on 'neutrality'—the view that the state should not reward or penalize particular conceptions of the good life but, rather, should provide a neutral framework within which different and potentially conflicting conceptions of the good can be pursued" (Kymlicka 1989, 883). In this regard, liberalism has universalistic aspirations in the sense of asserting that a just framework can be adopted regardless of one's culturally specific and historically contingent "thick" conception of the good.

Communitarian critics[6] have responded that liberalism is both wrong about the nature of people and the range of moral consideration. The individualist perspective of liberalism is said to presume that one can make sense of "a universal, stable, and to a large extent, pre-social individual identity" (Addis 1999, 633). But according to communitarian critics, people cannot be understood atomistically, separate from the communities and cultures that define them. Instead people are at least partially "constituted" by their social existence, culture, relationships, attachments, and affiliations (Sandel 1998, 150). Michael Sandel describes this theory of community as:

> A theory of community whose province extended to the subject as well as the object of motivations would be individualistic in neither the conventional sense nor in Rawls'. It would resemble Rawls' conception in that the sense of community would be manifest in the aims and values of the participants—as fraternal sentiments and fellow-feeling, for example—but would differ from Rawls' conception in that community would describe not just a feeling but a mode of self-understanding partly constitutive of the agent's identity. On this strong view, to say that members of a society are bound by a sense of community is not simply to say that a great many of them profess communitarian sentiments and pursue communitarian aims, but rather that they conceive their identity—the subject and not just the object of their feelings and aspirations—as defined to

> some extent by the community of which they are a part. For them, community describes not just what they *have* as fellow citizens but also what they *are*, not a relationship they choose (as in a voluntary association) but an attachment they discover, not merely an attribute but a constituent of their identity. (Sandel 1998, 150)

In what might be described as the "embeddedness thesis" (Caney 1992, 273), Sandel writes that a person is:

> indebted in a complex variety of ways for the constitution of [his] identity—to parents, family, city, tribe, class, nation, culture, historical epoch, possibly God, Nature, and maybe chance . . . assets are more properly described as common assets in some sense; since others made me, and in various ways continue to make me, the person I am . . . when "my" assets or life prospects are enlisted in the service of a common endeavor, I am likely to experience this less as a case of being used for others' ends and more as a way of contributing to the purposes of a community I regard as my own. (Sandel 1998, 143)

The community allegiances that shape and define who people are have a significant moral dimension (Sandel 1998, 179). Sandel argues that a person's "constitutive attachments" determine his or her moral obligations beyond justice, not as a matter of reason, or voluntary acceptance, but precisely because those attachments partly define them (Sandel 1998, 179). Contrary to the liberal's contention, a person without constitutive attachments is not an "ideally free and rational agent" but someone "wholly without character, without moral depth" (Sandel 1998, 179). This is because without "constitutive attachments," people's choices are simply matters of preference such that the ends people select are not themselves independently morally relevant (Sandel 1998, 180). When people act out of the "enduring qualities of [their] character, by contrast, [their] choice of ends is not arbitrary in the same way" (Sandel 1998, 180).

One implication of the moral relevance of "constitutive attachments" is a rejection of liberal universality—moral obligations are to some extent varied and particular because the community that shapes them varies. Another implication is a rejection of neutrality among competing conceptions of the good: some ends and aims are moral, such as those that support positive community building, and others are not, and the state need not be neutral between ends of different moral worth (Sandel 1989a, 521).

The difference in the liberal and communitarian approaches can be seen in differing interpretations of religious liberty rights. To a liberal, religious liberty might be worth protecting for the same reasons that personal liberty in general is worth protecting: so people are free to select and pursue values that matter to them (Sandel 1998, xii).[7] Such protections are grounded not in any particular respect for religion, or the content of people's religious values, but out of respect for the dignity of persons as independent selves able to define their own ends (Sandel 1998, xii). This account of religious liberty, however, is unable to distinguish protections for people choosing to engage in certain practices for religious reasons and people who would seek to engage in similar practices according to secular preferences (Sandel 1998, xii–xiii). Absent this distinction, there are no moral grounds for allowing a religiously based exception to a rule of general applicability while denying a secular preference to be exempted from the same rule (Sandel 1998, xiii).

Sandel argued that while this liberal account of religious liberty preserved neutrality among different conceptions of the good, it improperly "confuses the pursuit of preferences with the performance of duties" (Sandel 1998, xiii). A person's religious convictions are not simply chosen preferences but unchosen dictates of conscience (Sandel 1989b, 611). As such religious liberty ought to be protected not because it is *chosen* but because "address[es] the problem of encumbered selves" (Sandel 1989b, 611).

GROUP RIGHTS

A right can be defined as a group right "only if it is a right held by a group rather than by its members severally" (Jones 1999, 354). When rights are ascribed to individuals without consideration for their group membership, such as a right to free association that, if applied in the aggregate, might add up to a group, these rights are not group rights as such (Jones 1999, 354).

Darlene Johnston sketches out a number of different accounts of group rights following from the communitarian recognition that people can realize goods in common that they cannot recognize alone, drawing on the work of Owen Fiss (Johnston 1989, 22). First, Owen Fiss has described rights bearing groups as "social groups" that are more than a mere collection of individuals who happen to be in the same place at the same time (Fiss 1976, 148; Johnston 1989, 22). Two features distinguish social groups from mere aggregations. The first is that the group is an entity possessing a distinct existence separate from its members that it possesses an identity (Fiss 1976, 148; Johnston 1989, 22). The second is that the group is conditioned by its interdependence (Fiss 1976, 148; Johnston 1989, 22). As such, a social group is more than the mere sum of its parts (Fiss 1976, 148; Johnston 1989, 22).

As described by Johnston, McDonald has expanded on Fiss's conception of social groups as, unlike aggregations, being "self-collecting" in that members engage in rule following activities that constitute their shared collectivity (McDonald 1986a, 120; see also Johnston 1989, 23). Two forms of self-collecting groups are possible, those that are based on people's wills (W groups) and those that are based on "internal recognition of some significant commonality" (R groups) (McDonald 1986b, 41; Johnston 1989, 23). R groups are *natural* in this account whereas W groups are *artificial*. To McDonald, group interdependence is more a "matter of recognition than of choice" (McDonald 1986b, 41; Johnston 1989, 23).

R groups are for McDonald more important because they are "more basic or deeper" in determining the "identity and welfare of the collectivity and, through it, its individual members" (McDonald 1986b, 41; Johnston 1989, 23). Ronald Garet argues that the voluntariness of a group and its moral importance are inversely related such that the least voluntary groups are most morally significant, and the most voluntary are the least significant (Garet 1983, 1045; Johnston 1989, 24). Frances Svensson argues that the more multidimensional and less single-issue based a group is the stronger its claim to a special status (Svensson 1979, 434; Johnston 1989, 23).

According to Garet, group rights cannot collapse into individual rights organized associatively because "there are certain things that only groups, and not individuals, can have . . . there are a fortiori certain things that only a group can hold a right to have" (Garet 1983, 1045; Johnston 1989, 24). A group's existence is itself, for Garet, a basis for group rights as existence carries its own moral value and that value implies a corresponding right (Garet 1983, 1002; Johnston 1989, 25).

Adeno Addis has made several other arguments for group rights. When a person is discriminated against not because of their particular characteristics but due to their perceived group membership, the injustice is inflicted on the group rather than on a person as an individual (Addis 1999, 615.) This can be seen in the case of an African American job applicant who is rejected due to his race: the rejection of this one African American applicant is not a particular rejection of an individual but of a race (Addis 1999, 615.) In this way "the existence of group injustice must imply the possibility of collective rights and group duties" (Addis 1999, 615.)

Certain rights are then said to be only realizable by a group, in a group context. The right to speak one's language, for example, is only realizable in the context of a preserved community of people who speak the same language (Addis 1999, 615.) A market of free associative choices among different possible cultural practices in effect entails the destruction of some groups and the resulting deprivation of the cultural rights of their members. Addis describes this as "what a seemingly neutral state purports not to affirm, is affirmed for it by a market which acts as its surrogate. In matters of group affiliation, state neutrality, in the face of unequal circumstances between minorities and majorities, is nothing less than an affirmation of one particular way of life and a deconstitution of another" (Addis 1999, 645.)

EVALUATING GROUP RIGHTS

The moral implications of "constitutive attachments" or "encumbered selves" and group rights can be divided into several sets of claims. The first are claims about rights that attach to groups *qua* groups. These claims include a group's right to preservation and self-determination. Such rights might be vindicated through education policy aimed at encouraging group members to continue to identify with the group and its practices,[8] giving the group special power over its members, giving the group sovereignty or quasi-sovereignty or a right to secede, or giving the group resources in disproportion to its members. This set of claims concerns duties that groups owe to other groups, non-members owe to groups not their own, foreign states owe to other nation states and states owe to minority groups within their jurisdiction.

The second set of claims might be thought of as the assertion that some moral duties attach to individuals in virtue of their membership in a group, or their "constitutive attachments." Believing that someone has a duty to their country (apart from those duties that they voluntarily accept), or that conscription of a government's nationals may be justified for the preservation of that nation state while rejecting the notion that a warlord would be similarly justified in conscripting people in the territory he or she controlled would be examples of this type of claim. This set of claims concerns the duties that group members might owe to the groups they belong to. These duties imply a corresponding set of rights of groups enforceable against their individual members.

The third set of claims could be described as the assertion that what the state or third parties owe to other people might be modified by the way that those other people are encumbered by constitutive attachments or group membership. The belief that religious practices or culturally significant practices deserve special protection either by permitting exceptions to rules of general applicability not extended to non-religious practices[9] or that certain people should be granted additional resources to participate in community building practices that are not extended to people pursuing other aims, are examples of this sort of claim. These claims can be thought of as concerning the duties that people and the government owe to other people in virtue of those other persons' encumbrances and group memberships.

A fourth "meta-ethical" claim implicit or explicit in some group rights positions is that the shared values of a community determine the correct moral considerations for that community (Caney 1992, 274). In this way morality is not universal but is community contingent and relative to community norms. An implication of this fourth group rights claim is that liberalism is just another community norm, specifically the community morality of post-enlightenment Western culture, which has elevated the value of individual rights and interests above relational interests and to the exclusion of group rights. Although this set of values prevails in the West, other sets of equally compelling values prevail elsewhere, and there is no community-independent objective view from which a different community's values can be judged and held more or less sound than others.

While many proponents of group rights views do not subscribe to this last sort of claim, in certain ways it nonetheless forms an implicit background assumption of the proceeding three types of group rights claims. This is because they all seem to treat the alleged fact that groups adopt certain values as grounds for viewing those values as morally significant even by those who do not share those values. This implied view provides a central source of the underlying problem with group rights: that they rely on asymmetric assessments of values in a manner that cannot be sustained consistently.

PROBLEMS OF GROUPS AS RIGHTS BEARERS

Despite substantial efforts to explain what groups are metaphysically if not mere aggregations of individuals, there has not been a satisfactory account. Merely describing a collection of individuals as a group does not mean that the group gains a new ontology separate from the individuals who comprise it. A shared recognition among group members likewise does not without further explanation transform the group into a separate entity with a moral worth greater than the sum of its parts. The recognition individuals have of their groups remains bounded by their individual consciousness. There can be no separate distinct group consciousness to emerge from this because groups unlike people do not have subjective mental experiences. While Christian List and Philip Petitt have argued that a group can have agency and *operate* "in effect" as having a "mind of its own" (List and Petitt 2011, 8), this does not imply that groups experience the world separately from their members. Groups do not experience qualia. Only entities with brains do, as far as we know. Individualism requires nothing more than a common sense materialist metaphysics or a metaphysics that allows for the reality of physical things that appear to us in the world. For groups to be entities that have actual rather than metaphorical experiences giving rise to interests and moral considerations *separate from and distinct from* the individuals that compose them would require that they have a very different ontology than what typical proponents of group rights have presented. Instead, separate qualities of groups are merely asserted without the further explanation required to make such claims credible.[10]

A test for whether a group has an independent existence separate from its members is as follows. If no individual recognized the existence of a particular group, would the group still exist? If not, then individuals and their recognition of the group are constitutive of the group. If group membership is ascribed to people by more powerful individuals not part of that group (such as may be the case in a caste system, or apartheid system), then the group's social reality may depend on the narratives of individuals who are not themselves a member of the group, but it is nonetheless contingent on its recognition by some set of individuals.

If groups exist only insofar as they are recognized by individuals, then any ontological status of a group separate from its individual members requires additional explanation. If groups are not things in the world distinct from individuals and individuals' acts of recognition, then how can they have morally significant rights and interests that implicate obligations for actual people beyond the moral rights and interests of their individual members?[11]

The case Hayek presents of a person's knowledge and action is always limited in scope to their own sphere of awareness (Hayek 1948, 14) applies here. If people stopped acknowledging a group and enacting the performances that constitute the group, the group would not exist—groups are therefore better understood as constituted by individuals than constituting individuals. Interdependent sets of people, often with deeply overlapping interdependences, can be described as groups and can have experiences and relationships that would be impossible without those interdependences. However, they remain physically individuals at least in the sense that their minds remain separate: each has privileged special knowledge of their own thoughts and sensory experiences in a manner not shared immediately with others. This remains true whether interdependences are chosen or come about according to circumstances outside of individuals' control (Hayek 1948, 14).

As for the notion that there are some things that only groups and not individuals can have, it does not follow from this that groups have a *right* to possess them. It is also unclear where individual possession ends and group possession starts. The law might ascribe certain rights and possessions to a corporation, tribe, or other association. The exercise of those juridical rights, however, are always through the acts and declarations of identifiable individuals, either directly in executive actions, or through aggregations of their individual choices in votes.

Moreover, while some groups such as Native American tribes, corporations, political parties, and churches may be able to exert agency of the sort described by List and Petitt, most of the identity groups that group rights advocates are concerned with do not have institutions through which they take official actions. Ethnic groups, nationalities, and races are less like the agential corporate groups List and Petitt describe and more like social labels assigned to individuals.[12]

The claim that a group's existence is inherently good, and as such carries corresponding rights to exist, is problematic for a number of reasons. First, it is far from clear that all groups' existences, even deeply constitutive groups characterized by unchosen interdependence, is a good thing. People may have identified very strongly with the Confederate States of America and racist fraternal organizations and religious groups emerging from them, but their preservation could hardly be seen automatically as a good thing without some sort of further explanation. Second, a rule that all groups must be preserved would deny the possibility for the creation and development of other groups—and each ethnic and national group likely requires the dissipation (one way or another) of prior groups. The French could not be a group if the Galli and Aquitani were preserved not due to any founding state violence (although most ethnic and national groups have some element of that) but because their potential set of members would be overlapping.

The preservation of a group is not always in accordance with the wishes or interests of its constituent members. Secessionist movements implicitly deny that the survival of the group as a whole is in their interests—and may in fact wish to dissolve the parent group altogether. Bosnian, Serbian, Kosovar, and Croatian national aspirations are together incompatible with the preservation of Yugoslavia as a people and the national aspirations of Yugoslavia and vice versa. Newfoundland's people (by a narrow majority) preferred annexation by Canada over independence—such that the national self-determination of Newfoundlanders (as expressed through the aggregation of their individual voting preferences) was incompatible with their continued national existence.

Groups do not have a separate existence or minds with which to conceive of values and interests, or mouths to voice them, so accounts of "group values" and "group interests" must in fact refer to *someone's* values, and *someone's* interests. Ostensible group values are better understood as necessarily the values of some individual or set of individuals. Often the most powerful or established members of a group have the ability to define what is to *count* as the values of the group (Okin 1999, 12) but, in so doing, they merely elevate their own values rhetorically and conceal the fact that they remain the values of particular individuals. Similarly, when groups are ostensibly given power, because power is exercised by and through individuals, this amounts to granting individual people more power.

To grant groups special resources and powers or special deference to their values is, in effect, to have an unequal two-tiered system of personal values. People who only have pretentions to speak for themselves and act for themselves are accorded less rhetorical and moral weight than those who assert that their views and actions are not their own but those of their group. But this does not make it so. It instead means only that speech and claims of value couched in the language of group values and interests is granted rhetorical privilege over that which does not adopt such a rhetorical strategy. This unequal valuation of different people's conceptions of the good and values in accordance with whether or not their values allegedly coincide with group values is at odds with extending equal moral consideration to persons.

PROBLEMS OF CONSTITUTIVE ATTACHMENTS IMPOSING DUTIES ON THOSE ENCUMBERED BY THEM

Sandel has argued, as described earlier, that an autonomous individual unencumbered by constitutive attachment is not a rational agent but someone whose choice of ends is arbitrary (Sandel 1998, 180). But drawing one's ends from the alleged ends of a community, culture, family, religion, or other group whose membership is felt to constitute one's own identity does little to resolve this. Instead, it merely shifts the choice of ends back one step at best, or is much more arbitrary at worst.

Practically no one thinks that the putative values of their community are true or correct for themselves or anyone else *merely in virtue of the fact that their community selected those values*. Such a belief would entail a belief that individuals are bound by their community values, but that their community values have no justification beyond the circular assertion that they are the values of the community. While the "atomistic" liberal might at least be able to give a reasoned explanation to account for why he or she selected one value over another, the deeply "encumbered self" can give no more account than *because the community says so*. Such an account amounts to merely substituting some prior set of arbitrary valuations for one's own set of valuations.

Instead, people are more likely to think that the values of their community would have value even if their community did not choose to value them. For example, devout Southern Baptists might believe they are obliged to worship Jesus because they are Southern Baptists, but they are also likely to believe that worshipping Jesus Christ is valuable even if the Southern Baptist Convention reversed its policy on that matter or the community as a whole did not hold those beliefs. If posed the hypothetical, "would worshipping Jesus be obligatory if you had not been raised a Southern Baptist, but had instead been raised, say, a Hindu who was not exposed to Southern Baptist teachings," true believers would almost certainly answer in the affirmative.

This implies that the encumbered person's experience of their attachments as constitutive of their identity and implicating their duties does nothing to actually resolve the question of where those values, duties, and conceptions of the good come from. From the vantage point of the encumbered self, their feeling that a certain value or good is worthy does not provide the foundation for that value or good's worth. The value or the good in question is felt to remain worthy to them in the hypothetical case where they fail to "recognize" their encumbrance, or they failed to recognize that the content of the encumbrance constituted their identity.[13] This tends to be true even of values derived from one's constitutive attachments that are expressly non-universal and group limited. As such the question of *which* values to adopt, from the perspective of the encumbered self, is not resolved by the fact of their encumbrance. Instead, the reason for why one value is more worthy than another is based on something other than the fact of their constitutive attachments, the location of the value assessment is just shifted back one step, to an assessment made by a community (whose truth of falsity does not depend on the fact that the community made it) rather than an assessment made immediately by the individual.

If someone believes that the values of the community do not depend simply on the fact that the community values them, this implies that even an encumbered self has to perform an individual determination of what ought to be valued and judged good. This places them in precisely the same position as the unencumbered existentialist except that their reasons are not formulated along lines that might convince someone who does not share their constitutive attachments.[14] We should not, however, confuse the opaqueness and untranslatability of a moral system with "moral depth."

For example, a devout Orthodox Jewish person might believe that they have obligations to follow a set of Jewish laws that do not apply to non-Jewish people. However, they would likely believe that these special obligations would attach to them *even* if they did not understand them as constitutive of their identity and as special encumbrances (Yadan 2006).[15] To think otherwise would, in fact, be to return to the liberal "voluntarist" position that Sandel and others reject: to think that special obligations depend on a person's voluntary choice.

It is only from the perspective of the outsider looking in, that an encumbered person's values are contingent on their identity constituting community membership—from the internal vantage point, their values are not experienced as existing purely in relation to their community attachments. In this regard the communitarian proponent of group rights has adopted an external descriptive vantage point toward the constitutive attachments of other groups rather than describing a thesis that people can consistently apply to themselves and others. Although some might find this account convenient for representing to others why their particular values should be respected, it is not a satisfying account of where their particular values came from.[16] The idea that constitutive attachment explains personal values, therefore, requires an asymmetric account: constitutive attachments explain *other people's* personal values, but from a person's own perspectives, their values are not contingent on their constitutive attachments even though they happen to coincide with them.

There is also a separate problem of asymmetry arising in cases where an alleged group member does *not* recognize the values and goods of the group that she is allegedly part of. One option, a voluntarist option, is to simply say that her failure to recognize these values and goods means that they are not her own, and do not apply to her—she is free to choose whatever attachments she wants to have. This is, however, both a non-communitarian response and one unsatisfying to people whose view of their own group entailments includes a belief that their putative members must or should accede to the group interests whether they acknowledge them to hold a claim against them or not. Such a belief is likely necessary to claim a group right to self-preservation that is not purely derived from the aggregated preferences of individuals to perpetuate the group.[17]

If it is believed that a putative group member can owe a duty of loyalty to the values of their putative group whether or not they share those values or count themselves a member of that group, then it is implied that that person's subjective constitutive attachments are not decisive in determining the values that apply to them. Instead, such a view gives priority to other people's constitutive attachments and values: the values of the people who have the power and rhetorical ability to define the group's identity, boundaries, and values. This presents a conflict: if duties follow from group memberships and the corresponding group values, but there is disagreement about who is a part of the group or what its values are, then how can any person's constitutive attachments be taken to carry moral weight for others? To accept one person's account in these cases is to reject another's. To hold that a person is bound only by those attachments they feel bound to is to adopt a liberal voluntarist position and not a position that group values give rise to special duties independent of voluntary choice. To asymmetrically award decisive interpretive power over who is bound by the supposed values of a group to the group's majority, or its "leaders," and not the dissident members who reject it, is either a majoritarian position corresponding to the aggregate wishes of individuals and not a "group," or an appeal to the arbitrary power of group "leaders," respectively.

It is this appeal to the arbitrary authority of one person over another that violates the principle of equal concern and respect that both leftwing advocates of collectivism and group rights and liberal individualists share. It is to violate what Hayek describes as liberal individualism's "main principle," "that no man or group of men should have power to decide what another man's status ought to be, and it regards this as a condition of freedom so essential that it must not be sacrificed to the gratification of our sense of justice or envy" (Hayek 1948, 30). But if this egalitarian principle, shared by those group rights collectivists from the left, *must* be violated if constitutive attachments can impose duties on those encumbered by them, then only the individualist position is consistent with the values common to both positions.

PROBLEMS OF CONSTITUTIVE ATTACHMENTS MODIFYING THE MORAL OBLIGATIONS OF THOSE NOT PERSONALLY ENCUMBERED BY THEM

As described by Sandel, many people feel that their religion, ethnicity, or community *defines* them (Sandel 1998, 150). Many people think that who someone *else* is depends on their constitutive attachments. But the mere fact that someone believes that they possess certain properties or rights cannot be sufficient to grant them that property or right. A person's mere belief that they have certain entitlements does not provide others an independent reason to recognize those entitlements if they do not share those beliefs.

Consider the following scenario. X may believe (rightly or wrongly) that he is a member of the House of Bourbon. This belief could be based on elaborate inculcation by his immediate and extended family and central to his self-conception and identity. It might also be "true" in the sense that, according to the laws of inheritance of the Ancien Régime in force at the time of the French Revolution, X would in fact be a member of the House of Bourbon. This constellation of constitutive attachments may also make him feel very strongly that he has a divinely given right to command the French state, or at least be exempt from taxation and reclaim a number of lands seized from his ancestors—lands that might be crucial to his identity. At a minimum, X feels he should be addressed as "His Majesty." These rights claims, if recognized, necessarily impose corresponding duties on the government and other people.

Why should the modern French state, or French citizens, think that X's constitutive attachments and the moral claims that result from them have any moral force over them? If people could simply assert that their identity demands the recognition of rights particular to themselves or those who share their identity, and imposing corresponding duties on others, then there would be no way to adjudicate between mutually exclusive particular rights claims. That someone's particular rights claims are embedded in a community tradition rather than "self-declared" would only give reason to grant that person deference if that community tradition was already presumed to determine what was morally required, *even for those who do not share that tradition.*

This amounts to a form of question begging in the following way: if the question is why should a community tradition or religious belief impose moral demands on those who do not share it, it would be purely circular to think that the answer is because the tradition or belief demands it. Such positions would likewise lead to inevitable inconsistencies. X might believe that as a member of the House of Bourbon he should be addressed as "His Majesty" but if Y believes that as a citizen of the Fifth Republic she is to acknowledge no monarch, for Y to respect X's constitutive attachments she must deny her own. For either X or Y to respect and facilitate the other's set of duties deriving from their constitutive attachments would require subordinating their own to the other in an asymmetric fashion. In this regard a rule of *constitutive attachments should be respected* requires asymmetric enforcement if it is to modify anyone's moral obligations: some must adopt *others'* constitutive attachments as giving them moral reasons while not having the same deference returned to them.

Take for the sake of argument, a thought experiment where a secular person, Z, has sound, justifiable reasons for believing that dolphin hunting is morally prohibited. Z has, through use of the reader's preferred type of moral reasoning, come to the conclusion that it is cruel to hunt dolphins, that dolphins possess a right not to be hunted, and, for other reasons of general applicability, that there is a general duty to abstain from dolphin hunting. Z's reasoning is such that Z believes that even if she herself did *not* think it wrong to hunt dolphins, it nonetheless would be. Z is in this regard a cognitivist about the claim "it is morally impermissible to hunt dolphins"—and she believes such a position to be true, not just a matter of preference. Z has successfully lobbied her government to prohibit dolphin hunting.

R, a resident of Z's country, is a member of a religion that believes that it is not only permissible to hunt dolphins, but that it is a moral obligation to do so, and that dolphin hunting is a sacrament that brings R closer to her God. R explains that, although, absent her religious convictions, there might be a strong secular case against dolphin hunting, dolphin hunting is *right* for her because of her constitutive attachment to her religious beliefs. It is moreover her moral duty, and that duty should correspondingly be respected by the government in the form of a special religious exemption to the dolphin-hunting ban. To obey the general legal duty to *abstain* from hunting dolphins would require that R violate her conscience, which she feels in part defines her and constitutes who she is as a person.

Should Z find R's narrative of her particular moral obligations compelling? Well, R's religion gives R reasons to think it morally permissible to hunt dolphins . . . but how can R's religion give Z reasons for believing that it is morally permissible to hunt dolphins? Z does not believe in R's religion. R's faith might be constitutive of R's personal conception of morality, but it does not constitute Z's conception of morality. It does not engage with or respond to the moral reasoning that Z went through to come to her belief that dolphin hunting is morally impermissible, at least not in any way that secular Z could find persuasive such that she would be convinced of it as a general matter.

For Z to accept that R's religious reasoning is grounds for granting R a waiver to Z's law, Z must subordinate her own moral reasoning to unshared religious claims advanced by R. This would be necessarily asymmetric in the following sense: R's religious reasoning would be sufficient to impose duties on Z (to grant an exemption, to carve out space where her moral demands go unmet), but Z's secular moral reasoning would be insufficient to impose duties on R (for R in this case does not set her religious reasoning aside to accommodate Z's moral reasoning).

If Z is a liberal, then she has the option of saying that while the content of R's religious values are themselves morally irrelevant, the *fact* that R values them is morally relevant. This fact does not give those religious values any moral weight themselves. However, because R is a rights bearing person who should be free to pursue her view of the good, there might be flexibility to accord R some moral excuse if R would suffer to an unusual degree in fulfilling her moral duties. R's religion is relevant only insofar as it is bound up in R's aims. This is, however, to respect R as a person without offering any respect for R's religious reasoning—if R gets an excuse it is not because her aims are good but because of the priority of individual rights to the good; in other words, the precise sort of liberal reasoning that communitarians reject (Sandel 1998, xii)—one based entirely on generally applicable individual rights and not group rights or individual moral statuses modified by constitutive attachments.

The dilemma is even worse when it is not between a liberal and someone encumbered by community identity, but between two sets of people with constitutive attachments that entail precisely mutually exclusive claims. What if Aism holds that Aists are obliged to build a shrine to Apollo on Mount Olympus and any other shrines on Mount Olympus are intolerable blaspheme that must be destroyed, whereas Eism holds that Eists must build a shrine to Dionysus on Mount Olympus and are obliged to destroy any other shrines found there. Maybe Aism and Eism are both long-standing historically grounded traditions that are minority cultures, which have both been subject to historic persecution, if any of those factors might be thought morally relevant to the status of Aist and Eist group rights and moral claims.

A liberal might think through this dilemma by way of how to best respect each person's dignity as an individual able to determine their own goods in life, even if the goods they choose are not themselves independent moral reasons for other people. The pure cultural relativist who believes their own morality to be totally cultural bound also has a way out, albeit a philosophically unsatisfactory one: to disregard the other's culture-bound values and pursue their own exclusively. British imperialist Charles James Napier asserted a consistently applied cultural relativism when famously remarking that Hindu priests ought to act according to their national customs by burning widows just as he will act according to his national custom of hanging men who burn widows (Napier 1851, 35).[18] Napier was presumably being sarcastic in that he actually believed his constitutive attachment derived practice to be morally obligatory and the Hindu priests' practice to be morally impermissible regardless of its religious significance, but it would be unclear how his "logic" could be refuted without drawing from some moral theory with universalist aspirations.

Arguing that Napier was wrong because the Hindu priests represent an oppressed people and he represents a vicious colonial empire would require a moral theory implicating universal obligations: the principles for preferring the Hindu priest's values to Napier's would require that Napier set his constitutive attachments aside and embrace a moral theory of universal application in a manner not demanded of the priests. Arguing that Napier was right because the widows were suffering from oppression would be to simply assert that the priest's constitutive attachments are not morally decisive no matter how deeply felt when they conflict with other people's rights—a return to a liberal position that the right is prior to the good. Neither helps the group rights communitarian. Communitarian group rights theorists who both feel that their constitutive attachments give rise to their own moral obligations, and that constitutive attachments can generally give rise to moral obligations for other people, will find themselves in an internally inconsistent position when faced with another person whose constitutive attachments lead to moral obligations incompatible with their own.

CONCLUSION

If the central disagreement between the proponents of group rights and the proponents of liberal individualism is whether morality should consider the interests of individuals or the interests of groups, or both, then the critique of individualism offered by communitarians and group rights proponents has not succeeded in establishing that groups are proper subjects of independent moral consideration separate from their members. Ascribing moral or legal entitlements to groups, as Hayek suggested in "Individualism: True and False" and *Road to Serfdom*, requires coercing nonconforming individuals and ascribing some individual's values a higher status than others.

The normative project of group rights proponents, in insisting that individual interests can be displaced by what other individuals claim to be the interests of a group, imposing special liabilities on group members due to their group's ostensible values, or granting certain people greater privileges in virtue of their group membership, are all cases of group rights claims at their core failing to accord equal concern and respect to all persons regardless of who they are. If group rights morality and egalitarian principles are irreconcilable, then there is good reason for egalitarian-minded advocates for identity group rights to reevaluate their position and consider how their aims of reducing discrimination, oppression, and inequality might be better fulfilled through a liberal individualist framework.

NOTES

1. "Human beings always live in groups. Groups in turn cannot be understood, except in relation to other groups and in the context of the conditions in which they exist. We cannot isolate biological, social, cultural and economic factors, except by special abstraction . . . the distinction between group and individual psychodynamics is meaningless, except again by abstraction. We sometimes talk of group and individual separately, as we focus more on one or other aspect of what is in fact a single and inseparable process" (Foulkes 1990, 252).

2. For other expositions of the relationship between communitarian critiques of liberalism and group rights, see generally Darlene Johnston, "Native Rights as Collective Rights: A Question of Group Self-Preservation" (1989); Adeno Addis, "Individualism, Communitarianism, and the Rights of Ethnic Minorities" (1999).

3. What Hayek rejects as "false individualism" in "Individualism: True and False" (Hayek 1948, 23).

4. "Or, to put this fundamental contention differently, human Reason, with a capital *R*, does not exist in the singular, as given or available to any particular person, as the rationalist approach seems to assume, but must be conceived as an interpersonal process in which anyone's contribution is tested and corrected by others" (Hayek 1948, 15).

5. F. A. Hayek rigorously objects to the accusation of "atomism": "There can be no greater contrast to this [true individualism] than the false individualism which wants to dissolve all these smaller groups into atoms which have no cohesion other than the coercive rules imposed by the state" (Hayek 1948, 23).

6. There is very significant diversity in the views that are often characterized as communitarian responses to liberalism. It would be a mistake to speak of communitarianism as any kind of a unified philosophical position and many prominent critics of liberalism whose views are described as communitarian subscribe to only some of the views outlined here.

7. F. A. Hayek gives a defense of group attachments within the context of individualism as part of local autonomy and voluntary associations—to Hayek, an individualist does not reject such attachments, but instead requires that they be voluntary rather than coerced by the state (Hayek 1948, 23).

8. *Wisconsin v. Yoder*—although decided on the grounds of individual parent's rights to determine the child's education—could be interpreted as vindicating the group rights of the Amish to inculcate their cultural practices and self-understanding into their children so as to enable the preservation of the culture.

9. Such as provided for, in the case of religion, in the Religious Freedom Restoration Act.

10. While List and Petitt offer a compelling account of group agency, they argue that this does not provide any basis for thinking that groups have moral rights equivalent to the rights of individuals (List and Petitt 2011, 179–80).

11. Is there, for example, a duty to revive the Cult of Zeus, a group that has lost all its members? If the duty to keep a language alive is extinguished when its last speakers choose not to speak it anymore, or die out, then in what sense does the duty to preserve the language attach to the language group and not to the people who would like to speak it?

12. Language communities and religious communities as distinct from church institutions are not just labels assigned to individuals but also practices that individuals engage in with other individuals—still this is very different than the way certain corporate groups can take official actions that are more than the mere aggregation of individual actions, as List and Petitt described.

13. Though people as encumbered selves are likely (absent liberal respect for other person's beliefs due to a respect for those persons and not an intrinsic respect for those beliefs) to think this only of their own encumbrances.

14. They are not necessarily "public reasons."

15. At least provided that they were given sufficient knowledge of who they are and what their obligations are.

16. Few conservative American patriots identified with President Obama's statement that "I believe in American exceptionalism, just as I suspect that the Brits believe in British exceptionalism and the Greeks believe in Greek exceptionalism." They believe that they believe in American exceptionalism not because they have constitutive attachments to America, but because America is, in fact, actually exceptional (Zurcher 2013).

17. If group preservation is of importance only so far as individuals value it, then it is realized through the mode of individual rights, not group rights.

18. "The priests said it was a religious rite which must not be meddled with—that all nations had customs which should be respected and this was a very sacred one. The general affecting to be struck with this argument replied. 'Be it so. This burning of widows is your custom; prepare the funeral pile. But my nation has also a custom. When men burn women alive we hang them, and confiscate all their property. My carpenters shall therefore erect gibbets on which to hang all concerned when the widow is consumed. Let us all act according to national customs!'"

REFERENCES

Addis, Adeno. 1999. "Individualism, Communitarianism, and the Rights of Ethnic Minorities." *Notre Dame Law Review* 67: 615–76.

Caney, Simon. 1992. "Liberalism and Communitarianism: A Misconceived Debate." *Political Studies* 40 (2): 273–89.

Fiss, Owen. 1976. "Groups and the Equal Protection Clause." *Philosophy and Public Affairs* 5 (2): 107–77.

Foulkes, Siegmund Heinz. 1990. "Problems of the Large Group." In *Selected Papers of S. H. Foulkes: Psychoanalysis and Group Analysis,* 249–69. London: Karnac Books.

Garet, Ronald. 1983. "Community and Existence: The Rights of Groups." *Southern California Law Review* 56: 1001–75.

Hayek, Friedrich. [1944] 2007. *The Road to Serfdom: Text and Documents—The Definitive Edition*. Chicago: University of Chicago Press.

———. 1948. "Individualism: True and False." In *Individualism and Economic Order*, 1–32. Chicago: University of Chicago Press.

Johnston, Darlene. 1989. "Native Rights as Collective Rights: A Question of Group Self-Preservation." *Canadian Journal of Law and Jurisprudence* 2 (1): 19–34.

Jones, Peter. 1999. "Group Rights and Group Oppression." *Journal of Political Philosophy* 7 (4): 353–77.

Kymlicka, Will. 1989. "Liberal Individualism and Liberal Neutrality." *Ethics* 99 (4): 883–905.

Lilla, Mark. 2016. "The End of Identity Liberalism." *New York Times*, November 18.

List, Christian, and Philip Petitt. 2011. *Group Agency: The Possibility, Design, and Status of Corporate Agents*. Oxford: Oxford University Press.

McDonald, Michael. 1986a. "Collective Rights and Tyranny." *University of Ottawa Quarterly* 56 (2): 115–23.

———. 1986b. "Indian Status: Colonialism or Sexism?" *Canadian Community Law Journal* 9: 23–48.

Napier, William. 1851. *History of General Sir Charles Napier's Administration of Scinde*. London: Chapman and Hall.

Okin, Susan Moller. 1999. *Is Multiculturalism Bad for Women?* Princeton, NJ: Princeton University Press.

Rawls, John. 1980. "Kantian Constructivism in Moral Theory." *Journal of Philosophy* 77 (9): 515–72.

———. 2005. *Political Liberalism: Expanded Edition*. New York: Columbia University Press.

Sandel, Michael. 1989a. "Moral Argument and Liberal Toleration: Abortion and Homosexuality." *California Law Review* 77 (3): 521–38.

———. 1989b. "Religious Liberty—Freedom of Conscience or Freedom of Choice." *Utah Law Review* 3: 597–615.

———. 1998. *Liberalism and the Limits of Justice*. Cambridge: Cambridge University Press.

Svensson, Frances. 1979. "Liberal Democracy and Group Rights: The Legacy of Individualism and Its Impact on American Indian Tribes." *Political Studies* 27 (3): 421–39.

Taylor, Charles. 1989. *Sources of the Self: The Making of the Modern Identity*. Cambridge: Cambridge University Press.

Yadan, Yaron. 2006. "The Secular Jew's Place in Halacha." *Daat Emet*, October 17. http://daatemet.org.il/en/torah-science-ethics/religion-ethics/the-secular-jews-place-in-halacha/.

Zurcher, Anthony. 2013. "The Unlikely Story Behind the Phrase 'American Exceptionalism.'" *BBC News Magazine,* September 13.

Chapter 7

The Social Basis of Ultimate Legal Rules

Hayek Meets Hart

Mikołaj Barczentewicz

The bulk of the legal literature that either builds on or criticizes Hayek focuses on Hayek's work specifically devoted to law, in particular to the rule of law and to the common law (Beaulier, Boettke, and Coyne 2005; Skoble 2006). I want to go beyond Hayek's research on law, while still building on it. My aim is to explore what insights for thinking about ultimate legal rules may be taken from Hayek's more general discussion of rules and of spontaneous orders. I provide here a sketch of a synthesis of Hayek's thought with the current standard framework in general theory (philosophy) of law, that of H. L. A. Hart (Hart 2012). What is interesting in Hart from a Hayekian perspective, is that in Hart's model of law ultimate legal rules are by necessity customary social practices. Even in the most organization-like society, the law—including the state law and Hayek's "legislation"—ultimately rests on a social practice of identifying certain things as law.

Hart's model of the foundations of law is compatible with Hayek's work both specifically devoted to law and with that on social rules and spontaneous orders in general. Hayek's insights that may enrich Hartian general jurisprudence have not yet received sufficient attention. Part of the reason for this may be that for a contemporary legal philosopher the part of Hayek's work that was explicitly devoted to what he called "legal positivism" was already behind its times when it was published. Hayek did not cite and engage with the sophisticated jurisprudential literature contemporary to his *Law, Legislation and Liberty*. Hart's *Concept of Law* was one exception, but even here Hayek misapprehended some of Hart's core claims (especially about the nature of the rule of recognition as a social rule). Hence, my choice to focus on Hayek's other work not expressly concerned with legal philosophy. I aim to contribute to a rediscovery of Hayek for legal and social philosophy (see also Postema 2009), which hopefully will continue.

This chapter should be treated as an invitation to a bigger research project, hence my treatment is selective. I begin by presenting the outlines of Hart's model of the foundations of law with the ultimate rule of recognition at its core. Then, I explore two Hayekian themes that shed light on the foundations of law as understood by Hart. First, I consider the rule of recognition as an implicit (unconscious) social rule and a Hayekian spontaneous order. Second, I turn to Hayek's discussion of "common opinion" on which every official practice of law relies and argue that it should be seen as complimentary with Hart's model. Finally, I provide an illustration of how Hayekian insights can improve a Hartian account of one of the topical debates in US constitutional law—that of the merits of positive originalism.

HART'S MODEL OF THE FOUNDATIONS OF LAW

One of the central questions in general jurisprudence is: what is the best constitutive explanation of the content of law?[1] In other words, how to explain what makes it the case that, for instance, capital punishment is or is not legal under US law. It may be tempting to say that capital punishment is legal (or not) because the judges say so or because the text of the US Constitution says so. But why would what the judges say or what the Constitution says be considered *law*? General jurisprudence approaches this question as a conceptual, *philosophical* one. As a question of how to carve the empirical reality into *law* and *non-law*.

The currently dominant tradition in general jurisprudence maintains that, at its very foundation, all law is constituted by a social practice of a special kind (Hart 2012). For instance, on this view the legal fact of legality (or illegality) of capital punishment in US law has its final legal explanation in an ultimate legal rule; a rule about what is law and what is not. This rule, according to Hart, is also essentially a social rule (social norm). Such an ultimate legal rule *may have the content* that whatever the judges say is law, or whatever the text of the Constitution says is law. Importantly, it can also be whatever the Communist Party or the Dear Leader says is law. One should not underestimate how much bad, or even evil, law and law making historical societies accepted over long periods of time. The content of the ultimate rule varies across societies and legal orders, and may even be contentious within one legal order.[2] As it happens, there is considerable disagreement over the content of ultimate rules of US law (Himma and Adler 2009). The important upshot of the theory is that the criteria by which in a given society we distinguish law from non-law ("the society's ultimate legal rules") are socially constructed and grounded in social practices.

In his magnum opus, *The Concept of Law*, Hart proposed a new model of foundations of law, responding to what he saw as deficiencies in the earlier tradition of legal positivism intent on seeing laws as commands of a sovereign, a tradition that Hayek criticizes so forcefully (Hart 2012). On Hart's view, all law is "posited," in the sense of being a result of human thought and action. There is no requirement that the foundations of law are made deliberately. Thus, Hart's framework is perfectly compatible with law being a result of human action, but not of deliberate human will or design (Hayek 1973, 20). Hayek's criticism of what he called "legal positivism" (Hayek 1973, 28, 72–73; 1976, 44–56) is not applicable to Hart, as Hayek expressly noted (Hayek 1976, 56–57).

According to Hart, at the foundation (or at the top) of every legal system[3] there is a social practice he called "the rule of recognition." One way to explain it is through the following example developed by John Finnis and John Gardner (this is not supposed to be a historical case study; the formulation is mine) (Finnis 2011a, 238–51; Gardner 2013).

Imagine a society very much like ours. At some point the government breaks down, perhaps due to a revolution. A group of people, that I like calling "authority entrepreneurs," take charge and start acting as if they had authority to make law, authoritatively settle legal disputes, and so on. In Hartian terms, we call them "legal officials." Those people recognize each other as having such authority to make and apply the law.[4] What is also crucial is that they develop a social practice (social norm) within their group of identifying certain elements of reality as law (the rule of recognition). This practice may be partly designed, partly emergent, partly inherited (culturally transmitted), and in part newly constructed. The officials (authority entrepreneurs) are successful (in creating law) if the broader community at least conforms to their authoritative directives most of the time.

The rule of recognition normally does not have a canonical propositional formulation. Neither the US Constitution, nor any of its particular clauses, are *the* rule of recognition of the US legal system. That rule, just like any social rule, is constituted by attitudes of the members of the relevant social group. The attitudes that matter are normative attitudes consisting of a complex of dispositions to conform, criticize others for non-conformity, accept criticism of one's non-conformity as valid, and so on. In the case of the rule of recognition, those attitudes are directed toward something like the following proposition: "All legal officials have a duty to identify as valid law of our legal system the things that X."[5]

X is known in jurisprudence as "criteria of legal validity." Thus, it is the duty of the officials to identify valid laws according to the criteria of validity. The criteria can take many different forms. For instance, a US legal official could accept that the supreme criterion of validity in US law is whether the

US Supreme Court says something is law. A pontiff in the early Roman republic could have accepted that the supreme criterion of validity is whether a purported legal rule is consistent with natural justice while at the same time protecting interests of his social class (against the lower classes). The criteria of validity may "mix and match": including sources of law in general (whatever the king says, whatever Parliament enacts, whatever the custom is) and "lists" of specific legal rules. Moreover, and as I will discuss later on, to some extent there may be disagreement and uncertainty over what the criteria of validity are in the legal system. The reason for that is in uncertainty of the content of the underlying social rule (the ultimate rule of recognition).

WHAT CAN HARTIAN GENERAL JURISPRUDENCE LEARN FROM HAYEK?

It is understandable for a legal philosopher to see Hayek's foray into his or her discipline as at least anachronistic, if not unsophisticated. However, I aim to show that there is jurisprudentially valuable insight to be gained by reflecting on Hayek's broader work. While doing so I set aside most of Hayek's writings specifically on law. Also, I choose not to attempt to reconstruct what Hayek "really" thought about Hart and how far off the mark he was. I do so because I see that as a distraction from the positive project of bringing Hayekian insights into Hartian general jurisprudence.

In this section, I introduce two themes from Hayek that ought to have an important place in general jurisprudence. In varying degrees, the discipline has acknowledged those themes, but in all the cases there is still significant room for development. First, I consider the rule of recognition as a Hayekian implicit and spontaneous order. Second, I turn to Hayek's idea of the "common opinion" at the foundation of law and show how it can fill a gap in constitutive explanations of law.

The Rule of Recognition as an Implicit and Spontaneous Order

Hayek characterized "the law" as a spontaneous order (Hayek 1973, 85–86). However, what Hayek meant by "the law" is considerably different from how this term is used in general jurisprudence. Simplifying, by "the law" Hayek meant customary law and perhaps judge-made law, but not statutes and codified constitutions (Hayek 1973, 85–86, 134–35). I want to make a different point. Here, I argue that on Hart's view, law is *always* grounded in a foundation (the rule of recognition) that is in important respects an implicit and spontaneous order. I will first establish that the rule of recognition is an implicit rule in the Hayekian sense and then that it is a spontaneous order. Finally, I will consider what insights for jurisprudence can be derived from that.

An Implicit Social Rule

One of Hayek's important observations was that, from the perspective of an individual person, a rule may be a mere "propensity or disposition to act or not to act in a certain manner" manifested as a "practice or custom" (Hayek 1973, 75). Rules may be therefore "unconscious" (Hayek 1967, 56; see also Gaus 2006, 248). It does not follow that all rules are unconscious or that no rule may be specified (expressed) in words. Hayek only insisted that "we are not in fact able to specify *all the rules* which govern our perceptions and actions" (Hayek 1967, 60; emphasis added). He claimed that tacit knowledge ("knowledge how") relates to "rules of conduct" and he described such knowledge as a "habit" and a "skill" (Hayek 1988, 78).

Are Hartian rules of recognition Hayekian rules of conduct? Are rules of recognition unconscious (at least sometimes or in part)? There is a tendency, especially in less philosophically minded legal writing, to present rules of recognition as simple propositional standards fitting neatly into slogans like "whatever Queen-in-Parliament enacts is law." Hayek himself appears to have fallen into the trap of such simplistic reading of Hart, but this is not significant for my project of applying Hayek's broader agenda.[6] As I will show, there is space for much greater correspondence between Hayek's and Hart's views on the foundations of law.

Hart provided several reasons to think that rules of recognition are not, at least not straightforwardly, conscious and (fully) specifiable. He claimed that rules of recognition are not "stated," but their "existence is *shown*" in how they are used to identify valid laws (Hart 2012, 101, 108). Rules of recognition must be shared and used "as a public, common standard of correct judicial decision" (Hart 2012, 116). But at the same time "there are certainly situations in which questions as to the precise content and scope of this kind of rule, and even as to its existence, may not admit of a clear or determinate answer" (Hart 2012, 109). Nevertheless, Hart clearly considered it possible to provide useful propositional accounts of ultimate rules of recognition.[7] He himself is often cited for the slogan about the Queen-in-Parliament that I mentioned before.

It is a separate question to what extent such accounts can adequately represent the full reality of practices of recognition. Hayek's warnings about our capacity to understand such practices are apposite here (Hayek 1988, 75–85). Several commentators stressed Hart's intellectual debt to Peter Winch (1958), who advocated a very similar conception of rule-guidance of human action to Hayek's (see, e.g., Coleman 2001, 80–81; Fallon 2009, 56–57; Waldron 1999, 177–78).[8] Given the above, even if Hart wasn't as influenced by Winch as some suggest, on Hart's account rules of recognition are in essence implicit social rules that can be more or less correctly represented in propositional form.

A Spontaneous Order

Rules of recognition are not just implicit social rules, they are also spontaneous orders in the Hayekian sense. Gerald Postema (2009), following Sugden and Gaus (Sugden 1998, 487–88; see also Gaus 2006, 233–34), helpfully listed several features of Hayekian emergent orders: they are path-dependent, they approximate equilibrium, they are self-maintaining, and their spontaneity is a matter of degree.

Rules of recognition of legal systems like that of the United States or of the UK are spontaneous to a significant degree. No single actor (including governmental organizations) is likely to have enough power (in a social, causal sense) to induce major changes in them and they are not sustained by a continuing exertion of such power. Also in the historical dimension, the current content of those rules of recognition is mostly emergent, though with influence of deliberate norm entrepreneurship.[9] Hart himself noted that even if someone tries deliberately to change the rule of recognition by legislation (by a statute), the rule of recognition will not become a statutory rule (Hart 2012, 111). That is, there always is a social rule (social practice) at the foundation of law and it cannot help but to be spontaneous (emergent) to an extent.

Furthermore, the rules are heavily path-dependent. This may be seen in reliance on English constitutional ideals in the emergence of the new US legal system. It is also true about the history of the British legal system itself—even the most severe shocks like the Glorious Revolution did less to the foundations of the legal system (to the criteria of validity) than it may seem. Of course, path-dependence is compatible with gradual change and it therefore should not be surprising if, for instance, the US rule of recognition in 2016 does not give as much (any?) weight to the sense of natural justice or to expectations of natural rights as the US rule of recognition in 1800.

Insights for Jurisprudence

Perhaps the most important lesson that both general jurisprudence and legal practice can take from Hayek's work on implicit social rules and spontaneous orders is a lesson of humility. Humility in two spheres: (1) knowledge of the content of ultimate legal rules and (2) capacity to affect the change of ultimate legal rules.

Considering the first, even though Hart noted that rules of recognition exist in how they are being used and that it is problematic to provide their canonical formulations, he decreed that "whatever Queen-in-Parliament enacts is law" was the UK rule of recognition of his time. This was probably too quick (Tucker 2011). Hart did not do a serious empirical study of the social practice, but relied on his intuition as its competent participant and observer. However, Hayek's notion of following rules as a skill not necessarily connected to propositional knowledge casts doubt on Hart's conclusion. Competent participants of legal practices may be able to identify what counts as valid law within the practice, but it does not follow that they can reliably give satisfactory propositional accounts of the rules governing what counts as valid law. In fact, "the process of articulation of pre-existing rules will . . . often lead to alterations" (Hayek 1973, 78). This may seem suboptimal—after all, should we not be able to know the content of all legal rules? The Hayekian response would be that sophisticated emergent social orders can only exist if they have some degree of unknowability. Like a market economy, a legal system may function without anyone having a God's eye view.

The second sphere in which humility is called for is that of change in ultimate legal rules. That rules of recognition are spontaneous orders means both (a) that it may be difficult to change them by deliberate attempts to do so and (b) that they may change without anyone trying to change them. On one hand, a lawmaker hoping to change the rule of recognition can only really make a proposal, so to speak. Or, in other words, lawmakers can try to introduce exogenous shocks on the emergent system that is the rule of recognition. If the shock is not strong enough (e.g., an insufficiently credible threat of use of raw coercion), then the system may not respond at all.

On the other hand, the system may respond to changes in the environment like technological change. It may also respond to norm entrepreneurship from within the system by people who are not law-sanctioned lawmakers. The last point may be particularly applicable to the role of judges in times of political revolutions (e.g., the history of Pakistan delivers several interesting cases like *Dosso* from 1958) (Tayyab 1994).

Common Opinion at the Foundation at Law

The other theme from Hayek's work significant to general jurisprudence is part of Hayek's unified account of emergence of law and society. Contemporary general jurisprudence has a strong inclination for delimiting its remit from that of sociology and even other areas of philosophy. However, at least among legal philosophers heavily influenced by Hart, it is common to think that some crucial features of law are grounded in extra-legal social reality (Barczentewicz 2018a; Finnis 2011b, 428–29; Gardner 2012, 284; Raz 2009,

100–02). For instance, it is claimed that continuity of legal systems throughout time is a function of continuity of communities they are law of. The same is said to be the case with unity of the law, that is with what makes it the case that various individual laws are part of one legal system. The big question, as yet insufficiently considered in general jurisprudence, is what are those connections between the practice of law and the society at large. In *Law, Legislation and Liberty*, Hayek wanted to show that supreme legislative power does not have to be unlimited (Hayek 1973, 91–93). While doing so, he made an argument that is potentially very relevant to the big question just mentioned.

Leading legal positivists claimed that legal power to legislate is limited by its nature before Hayek published Volume 1: *Rules and Order* (Hart 2012, 106; Raz 1980, 27–32). An important part of Hart's account was that every legal system has at its foundation a social practice grounding the ultimate rule of recognition, which determines what counts as law and what does not. The ultimate rule controls effects of deliberate law making. No command of a legislator (act of legislation) can become valid law if this is not provided for in the ultimate rule of recognition.[10] However, the ultimate rule is not itself under direct control of deliberate law making. A legislature could *try* to change the ultimate rule by enacting a new law, but whether the rule actually changes depends on whether the underlying social practice shifts.

Hayek's solution has a similar structure. He claimed that "the authority of a legislator" has a "source" from which it is "derived":

> This source is a prevailing opinion that the legislator is authorized only to prescribe what is right, where this opinion refers not to the particular content of the rule but to the general attributes which any rule of just conduct must possess. (Hayek 1973, 92; see also Hayek 1976, 61)

Hayek defined "opinion" as:

> a common tendency to approve of some particular acts of will and to disapprove of others, according to whether they do or do not possess certain attributes which those who hold a given opinion usually will not be able to specify. (Hayek 1973, 92; see also Hayek 1976, 13–14)

How would such disapproval be manifested? Hayek is not very specific on this point. He referred to "allegiance" on which legislative power "rests," which may "vanish," as well as to "refus[al of] obedience" (Hayek 1973, 92). He also said:

> This power of opinion does not rest on the capacity of the holders to take any course of concerted action, but is merely a negative power of withholding that support on which the power of the legislator ultimately rests. (Hayek 1973, 93)

Finally, Hayek noted that it would be good "if the criteria were explicitly stated by which it can be determined whether or not a particular decision can be a law" (Hayek 1973, 93). However, such criteria "have hardly ever been adequately expressed in words" (Hayek 1973, 93). Hayek set for himself the goal of providing such an adequate account.

Hayek was not overly preoccupied with practices of legal officials and with systematic features of law that Hart focused on. Hart, however, did not devote much attention to the wider societal basis or social constraints of legal systems—one of Hayek's chief concerns. We could take from Hayek the account of how social practices of legal officials are constrained by common opinion. And from Hart, the account of practices of legal officials and how they ground law as an institutionalized normative system. In this sense, Hart and Hayek are interested in different levels of constitutive explanation of law. Before I can move further, I need to address a potential source of significant tension, if not latent incompatibility: which level is more fundamental?

I will consider two alternative constitutive explanatory accounts of law. According to the first, Hayekian common opinion is the truly fundamental ground of law. If some purported directive (law) created by legal officials or some other feature of official practice does not meet with approval of the common opinion, it is not law. It does not matter what the officials themselves think about this. The officials may think that whatever is enacted in the proper procedure is law, end of story. But they would be mistaken, because the non-official, public opinion is determinative.

The second account takes the official practice as fundamental. If the official practice of recognition sees procedural propriety as the only criterion for validity of new laws, then it is so. Whenever the public at large "refuses support," they disobey the law.[11] Any role for common opinion in determining what counts as law must be mediated through official practice. In other words, it may be the case in a given legal system that officials accept that procedural propriety is not enough and that nothing counts as law unless it is approved of by common opinion, in Hayek's technical sense (Lamond 2013). But even here, the significance of common opinion to what counts as valid law is at the mercy of officials.

At this stage, I must investigate more closely what Hayek's "refusal of support" is supposed to mean. Does it mean failure to conform (most of the time) to a specific individual law? Was Hayek saying that individual laws face the tribunal of common opinion; in other words, if they are disapproved of they do not count as law (are not taken, or perceived, as law)? This would be very hard to substantiate as a descriptive claim and Hayek does not provide evidence for it.

Hayek's discussion suggests a more general kind of disobedience: a comprehensive refusal to conform to all of law. In his words: "withholding that support on which the power of the legislator ultimately rests" (Hayek 1973, 93). Hayek has also written: "[a]s dictators themselves have known best at all times, even the most powerful dictatorship crumbles if the support of opinion is withdrawn" (Hayek 1973, 92). It is a pity that he does not provide examples of what "crumbling dictatorships" he has in mind, which could provide a clue to what sort of common opinion is he concerned with. A part of the interpretative difficulty stems from the fact that some of the history's most notorious dictatorships persisted for a long time and did not crumble due to disobedience. What is more, as Dennis Galligan noted:

> The more we learn about those qualifying as the most repugnant [legal orders] of recent times, the Germany of Hitler, the Soviet Union of Stalin, or the China of Mao, the clearer it becomes that they had not just the obedience but the positive support of large sections of the population. If examples of regimes that lacked popular support could be found, the chances are their life was short. (Galligan 2006, 128)

In one sense, Galligan confirms Hayek's core intuition that all legal systems that persist over time are characterized by public support. However, if—by Hayekian standards—common opinion approved of Stalinist, Maoist, and Nazi law, then a serious question arises of how much of a constraint Hayekian common opinion really is? Even though a legislator's "power is not unlimited," it still may be that the limits are so broad that even the real-socialist governments stayed within them. This is not a criticism of Hayek's descriptive account, but it helps to illustrate the distance between his positive description and his favored classical liberal law.

This is also not a *reductio ad absurdum* in the sense that common opinion so construed may have explanatory value. For instance, the Soviet Union did not fully eradicate private property, which is Hayek's favorite example of a rule of just conduct (see, e.g., Hayek 1973, 107). Private property in a restricted form of "personal" property continued, even under Stalin. Hence, once we accept that common opinion is likely to disapprove of and "refuse support" (in the relevant, technical sense) only to extreme infringements of the common sense of what is right and just, then Hayek's account remains unaffected and produces an interesting hypothesis. Perhaps a more significant restriction of private property than was the case in the Soviet Union would have met with public disapproval leading to "refusal of support" in the relevant sense.

It hardly follows that the constraint of common opinion leads to Hayek's preferred classical liberal law. If common opinion really requires that "the same rules should apply to all men" (the principle of generality), then why is there no policy of open borders in all long-lasting legal systems (Hayek 1976,

58)? To answer this, Hayek distinguished between limits of "the powers of the legislator" and limits of "the extent to which the application of recognized principles of the law can and should be carried" (Hayek 1976, 57). This distinction is very unclear. What Hayek probably should have said is simply that common opinion in actual historical societies has been giving significant latitude to the power of the legislator (so broad that it included Stalinist legislation). Hayek could have still insisted that "persistent application" of the negative test of injustice might in distant future preclude such egregious cases (see, e.g., Hayek 1976, 54). But he would have had to admit that given that justice is an entirely cultural phenomenon (not some "external and eternal order of things"), whether such convergence on specific classical liberal constraints ever obtains is a contingent matter (see Hayek 1976, 59–60).[12]

I will now turn back to the question of which account is more fundamental. Once we accept the above interpretation of "refusal of support," the first account—viewing common opinion as constraining what counts as law in a non-derivative way—becomes quite plausible. As I argue elsewhere (Barczentewicz 2018a), if we are interested in providing an account of law as it exists for a society, and not just of law-among-officials, then we have very good reasons to treat social rules of non-officials (regulating non-official support for law) as non-derivatively contributing to (constraining) the content of law. Otherwise we must accept the possibility I already mentioned: that the officials, and only them, see something as law, and that the public disapproves of it so much that they "refuse to support" the legal system as a whole. We thus could end up with a legal system that only meaningfully exists for legal officials, but does not exist for the whole society.

Admitting the fundamental and content-constraining role of non-officials requires a modification of the standard Hartian model, which takes the official practice as fundamental. However, it is certainly a possibility to be taken seriously and that calls for further study (see Barczentewicz 2018a; Southwood forthcoming).

Importantly, even if common opinion counts only derivatively, through affecting what officials think and do, it may still be very significant for the study of law (see, e.g., Postema 1982, 192). True, if this is the case, then for methodological reasons an account of common opinion no longer belongs to general jurisprudence, at least as Hart saw it. However, neither Hart nor anyone working in this tradition denied the importance of studying the causal factors of social practices of legal officials. Thus, it matters whether Hayek was successful in his attempt to adequately express in words the restraints of common opinion "which in fact have long operated on the legislatures" (Hayek 1973, 93).

I will not attempt here to assess whether he was. I will only give an illustration of what an adequate account could look like. One of the very few concrete examples[13] that Hayek gives of a plausible constraint on public "allegiance" or "support" in the relevant sense is that of establishing a new government after a revolution (Hayek 1973, 135). He correctly observed that even though public law (constitutional law, administrative law) is very susceptible to change in such circumstances, private law (tort, contract, etc.) tends to persist without much alteration. His explanation was that "only by satisfying general expectations can a new government obtain the allegiance of its subjects" (Hayek 1973, 135).

HAYEK AND THE POSITIVE ORIGINALISM DEBATE

The current debate on the merits of the so-called "positive originalism" in US constitutional law provides a good case to illustrate the explanatory potential of Hayek's framework. Positive originalism, as advocated by Stephen Sachs, relies on the Hartian model of the foundations of law, which I presented above (Sachs 2014, 2015; see also Baude 2015; Baude and Sachs 2017). On this view, every change in US law since the enactment of the Constitution in 1787–1788 must be explained in terms of the rules of legal change in force immediately after the making of the Constitution. In other words, positive originalism's central thesis is that there has been no unlawful or revolutionary (in a legal sense) change in US law since 1788. What follows is that if it can be shown that something was law in 1788 (e.g., a rule on how the constitutional text is to be interpreted), then it is law today, *unless* it can be shown that the law was lawfully changed in the meantime. It also follows that if it can be shown that some alleged legal rule cannot be traced back through a chain of lawful changes all the way to 1788, then this alleged rule is no part of today's US law.

The problem with this argument is that it seems easy to show examples of how, for instance, the Supreme Court departed from the established law in ways that were not allowed as lawful legal change (see, e.g., Barnett 2004). And it may appear that today the judges and other US legal officials follow many legal rules that should not be part of US law if positive originalism were true (Barzun 2017; Greenberg 2017; Primus 2016; Pojanowski and Walsh 2016). The main response of a positive originalist is that the rule that all US law must be traced back through a chain of lawful changes to 1788 *is more fundamental* or *hierarchically higher* than all the apparent departures from the rule. Hence, those who follow the unlawfully created legal rules are mistaken as a matter of law.

This response may appear to be in tension with the core feature of the Hartian model of the foundations of law, namely that at every point in time the content of law is grounded in a social practice of recognizing certain things as law *at that time* (and thus in the ultimate rule of recognition). Hence, if US officials recognize as law some rules that cannot be traced back to 1788, then why not admit that those rules are law today just because they are accepted as law today, irrespective of their pedigree?

A positive originalist may respond, first, that the same officials accept the no-unlawful-change-since-1788 rule and accept it as more fundamental (higher-order). Hence, the officials are acting unlawfully on their own terms. Second, a positive originalist may also respond that even if US officials do not accept the no-unlawful-change rule, the public at large does and the social rule of all citizens is what truly grounds the content of law. Thus, it could be that all the officials are rebelling against what is really law.

Does either of the two responses succeed? I see two ways in which Hayek's discussion of law and rules may bear on this problem.

What Is the Content of the US Rule of Recognition?

If we see ultimate rules of recognition through the Hayekian perspective as concerned with classification of behavior as right and wrong, then this strengthens the case against the positive originalist interpretation of the US rule of recognition. To recapitulate, on this perspective behavior to be classified as right or wrong consists of official actions of recognizing certain things as law. If it is indeed the case that the officials recognize as valid law things that violate the no-unlawful-change-since-1788 rule, then this is very significant evidence that the rule of recognition does not contain that rule.

In response, a positive originalist may invoke public statements given by the same officials (e.g., in reasoned judgments), which suggest commitment to the no-unlawful-change rule. The problem with this counterargument, on Hayekian terms, is that the reality of convergent behavior is privileged over verbal accounts provided by the participants of the practice. A better answer would be to try to show that the cases of inconsistency with the no-unlawful-change rule are only apparent and that in fact they are consistent with the rule (Baude 2015).

However, positive originalists may also get some indirect support from the Hayekian perspective. One of the features of the rule of recognition as a spontaneous order is that it is path-dependent. Hence, we have a reason to believe that it persists with unchanged content. Path-dependence shifts the burden of proof, so to speak, on those who claim that a change took place. If a positive originalist can show that the no-unlawful-change rule was a part of the US rule of recognition at some point in the past, then this would be a reason to believe that it is still a part of it now. Interestingly, at least Sachs prefers to rely on the content of the current rule of recognition expressly distancing himself from any claims about the no-unlawful-change rule being accepted in the past (Sachs 2015, 848–49).

Hayek on Common Opinion at the Foundation of Law

As I noted above, Hayek stressed that a social practice of all members of a society constrains the content of law (by constraining what the officials may get away with in recognizing as law). Assume that it is part of the common opinion, in the relevant sense, in the United States today, that all current US law may be traced back to the Constitution as enacted. It would mean that the people at large would "refuse support" to the US legal system if they learned that the government (broadly understood) acts according to rules that cannot be traced back to the Constitution.

If the government does act according to rules that cannot be traced back to the Constitution, then on the first of my two accounts, it acts *unlawfully* (because what common opinion disapproves of, in the technical sense, is not law). What would follow is that the correct legal argument, which could be made and should succeed in court, is that such purported laws are invalid (unconstitutional).

However, even on the second account—where common opinion only counts derivatively (because officials accept that it does)—the stipulated fact of the US common opinion would matter a good deal. It would matter, because it is reasonable to assume that officials do in fact accept the constraint of common opinion (see, e.g., Fallon 2009, 61–62). Hence, if we know what common opinion requires, this could still feature in a proper legal argument.

Is the starting assumption about the content of the contemporary US common opinion plausible? It may be, but several significant caveats are in order.

First, it is difficult to ascertain what the common opinion requires. Hayekian common opinion is not the public opinion from Gallup polls. Just because people respond affirmatively to a survey asking them an abstract question about laws having to be traceable to the Constitution, it does not follow that they truly accept a rule that would result in "refusal of support" to the state law in general if some purported laws applied by the officials are unconstitutional in this sense.

To make matters worse, the personal attitudes (or dispositions, as Hayek would prefer) that together constitute common opinion are likely to be implicit. They may not exist in people's minds in propositional form. Even if they are specifiable, this may require considerable effort and carry a risk of error.

Second, there may be significant indeterminacy or disagreement on whether any particular law can be traced to the Constitution as enacted. In other words, the worry is that even if the US common opinion requires traceability to 1788 law, it does not follow that it requires a technical legal test of going back through a chain of lawful legal changes. Instead, the common opinion may require for current law to reflect the "ethos" of 1788 or some other non-technical consideration (see, e.g., Kesavan and Paulsen 2003; McGowan 2001).

Finally, even if it is one of the requirements of common opinion, it could be that there are other requirements pulling in a different direction. Perhaps, the contemporary US common opinion also approves of all laws that are generally perceived to have good effects, whatever they may be. If the public takes some specific law as beneficial, would they really consider it as a cause to "refuse support" to the law in general if they learned that this specific law cannot be traced back to the Constitution as enacted?

Jeffrey Pojanowski and Kevin Walsh recently proposed an argument that may be read as a defense of the claim that Hayekian common opinion in the contemporary United States requires no-unlawful-change-since-1788 (Barczentewicz 2018b; Pojanowski and Walsh 2016). The authors' rhetoric of traditional understandings and of what justice requires does sound like what Hayek would have said. However, Pojanowski and Walsh are not conventionalists about law and morality in the sense Hayek was, they are full-bloodied natural lawyers. Hayek would have probably agreed that arguments from history of ideas help to understand the current common opinion. But he would have been forced also to admit that they are no more than epistemic proxies and that the true question is about current patterns of thought and behavior, which may not reflect historical elite ideas (see, e.g., Hayek 1976, 50–51, 59–60).

CONCLUSIONS

Hayek wrote (1973, 114): "It is not in the descriptive branches of sociology but only in the theory of the overall order of society that an understanding of the relations between law and social order can be found." Many legal philosophers would agree with this statement. However, few among them attempt to move across disciplinary boundaries, leaving all "society stuff" to social scientists. It is also true that few social scientists or philosophers of social sciences share the interest in constitutive explanations of law (a recent exception is Epstein 2015). This isolation is unfortunate, but it is understandable.

How can general jurisprudence benefit further from Hayekian insights? One important area I suggested in this chapter is in stressing the limits of knowledge of law (at least at the most foundational level of ultimate legal rules). For an outsider, it may be surprising how much credence both legal theorists and lawyers assign to their armchair accounts of ultimate legal rules, even if—when pressed—they admit that such rules are grounded in implicit and emergent social practices.

Legal change is another issue. Designing legal institutions, including constitutional orders, is very much in fashion today. Thinking of ultimate legal rules as Hayekian spontaneous orders should curb some of the enthusiasm (Felin et al. 2015). But knowledge of the limitations can also lead to better design (Calabresi 2016; Levinson 2016; Smith 2016). From a more theoretical perspective, an important question requiring a better answer is how law changes outside of formal processes of change (legislation) and whether anything general may be said about constraints of such legal change.

Hayek's view that common opinion is foundational to the existence of law could provide one such constraint on the possibilities for legal change. However, admitting that some non-officials and even non-lawyers stand in a constitutive relationship to the law—their attitudes limit what law can be and become—entails a significant change from the currently dominant Hartian view that all that counts in constituting the law is thought and actions of legal officials. If the common opinion account holds, then it would also provide an answer to the big question of a constitutive connection between law and society. As I noted above, there are many further issues to be resolved before one could confidently endorse this account. For instance, what is the process by which potential "withholding of support" affects legal practices? Is it a constraint of any practical relevance? These are the sort of issues that would benefit from collaboration of social scientists and philosophers.

NOTES

1. To be clear, I use "law" as the term is understood in modern jurisprudence, i.e. including all of state law, legislation, etc.—not in Hayek's narrower, technical sense (Hayek 1973, 85–86).

2. See the discussion of dictatorships below and the observation made by Dennis Galligan cited there.

3. More precisely: every legal system that is akin to what we call "the law."

4. It could be that everyone in the community sees everyone else as having equal authority in that sense. Then the group of officials would be identical with the community. There are good reasons why this does not happen in bigger communities (think: tribal elders, pontiffs of early Roman republic, the Lawspeaker in Icelandic Commonwealth).

5. I am not saying those attitudes are necessarily propositional, as discussed below.

6. Hayek explicitly refers to Hart's concept of the rule of recognition in *Rules and Order* (Hayek 1973, 135). On Hayek's view a rule that "defines the formal

properties which a law must possess in order to be valid" ("a definition of rules of just conduct") is not itself a rule of conduct. The rule of recognition only enables "the courts to ascertain whether particular rules possess those [formal] properties." Hayek misunderstood Hart in thinking that the rule of recognition is an "attempt to articulate conceptions underlying an existing system of norms" by legislation (e.g., by enacting a rule of recognition in a codified constitution). Hayek entirely missed Hart's main point that rules of recognition are essentially social rules and they cannot be "attempts" of persons or organizations. As I already noted, the rule of recognition cannot be grounded in a codified constitution. A codified constitution may only approximate or provide an epistemic proxy of the real thing, i.e., of a social rule (Hart 2012, 111; Kramer 2008, 110–11).

7. For instance, in the United Kingdom, Acts of Parliament are law because of the ultimate rule of recognition (there is no other legal explanation for them being law). The same is true for the common law. This picture is consistent with the fact that judges sometimes present, self-servingly, parliamentary legislation as a source of law derivative from the common law. Such pronouncements can be discounted, because they are rare and because they are inconsistent with how law is normally applied in the UK.

8. Consider this characteristic statement of Winch's position:

> the test of whether a man's actions are the application of a rule is not whether he can *formulate* it but whether it makes sense to distinguish between a right and a wrong way of doing things in connection with what he does. Where that makes sense, then it must also make sense to say that he is applying a criterion in what he does even though he does not, and perhaps cannot, formulate that criterion. (Winch 1958, 58)

But see (Galligan 2006, 98).

9. For instance, I see it as plausible to regard the making of the US legal system through the making of the US Constitution and related events more as norm entrepreneurship than as an act of deliberate design. This is so even though some of the "agents of change" may have thought they were engaged in designing institutions—if so, they overestimated their power (Felin et al. 2015; but see Calabresi 2016).

10. Or in lower-level legal rules, which themselves are valid law due to ultimate rules of recognition.

11. On the first account, they do not disobey the law, because what they disapprove of is not law, by definition: it does not count as law because common opinion disapproves of it.

12. There is an interesting tension between Hayek's conventional (cultural) view of justice and morality, and his rhetoric of what he thought was just and should be so accepted. His discussion of law may be perceived as bordering on a sleight of hand—that some of his claims cannot be substantiated by his own grounding story of normativity (what ought to be the case).

13. That Hayek does not have many concrete examples is consistent with my interpretation of how permissive is Hayekian common opinion. We may reasonably expect that only very rarely lawmakers (authority entrepreneurs) try to do things that do not fit within what common opinion would approve of (in the technical sense, where disapproval would mean comprehensive refusal to conform).

REFERENCES

Barczentewicz, Mikołaj. 2018a. "The Illuminati Problem, Rules of Recognition, and What Distinguishes Law from Non-Law?" *Oxford Journal of Legal Studies*. https://ssrn.com/abstract=2915564.

———. 2018b. "The Limits of Natural Law Originalism." *Notre Dame Law Review Online* 93: 115–30. https://ssrn.com/abstract=2955184.

Barnett, Randy E. 2004. *Restoring the Lost Constitution: The Presumption of Liberty*. Princeton, NJ: Princeton University Press.

Barzun, Charles L. 2017. "The Positive U-Turn." *Stanford Law Review* 69 (5): 1323–88.

Baude, William. 2015. "Is Originalism Our Law?" *Columbia Law Review* 115: 1–86.

Baude, William, and Stephen E. Sachs. 2017. "The Law of Interpretation." *Harvard Law Review* 130 (4): 1079–147.

Beaulier, Scott A., Peter J. Boettke, and Christopher J. Coyne. 2005. "Knowledge, Economics, and Coordination: Understanding Hayek's Legal Theory." *NYU Journal of Law and Liberty* 1: 209–23.

Calabresi, Steven Gow. 2016. "Friedrich A. Hayek, the U.S. Constitution, and Institutional Design." *Arizona State Law Journal* 48: 231–40.

Coleman, Jules. 2001. *The Practice of Principle*. New York: Oxford University Press.

Epstein, Brian. 2015. *The Ant Trap: Rebuilding the Foundations of the Social Sciences*. Oxford: Oxford University Press.

Fallon, Richard H. 2009. "Precedent-Based Constitutional Adjudication, Acceptance, and the Rule of Recognition." In *The Rule of Recognition and the U.S. Constitution*, edited by Matthew Adler and Kenneth Himma, 47–67. Oxford: Oxford University Press.

Felin, Teppo, Caryn Devins, Stuart Kauffman, and Roger Koppl. 2015. "Against Design." *Arizona State Law Journal* 47 (3): 611–81.

Finnis, John. 2011a. *Natural Law and Natural Rights*. 2nd ed. Oxford: Oxford University Press.

———. 2011b. "Revolutions and Continuity of Law." In *Philosophy of Law: Collected Essays Volume IV*. Oxford: Oxford University Press.

Galligan, Denis. 2006. *Law in Modern Society*. Oxford: Oxford University Press.

Gardner, John. 2012. *Law as a Leap of Faith*. Oxford: Oxford University Press.

———. 2013. "Why Law Might Emerge: Hart's Problematic Fable." In *Reading HLA Hart's "The Concept of Law,"* edited by Luis Duarte d'Almeida, James Edwards, and Andrea Dolcetti. Oxford: Hart.

Gaus, Gerald F. 2006. "Hayek on the Evolution of Society and Mind." In *The Cambridge Companion to Hayek*, edited by Edward Feser, 232–58. Cambridge: Cambridge University Press.

Greenberg, Mark. 2017. "What Makes a Method of Legal Interpretation Correct? Legal Standards vs. Fundamental Determinants." *Harvard Law Review Forum* 130 (4): 105–26.

Hart, Herbert L. A. 2012. *The Concept of Law*. 3rd ed. Oxford: Oxford University Press.

Hayek, F. A. 1967. *Studies in Philosophy, Politics and Economics*. Chicago: University of Chicago Press.

———. 1973. *Law, Legislation and Liberty*, Vol. 1: *Rules and Order*. Chicago: University of Chicago Press.

———. 1976. *Law, Legislation and Liberty*, Vol. 2: *The Mirage of Social Justice*. Chicago: University of Chicago Press.

———. 1988. *The Fatal Conceit*. Chicago: University of Chicago Press.

Himma, Kenneth, and Matthew Adler. 2009. *The Rule of Recognition and the U.S. Constitution*. Oxford: University of Chicago Press.

Kesavan, Vasan, and Michael Stokes Paulsen. 2003. "Interpretive Force of the Constitution's Secret Drafting History." *Georgetown Law Journal* 91: 1113–214.

Kramer, Matthew H. 2008. *Where Law and Morality Meet*. Chicago: University of Chicago Press.

Lamond, Grant. 2013. "The Rule of Recognition and the Foundations of a Legal System." In *Reading HLA Hart's "The Concept of Law,"* edited by Luis Duarte d'Almeida, James Edwards, and Andrea Dolcetti. Oxford: Hart.

Levinson, Sanford. 2016. "On the Inevitability of 'Constitutional Design.'" *Arizona State Law Journal* 48: 249–56.

McGowan, David. 2001. "Ethos in Law and History: Alexander Hamilton, The Federalist, and the Supreme Court." *Minnesota Law Review* 85: 755–896.

Pojanowski, Jeffrey, and Kevin C. Walsh. 2016. "Enduring Originalism." *Georgetown Law Journal* 105: 97–158.

Postema, Gerald J. 1982. "Coordination and Convention at the Foundations of Law." *Journal of Legal Studies* 11 (1): 165–203.

———. 2009. "Nature as First Custom: Hayek on the Evolution of Social Rules." https://ssrn.com/abstract=1505430.

Primus, Richard. 2016. "Is Theocracy Our Politics?" *Columbia Law Review Sidebar* 116: 44–60.

Raz, Joseph. 1980. *The Concept of a Legal System*. 2nd ed. Oxford: Oxford University Press.

———. 2009. *The Authority of Law*. 2nd ed. Oxford: Oxford University Press.

Sachs, Stephen E. 2014. "The 'Constitution in Exile' as a Problem for Legal Theory." *Notre Dame Law Review* 89 (5): 2253–98.

———. 2015. "Originalism as a Theory of Legal Change." *Harvard Journal of Law and Public Policy* 38 (3): 817–87.

Skoble, Aeon J. 2006. "Hayek the Philosopher of Law." In *The Cambridge Companion to Hayek*, edited by Edward Feser, 171–81. Cambridge: Cambridge University Press.

Smith, Teppo. 2016. "Design Is the Source of Variation: Selection Is the Filter." *Arizona State Law Journal* 48: 257–60.

Southwood, Nicholas. Forthcoming. "Laws as Conventional Norms." In *Legal Norms, Ethical Norms: New Essays on Meta-Ethics and Jurisprudence*, edited by David Plunkett, Scott Shapiro, and Kevin Toh. Oxford: Oxford University Press.

Sugden, Robert. 1998. "Spontaneous Order." In *The New Palgrave Dictionary of Economics and the Law*, edited by Peter Newman, 485–95. London: Macmillan Palgrave.

Tayyab, Mahmud. 1994. "Jurisprudence of Successful Treason: Coup d'Etat & Common Law." *Cornell International Law Journal* 27: 49–140.

Tucker, Adam. 2011. "Uncertainty in the Rule of Recognition and in the Doctrine of Parliamentary Sovereignty." *Oxford Journal of Legal Studies* 31 (1): 61–88.

Waldron, Jeremy. 1999. "All We Like Sheep." *Canadian Journal of Law and Jurisprudence* 12: 169–88.

Winch, Peter. 1958. *The Idea of a Social Science and Its Relation to Philosophy*. London: Routledge.

Chapter 8

F. A. Hayek and the Administrative State

Daniel Gibbs

This chapter examines the role of the administrative state in F. A. Hayek's analysis of political institutions. Its primary purpose is to make explicit an implicit positive theory of the administrative state that runs throughout Hayek's writing on political economy. This theory is composed of three related claims. The first states that the separation of powers is vital to ensuring that the actions of the administrative state are bound by the rule of law. The second claim states that unrestricted democratic control of the administrative state leads to the expansion of the scope and complexity of its activities. The third claim states that this expansion of activity makes democratic control of administration increasingly difficult.

In clarifying this theory of the administrative state—that is, a theory of what government agencies do and why they do it—this chapter also argues that Hayek's theory is worth being taken seriously by contemporary bureaucracy scholars. His theory is readily intelligible to contemporary institutional analysts in its methodological emphasis on individual action under rule-like constraints. Its contribution to contemporary scholarship is to provide a framework for rigorously analyzing one of the classic yet recently understudied problems in the study of administration: how, if possible, to separate politics from administration. This classic problem of separating professional yet accountable administration from the whims of politics and ideology has largely been abandoned by contemporary students of bureaucracy. Scholars now tend to accept a "policy-neutral bureaucracy" (Brehm and Gates 1999, 4) or the possibility of "neutral compliance" with statute (Gailmard and Patty 2007) to be a chimera. This is not without good reason as scholars have come to understand how information asymmetries (Crawford and Sobel 1982; Niskanen 1971), inherent biases of bureaucrats (Prendergast 2007), problems incentivizing bureaucrats to acquire expertise (Bendor and Meirowitz

2004; Callander 2008; Gailmard and Patty 2007), imperfect screening and monitoring technologies (Brehm and Gates 1999; Huber and Shipan 2002), the potential for agency capture (Wilson 1989), and political processes associated with the design and operation of agencies (Arnold 1979; Gailmard 2009; Lewis 2008; McCubbins, Noll, and Weingast 1987; Moe 1989) combine to make the possibility of separating the administrative sphere from the political sphere seem impossible. These features of bureaucrats, bureaucracies, and the political environments they inhabit, however, should not lead scholars to neglect the theoretical importance of the apolitical bureaucracy in a democratic society. Suleiman (2003) observes that as the apparatus charged with implementing public policies and delivering public services in an effective and just manner, a nonpolitical and professional bureaucracy is an indispensable institution for both the development and maintenance of the democratic state. Hayek's theory of the administrative state provides an entry point for reexamining this important question with the tools of contemporary institutional analysis. The next three sections address in turn each of the three major claims that make up Hayek's theory of the administrative state. A final section discusses how Hayek's three claims together offer contemporary scholars of bureaucracy a model for revisiting the separation of politics and administration in a rigorous fashion.

SEPARATION OF POWERS AND ADMINISTRATION UNDER THE RULE OF LAW

This section identifies and discusses the first of three claims in Hayek's theory of the administrative state. This first claim is that the strict separation of legislation and governance, provided that there exists a strong judiciary to enforce the separation of powers, is sufficient to support administration that is bound by the rule of law.

In *The Political Ideal of the Rule of Law* (1955) and *The Constitution of Liberty* (1960), Hayek offers a general analysis of political institutions. His third lecture in *The Political Ideal of the Rule of Law* is devoted to identifying institutional arrangements that are capable of supporting the rule of law. For Hayek, the separation of powers is a crucial feature of a free society's political institutions. In particular he emphasizes the importance of an independent judiciary to check the powers of the legislature:

> The significance of the demand for the separation of powers is fairly clear in so far as the relation between legislature and judicature is concerned. The principle that the general rules should be laid down apart from their application to particular instances almost requires that these distinct tasks should also be performed

> by distinct groups of people. This is perhaps not the only conceivable but almost certainly the only practicable safeguard that the rules are not made to fit particular instances but because of their general significance. (Hayek 2014, 168)

Hayek doubts whether an independent executive branch of government coequal with the judiciary and legislature is compatible with the rule of law. In order for an independent executive branch to fit into a political institutional framework that supports the rule of law, all coercive acts that the executive takes against citizens must be subject to judicial review and bound by general rules laid down by the legislature. Whether such an executive can justifiably be given the power to create and enforce rules is a matter that concerns democracy more than the rule of law. So long as executive branch agencies make general rules that can be reviewed by the judicial branch, delegation poses no threat to the rule of law, although delegation of rulemaking authority by the democratically elected legislature to unelected bureaucrats may be objectionable as antidemocratic. Delegation becomes problematic for the rule of law when an administrative agency is given discretion such that its actions take the force of law. Under such a delegation scheme, "authorities are in effect given power to wield coercion without rule, because no general rule can be formulated for the exercise of the powers in question" (2014, 170).

The Constitution of Liberty develops at greater length the arguments Hayek makes in *The Political Ideal of the Rule of Law*. Hayek reiterates the importance of the separation of powers for preserving the rule of law and the need to ensure that administrative actions are both reviewable by the courts and limited to rule making and rule enforcement. He adds to this a clarification of the type of judicial review of agency action that supports the rule of law. Hayek observes that most countries have legal provisions by which individuals can dispute administrative action through the court system. These provisions, however, often confine the scope of appeals to the question of whether or not the agency had the authority to act in the way that it did. If the law said that everything a certain authority did was legal, it could not be restrained by a court from doing anything. What is required under the rule of law is that a court should have the power to decide whether the law provided for a particular action taken by an agency.

In the *Constitution of Liberty*, Hayek provides a partially institutional account of the decline of the rule of law in Europe and the United States in the late nineteenth and early twentieth centuries. An important part of this narrative is the rise of the autonomous administrative state. In the American case, Hayek argues that progressive thought on public administration and governance combined with efforts by administrators to expand their agencies accounts in part for the growth of government and the increasing degree of arbitrary discretionary authority granted to the bureaucracy. The tendency for the bureaucrats to attempt to acquire greater discretion and command of resources from the government follows from the incentives that the task of administration provides for them. In directing and allocating its resources to the needs of the community, an agency must decide on what tasks are most important and on the means of executing these tasks. Hayek writes that

> the tendency of the professional administrators concerned with these tasks is inevitably to draw everything they can into the service of the public aims they are pursuing. It is largely as a protection of the private citizen against this tendency of an ever growing administrative machinery to engulf the private sphere that the rule of law is so important today. (Hayek 2011, 324)

Hayek refines his analysis of the separation of powers in *Economic Freedom and Representative Government* (1973) and volumes one and three of *Law, Legislation, and Liberty* (1973; 1979). In his earlier work, Hayek emphasizes the importance of subordinating administration to legislative constraint and judicial review. He is agnostic as to whether administration is a responsibility of the government that should be carried out by a body independent of the legislature in a society governed by the rule of law. Where this is a separate executive branch, delegation of rulemaking power is compatible with the rule of law as long as such rules are reviewable.

In his writing in the 1970s, Hayek argues for a much more explicit separation of administration and legislation. As he did earlier in *The Constitution of Liberty*, Hayek attempts to identify the characteristics of a political institutional framework capable of supporting the rule of law. He takes the position that the tasks of laying down general rules and of directing the particular activities of government should be carried out by separate elected bodies. One elected body, a legislative assembly, should be made responsible for making law in the form of general rules. This power to make rules should be exclusively carried out in the legislative assembly. Delegation of rulemaking authority to the bureaucracy, a potentially expedient option for the legislature in Hayek's earlier writing, is now impermissible in his model constitution. Where Hayek was similarly ambivalent regarding the role of the legislature in governance in his earlier writing, his updated position is that the legislature should have no direct executive authority. A separate elected body, a governmental assembly, would be responsible for everyday administration. Having no rulemaking authority of its own, the governmental assembly would determine the organization of government, how to use the means placed at its disposal, and the character of the services to be rendered by government (1973, 21). The governmental assembly would have authority to raise revenue through taxation but this action, like all of its permissible actions, would be limited to the enforcement of general rules passed by the legislative assembly. Legislative acts and administrative actions would both be reviewable by an independent judiciary.

This strict separation of legislation and governance accomplishes two primary objectives vital to the preservation of the rule of law. First, separation of these two functions allows for the two branches of government to specialize in their respective areas. When the two tasks are combined in the same body as they are in most Western democracies, legislators are not able to devote sufficient time and resources to acquiring the detailed expert knowledge required to make law. Relieving the legislature of its administrative obligations allows its members to specialize in the difficult task of crafting general rules. Second, separation of powers provides a check on the expansion of state authority. Bound by legislation and deprived of the authority to craft law itself, the governmental assembly acts as an independent agent of the legislative assembly. The legislature has no say in the performance of specific actions that the governmental assembly takes. The governmental assembly has no say in determining the bounds on its coercive activities or the broad social objectives that it is to pursue. Were either of these constraints on the authority of the two bodies to be relaxed, law could easily be produced to serve the momentary purposes of the government. If those who decide on particular issues can make for any purpose whatever law they like, they are clearly not under the rule of law.

Compared to this later work, Hayek's analysis of how political institutions support the rule of law in *The Constitution of Liberty* is rather broad. The rule of law is protected by constitutional provisions that mandate that all rules made by legislators or their bureaucratic agents be stated as general rules. The pivotal institution that constrains these actors is an independent judiciary with the authority to review and nullify legislative acts or government actions that violate the constitution. There is little to be critiqued about the capacity of this institutional configuration to support the rule of law on its own terms. The constitution essentially says that the rule of law is the principle by which society is to be governed and a strong apolitical judicial branch ensures that the government is prevented from getting away with actions that violate the constitution. Without relaxing the assumption that the judiciary's rulings are strictly enforced or that it acts apolitically, this institutional framework may potentially fail to work effectively if the judiciary's resources are outpaced by government violations of the constitution. Outside of this concern, however, the assumption of a strong judiciary and a rule-of-law constitution are trivially sufficient to support the rule of law. What happens to the rule of law when these relatively strong assumptions are relaxed? Hayek's subsequent institutional analysis explores just this.

In volume three of *Law, Legislation, and Liberty* Hayek appears to relax the assumption that the constitution restricts all state action to the making and enforcing of general rules. Although Hayek does not explicitly frame his analysis in terms of relaxing this assumption, it is clear that the need for separation of powers to extend to executive and legislative responsibilities arises from modifying this assumption about the constitution. The point of strictly separating legislation and governance is to prevent one body from having the power to make its own actions lawful. If a non-amendable constitutional principle exists limiting government to general rule making and rule enforcement, there is no risk of one branch establishing arbitrary rule in the presence of a strong judiciary. The court would strike down any arbitrary rule or action and the political environment characterized by stable rule of law from *The Constitution of Liberty* prevails. The effect of relaxing the strong judiciary assumption, however, is ambiguous. If either the government or the legislature can violate the constitution, then a constitutional requirement preventing either branch from taking particular actions is meaningless. The institutional analysis is held together by the ability of the judiciary to enforce the law.

By relaxing the strict assumption that the constitution binds the state to make and enforce general rules, Hayek relies on the separation of powers between the legislative assembly and government assembly to maintain the rule of law. Here Hayek needs to assume that the division of responsibility between the two branches can be enforced. The legislature is prohibited from taking action against or in the service of private citizens and the government cannot write rules. Without the power to create rules, the governmental assembly should work as Hayek intends it to. Its actions can never take the force of law and are always reviewable by the court. Arbitrary action by the governmental assembly is prevented by construction given a strong judiciary. The tendency of administrators to attempt to expand the scope of their own authority is similarly checked by the constitutional separation of bureaucrats from the rulemaking process.

It is less clear whether a strong judiciary can similarly constrain a legislature whose actions are strictly confined to writing rules. Even if a court could prevent the legislature from engaging in direct governance, would there be anything preventing the legislature from indirectly using the government to achieve its momentary arbitrary aims? Presumably an arbitrary rule could be written by the legislature that the government would be compelled to enforce. The rule could potentially be struck down on the grounds that the constitution mandates that the legislative assembly only make general rules. This cause for prohibiting arbitrary rule crafting, however, throws out the reason for having separation of powers in the first place. If the courts can force the legislature to only make general rules, then the political environment is essentially the same as that of *The Constitution of Liberty*. In such an environment, separating legislation and governance may still have desirable effects on law and policy by allowing specialization, but there would be no additional need to use separation in order to support the rule of law.

Alternatively, a non-general rule drafted by the legislative assembly may be struck by the court on the grounds that it is a violation of the separation of powers. A specific rule is an effective act of governance that the legislature is constitutionally forbidden from taking. The core assumption here is that separation of powers is a constitutional provision that courts can enforce. Hayek's accomplishment in the model constitution of *Law, Legislation, and Liberty*, therefore, is to find an institutional or procedural solution to a constitutional problem. If the state is not constitutionally bound to explicitly obey the rule of law as such, the separation of rulemaking and rule enforcement provides procedural conditions that prevent the creation of arbitrary rules.

From a theoretical perspective, replacing one strong assumption about the enforceable content of the constitution with a similarly strong assumption may be problematic. If courts are assumed to be strong enough to enforce constitutional provisions, why write a more institutionally complicated constitution? A reasonable answer to this concern is that there are many imaginable circumstances in which a constitution that mandates the rule of law may not be available to an institutional designer. Politics is a messy conflict-ridden process. The first-best trivial solution to establishing the rule of law, even in an unrealistic world in which courts can perfectly enforce the constitution, is unlikely to emerge from any noncooperative process of constitutional design. Institutional or constitutional reforms that procedurally amend lawmaking and governance in a society may also be more likely than deeper constitutional changes that redefine the role of government. Moreover, separation of powers is an institutional arrangement that across time and space has been found to function as more than mere constitutional window dressing. A large literature in comparative politics examines the ways in which different varieties of the separation of powers substantively influences political processes and outcomes across democracies (Laver and Shepsle 1999; Linz 1994; Londregan 2000; Samuels 2009; Shugart and Carey 1992). It may also be realistic to think that courts can be strong enough to resolve disputes between two branches of government according to procedures specified in a constitution but not strong enough to bind the government as a whole. However it specifically comes about, a circumstance in which separation of powers can be established in a constitution and actually enforced is hardly unimaginable. Although executive and legislative authority is not separated specifically along the lines that Hayek suggests in any contemporary democracy, there exist numerous stable democracies with strong judicial branches in which executive and legislative powers are constitutionally separated (Lijphart 1999; Widner 2001). Similar working examples of societies in which government is effectively bound to adhere to the rule of law or a similar general principle by constitutional provisions are difficult to find.

The conclusion regarding administration and the rule of law that can be drawn from this analysis is relatively straightforward. Setting aside the issue of whether government and legislation are carried out through democratic means or not, Hayek's claim is that the constitutional separation of these two activities and a strong judiciary are sufficient to support non-arbitrary public administration. The strict separation of government and legislation in Hayek's model constitution that engenders non-arbitrary administration is essentially the same politics-administration dichotomy that appears in Woodrow Wilson's (1887), Frank Goodnow's (1900), and Max Weber's (1948) foundational theoretical analyses of bureaucracy. Wilson (1887) draws an analytical distinction between government and administration that closely maps onto Hayek's distinction between legislation and governance. For Wilson, "the broad plans of governmental action are not administrative; the detailed execution of such plans is administrative" (1887, 212). Goodnow echoes this distinction, separating the elected legislative government from the professional executive government (1900, 17). With this distinction, Wilson makes an argument similar to Hayek's regarding the role of a constitution in checking the potential threat posed to liberty by the administrative state. "Liberty," he writes, "cannot live apart from constitutional principle; and no administration, however perfect and liberal it methods can give men more than a poor counterfeit of liberty if it rests upon illiberal principles of government" (Wilson 1887, 212). Constitutions and the institutional arrangements they define structure the extent and nature of government activity. The separation of politics and administration—or in Hayek's terms the separation of legislation and government—is an important arrangement for the preservation of liberty. Voters and their representatives are too ill-informed or improperly incentivized to be trusted with the power to directly manage administration. Wilson concludes that "although politics sets the tasks for administration, it should not be suffered to manipulate its offices (1887, 210)."

Hayek and Wilson differ somewhat regarding the appropriate way that administration should be organized. While not denying that economies of scale in some domains of administrative action could make centralization an efficient use of resources, Hayek speaks favorably about the potential benefits of delegating certain tasks to local administrative authorities ([1994] 2007, 107). Wilson, however, saw centralization as a key structure in the executive of efficient administration (Ostrom 2008, 24). The two also place different limits on the scope that government activity should take in a free society. These disagreements aside, Hayek and Wilson can both be read as engaged in the problem of fostering effective rule-bound administration by separating the administrative sphere from the political sphere.

In Weber's ideal-typical bureaucracy, the separation of politics from administrative activities emerges from the core features of the bureaucracy. Merit-based recruiting standards, the treatment of government service as a vocation or career, clear hierarchies, written operating procedures, and the vesting of authority in specific positions rather than specific individuals are features of administrative organizations that foster apolitical professionalism. As Suleiman (2003) notes, for Weber, "the politics-administration dichotomy is based on a division of labor that assumes the bureaucracy's loyalty to the government of the day as well as to the even-handed, professional implementation of policies."

Like Hayek, Weber understood that this class of nonpolitical professional administrators could develop and defend interests of its own that may conflict with the requirements of democracy. The two differ, however, in their analysis of this problem. Hayek begins with administrative self-interest and prescribes separation of powers as a check on the capacity of bureaucrats to pursue these interests. For Weber, the separation of powers helps to define the parochial interests of the bureaucracy by creating a class of professional administrators. Despite this potential problem created in part by the politics-administration dichotomy, Weber ultimately concludes along with Hayek that the separation of powers is a necessary condition for the preservation of both democracy and a market economy.

The consequences of the self-interest of professional administrators is a topic that economists and public choice theorists attempted to understand after Weber. The behavioral assumption in most of these studies before the late 1970s matches Hayek's (Gailmard and Patty 2012). Whether for the purpose of self-enrichment or to aid in the execution of tasks in their domain of administrative responsibility, bureaucrats were often assumed to want to maximize the total amount of resources allocated to them. Mises (1962, 87), for example, asserts that "the bureaucrat as voter is more eager to get a raise than to keep the budget balanced." Tullock (1965, 147) similarly writes that "all bureaucrats, whether successful or not, thoroughly approve of an expansion of the whole bureaucracy." Downs (1967) shares this assumption for most types of bureaucrats. In the most systematic and influential early rational-choice approach to bureaucracy, Niskanen (1971) assumes that bureaucrats maximize the size of their agency's budget.

This behavioral assumption has received considerable criticism (Blais and Dion 1991; Migue and Balanger 1974). Accordingly, contemporary models of bureaucracy generally treat bureaucrats as policy preference maximizers rather than resource maximizers (Gailmard and Patty 2012). The implications of this for how bureaucrats prefer to expand their resources and domain of activity can be ambiguous. Working outside of a strict rational choice approach to bureaucracy, James Wilson (1989) observes that there is little evidence that agencies universally seek to expand their size or resource base. Some agencies do this and these agencies receive considerable attention. Plenty of agencies, however, quietly go about their business without attempting to increase their discretion or command of government resources. Larger budgets and greater responsibilities can reduce an agency's autonomy (Carpenter 2001) as this expansion brings about higher expectations and oversight from political principals, draws more public attention to agency activities, creates new sources of conflict with other agencies or private actors, and often makes the tasks the agency is charged with carrying out more complex. If an agency desires political support and the autonomy that comes with it, the agency is best off keeping its tasks simple, its rivals nonexistent, and constraints to a minimum.

How sensitive is Hayek's analysis of the separation of politics and administration to the problematic assumption that administrators have a tendency "to draw everything they can into the service of the public aims they are pursuing?" It appears to be hardly important at all. The rule of law is threatened by the combination of legislation and governance in the same body regardless of the goals of administrators. If an agency is asked to execute an arbitrary police action against a specific class of citizens, for example, and it carries out this task perfectly without pressing for more resources or discretion, the rule of law is nonetheless violated.

As this discussion has made clear, Hayek's theory of the administrative state features at its core an understanding in common with seminal early theories that the separation of politics and administration is a causally relevant institutional arrangement for fostering professional, rule-bound, and nonpolitical administration. Hayek expands on these foundational works by moving his analysis back one step further. Rather than simply working out the consequences of the politics-administration dichotomy on what government agencies do and why they do it, Hayek takes the sustainability of this dichotomy as problematic in the presence of rational self-interested actors and provides an institutional mechanism—the separation of powers in the presence of a strong judiciary—that allows the separation of politics and administration to arise endogenously. Unlike similar rational-institutional theories of administration that emerged around the time Hayek published *Law, Legislation, and Liberty*, Hayek's argument withstands the weakening of a problematic assumption that it had in common with these early theories, namely, the assumption that bureaucrats seek to maximize their budgets and expand the scope of their responsibilities. The following two sections discuss what becomes of administration when separation of executive and legislative authority breaks down. In particular, they examine what Hayek sees as the consequences combining both powers in a single democratic body.

UNLIMITED DEMOCRACY AND THE EXPANSION OF THE ADMINISTRATIVE SPHERE

This section and the following section address the issue of democratic control of government separately from that of maintaining the rule of law. While the two concerns are closely related in Hayek's writing, they are conceptually separable.[1] The focus of this section specifically is Hayek's claim that in the absence of the separation of powers, majority rule enables the arbitrary expansion of administrative authority.

Hayek's earliest analysis of political institutions comes out of his writing on the political economy of planning and deals directly with the complicated relationship between democratic governance and the execution of administrative objectives. In "Freedom and the Economic System" (1939) and *The Road to Serfdom* ([1944] 2007), Hayek argues that democratic governance and economic planning are incompatible. Democratic political institutions only function effectively where there is considerable room for agreement among elected representatives. Accordingly, the scope of government activity in a democracy is best confined to those domains over which agreement can be reached. Democratic planning demands that individuals and their representatives agree on the relative importance of different social ends. This requires citizens and their representatives to agree on almost everything. As a consequence of the inability of democratic assemblies to produce a unitary plan to centrally organize the economy, political pressure arises for discretionary authority to be delegated to administrative officials. The nature of the task of planning, moreover, places strong centralizing pressure on the state bureaucracy. Delegation of specific planning powers to separate agencies creates a potential coordination problem between agencies. The most readily available solution to this problem is to make a single agency responsible for the entire plan.

Hayek notes that delegation in general by a democratic assembly to an agency is not inherently antidemocratic. Central planning, however, is not a responsibility that can be delegated to an agency without endowing it with decision-making powers that undermine democracy:

> So long as the power that is delegated is merely the power to make general rules, there may be very good reasons why such rules should be laid down by local rather than by the central authority. The objectionable feature is that delegation is so often resorted to because the matter in hand cannot be regulated by general rules but only by the exercise of discretion in the decision of particular cases. In these instances delegation means that some authority is given power to make with the force of law what to all intents and purposes are arbitrary decisions. (Hayek [1994] 2007, 107)

In *The Road to Serfdom*, Hayek shows that even when freed from the constraints of the rule of law, a government is incapable of central economic planning by democratic means. Arbitrary authority may be exercised, but only under highly unrealistic conditions can majority consensus be formed over the set of arbitrary actions that should be taken to organize all production that takes place in a society. Hayek's jump from the impossibility of democratic planning to the inevitability of delegated planning in *The Road to Serfdom* follows from the structure of his analysis. His task is to take a particular goal, state economic planning, and identify which institutional arrangements are capable of supporting this goal and which are not. Whether the response of a democratic government to its inability to centrally coordinate production would be to leave its goal unchanged and delegate planning authority to an agency or to abandon the goal of planning in the interest of maintaining democracy were it free to do so is not clear in *The Road to Serfdom*. His subsequent writings on democracy in the absence of the constraints of the rule of law focus on the latter case in which planning is no longer the objective.

In volume three of *Law, Legislation, and Liberty*, Hayek argues that the expansion and bureaucratization of democratic governments in the nineteenth and twentieth centuries follows from this failure to institutionally separate law making and governance. Legislators in possession of the authority to make law and direct specific administrative actions are pressured by electoral concerns to cater to specific interests. In the absence of a check on their ability to make a government action legal or to take such an action in the first place, there is little to prevent democracy from becoming all-encompassing.

Although detrimental to the rule of law, arbitrary government action is not necessarily antidemocratic if democratic actions are defined as those authorized by a majority of citizens or their representatives. Moreover, the delegation of the authority to act arbitrarily within a particular domain to an unelected bureaucracy is compatible with democratic administration as long as the majority retains final authority to override the bureaucracy's action. Assuming that this possibility of override is maintained, what are the effects of democratic administration? If legislation and governance are not separated, the primary consequence of democratic administration is the expansion of the size of the state and the scope of its activities. Representatives of various constituencies and interest groups can legally carry out whatever government action they so choose as long as a temporary majority can be secured. The growth of government is still checked by the requirement that government action and legislation be approved by majority consensus. As Hayek observes in *The Road to Serfdom*, there is a limit to how all-encompassing the domain of democratic government action can be. However, the constraint on the growth of government imposed by democracy is likely to be far less restrictive than that implied by the strict separation of governance and legislation in Hayek's model constitution.

Whether the expansion of arbitrary state authority is more pronounced in a democracy than in other types of polities when legislation and governance are combined is not clear in Hayek's writing. Regardless of the choice rule by which laws and government actions are legitimized, the combination of governance and legislation in the same body opens the door for the unchecked growth of arbitrary state administration. Autocrats and oligarchs would likely be just as ambitious as democratic majorities to use political means to attain their preferred ends. How limited the growth of government would be across political regimes in the absence of strict separation of powers will depend presumably on the specific procedural rules used to generate lawful government action. This interaction between decision-making rules and the scope of government activity has received considerable attention from political scientists and economists (Agranov and Palfrey 2015; Buchanan and Tullock 1962; Meltzer and Richard 1981; Roberts 1977; Romer 1975). Hayek's institutional analysis, while not directly contributing substantively to this literature, may provide a qualification for some of its main conclusions by pointing out that the effect of decision-making rules on the size of government is conditional on the effective combination of legislative and governmental authority in the hands of decision makers.

This second claim, like his first claim, is readily intelligible to contemporary institutional analysts. It is a causal claim that takes self-interested actors as given and connects an institutional arrangement—democratic administration—to a political outcome—growth of administrative responsibility. The institutional causal structure of Hayek's claim makes it possible for contemporary analysts to apply contemporary methodological tools, in particular formal theory, to assess the veracity of his claim under various conditions.

DEMOCRATIC CONTROL OF COMPLEX ADMINISTRATION

This section considers Hayek's third and final major claim regarding the administrative state: the expansion of administration into more complex and all-encompassing domains makes democratic control of administration impossible. In *Law, Legislation, and Liberty*, Hayek works out the consequences of the unchecked expansion of administrative responsibility into any feasible domain of private life so long a temporary majority can be assembled to charge the bureaucracy with a new task:

> Democracy, at the same time at which it seems to become all-engulfing, becomes on the governmental level an impossibility. It is an illusion to believe that the people, or their elected representatives, can govern a complex society in detail. Government relying on the general support from a majority will of course still determine the major steps, so far as it is not merely driven to these by the momentum of its previous proceedings. But Government is already becoming so complex that it is inevitable that its members, as heads of the various departments, are increasingly becoming puppets of the bureaucracy, to which they will still give "general directions," but on the operation of which the execution of all details depends. It is not without reason that socialist governments want to politicize the bureaucracy, because it is by it and not in any democratic body that more and more of the crucial decisions are made. (Hayek 1979, 144–45)

While Hayek's claim that government expansion makes effective control over administration increasingly difficult is made as a warning regarding the consequence of democratic administration in the absence of the rule of law, the central logic of his claim appears to be much broader, applying to non-democratic regimes as well. The logic of his claim is rooted in an informational problem in which citizens or their representatives cannot possess the knowledge needed to democratically control the administrative state once the tasks it is charged with become sufficiently complex. This resembles a fairly standard principal-agent problem. If an agent is more well-informed than his or her principal about an underlying state of the world on which policy outcomes depend, this creates space for the agent to strategically manipulate the information he or she shares with a principal to obtain outcomes more favorable to him- or herself than those that would prevail were the principal able to make a decision with the same information possessed by the agent. In other words, an information asymmetry creates conditions for bureaucratic drift—that is, a circumstance in which the bureaucracy's actions diverge from those that the principal prefers it takes. Intuitively, as policy complexity—modeled as the severity of the informational asymmetry or the variance of the underlying state of the world—increases, informed policymaking comes at the price of greater bureaucratic drift and therefore less principal control over ultimate policy outcomes. Under certain regularity conditions, this intuition is largely corroborated in formal models of legislative-agency relations (Alonso and Matouschek 2008; Bendor and Meirowitz 2004; Epstein and O'Halloran 1999; Gailmard 2009; Gailmard and Patty 2007; Huber and McCarty 2004; Huber and Shipan 2002). These basic results clearly hold for any principal, regardless of whether he or she is a median voter or an autocrat.

A more nuanced separation of democracies and non-democracies may concern whether or not direct policy-making authority can be delegated to an agent. Following Hayek, democratic majorities would need to retain the power to ultimately choose policy while non-democratic decision makers would be allowed to delegate the policy choice to an unelected agent. Alonso and Matouschek (2007) and Callander (2008) provide thorough formal treatments of this distinction. Callander's model in particular works out its implications for legislative control of government action and resulting policy. While the results of the model do not directly address bureaucratic drift as a function of policy complexity or the ability of the principal to commit to delegation, its results imply that if principals are free to choose the policy preferences of the agency, bureaucratic drift can be more problematic for democracies than non-democracies. A more direct formal analysis of this problem across regimes is needed to provide a more definitive answer to this question. Such a comparative formal analysis of institutions will also help to clarify the logic underlying Hayek's claim that democracy becomes impossible when it becomes all-encompassing. As for his previous two claims, the institutional logic of Hayek's informal claims makes his claims highly amenable to formalization.

It should be noted that Hayek's third claim requires some degree of conflict between the will of a democratic assembly and the interests of administrators. If bureaucrats and politicians had the exact same interests, bureaucratic drift would generally not be an issue. The conflict he identifies as particularly salient is the ambition of bureaucrats to expand their responsibilities and resources. Like the first claim, the third claim is not dependent on the potentially weak assumption that conflict over budgets and the scope of administration prevails. As the above discussion of principal-agent problems makes clear, conflict over most preferred policy outcomes is sufficient to allow bureaucratic drift to increase as the complexity of the tasks an agency is charged with executing grows. Following Wilson (1989), it is quite conceivable that bureaucrats who exclusively value policy outcomes would prefer to leave their agency's budget alone. Greater oversight, criticism, and responsibility may prevent the agency from bringing about its most preferred outcomes in a narrower and less conflictual domain of policy.

While Hayek's third claim is generally corroborated by the formal bureaucracy literature, a series of influential papers in the American politics literature suggests that the significance of this drift may be muted by oversight institutions and administrative procedures. Weingast and Moran (1983) argue that the institutions of Congress such as committees, interests groups, and ex post sanctions enable Congress to effectively provide strong incentives for bureaucrats to obey legislative orders. McCubbins and Schwartz (1984) identify two types of bureaucratic oversight, "police patrols" and "fire alarms." The former refers to active monitoring of the bureaucracy by Congress. The latter describes an institutional structure of oversight in which citizens and interests groups can file complaints against the bureaucracy when it violates a legislative statute. Police patrols are costly for Congress, particularly as the scope of government expands. Fire alarms, however, distribute the cost of oversight on citizens. Hayek's concerns about oversight seem to strictly regard police patrols. By removing the burden of direct oversight from the legislature and placing it in the hands of citizens, fire alarm oversight is a procedural fix for the problem of democratic control of complex administration that Hayek identifies. McCubbins, Noll, and Weingast (1987, 1989) advance this institutional analysis further, arguing that Congress can and does design administrative procedures as a way of controlling the actions of the bureaucracy. By requiring administrative agencies to follow specific procedures, Congress shapes the institutional environment that agencies operate within. This effectively limits the feasible set of policy actions that the agency can take.

These papers were criticized by Moe (1989, 2013) and others for neglecting to seriously take into account both the role of the president and the forward-looking strategic concerns of temporary legislative majorities. In the US system, the administrative state serves two separate democratically elected masters who often have opposing interests (Moe 1989; Wilson 1989; Bolton and Thrower 2015). Democratic control of administration is clearly complicated on both a practical and conceptual level in such an environment. Moreover, legislative majorities or presidents who want the administration to carry out a set of policies understand that their continued control of government is uncertain. In response to this uncertainty, administrative procedures are used to insulate agencies from attempts by future majorities to reverse policy.

This criticism of the "Congressional dominance" literature highlights one of Hayek's core insights into how political institutions operate. Hayek's work points out that separation of powers itself is not sufficient to guarantee limited or democratically controlled government. The specific manner in which powers are separated is crucial to achieving these tasks. In the US case, powers are separated between executive and legislature, but both branches effectively retain power to legislate and govern. The result is a bureaucracy that is strategically designed to be insulated from political control.

Overall, while Hayek's thought on administration has received little attention from political scientists and is generally not viewed as a contribution to the literature, his work anticipates some of the major themes that will be explored more rigorously in political science beginning in the early 1980s. Moreover, his way of thinking about political institutions and administration in particular has in common with this later literature a broad methodology of institutional analysis. Hayek clearly views institutions as vital to structuring individual behavior and thereby shaping political outcomes. This causal structure allows his work to be revisited and analyzed with contemporary formal methods.

One potential ambiguity in Hayek's theory that formal analysis may help to clarify concerns the relationship between his third claim and his second. It appears that in order for his second and third claims to operate simultaneously with sufficiently informed voters, these claims must to some extent be partial equilibrium claims. If claim three is correct, democratic majorities will presumably understand the effect of expanding the domain of administration and therefore be more hesitant to expand the complexity of administrative tasks than they would be if they were ignorant of the consequences of such an action. In other words, understanding of the third claim should temper the salience of the second claim in a democracy.[2] Some additional mechanism such as a collective action problem or a cost-benefit asymmetry needs to be added to Hayek's theory for claim two to hold at the same time as claim three.

REVISITING THE POLITICS-ADMINISTRATION DICHOTOMY

Together, Hayek's three claims provide contemporary scholars with a theoretical framework for revisiting the question of how politics and administration can be separated. Hayek's first claim provides a potential answer to this classic question. By separating rule making and rule enforcement into two completely separate democratically elected bodies, the administrative state can effectively be bound by general rules that insulate administration from the influence of parochial interests. Hayek's second claim identifies why this separation of powers is vital to the separation of politics and administration. If those who design rules are also given the power to administrate, administrators can make their arbitrary actions lawful. This legal arbitrariness paves the way for parochial interests to prevail in administration. Hayek's third claim provides another avenue through which politics may enter administration. When administrative tasks become sufficiently complex, the difficulty of overseeing administrative activity creates space for unchecked administrative action. Where administrators work effectively unsupervised, arbitrary action becomes possible. While such arbitrary action may accord with the best judgments of professional bureaucrats, it is also quite feasible that parochial interests influence administrative action in these unsupervised spaces.

The implications of Hayek's theory for the politics-administration dichotomy invites scholars to look at the broader institutional environment in which bureaucracies and bureaucrats act. Often the relationship between administration and politician is a simple abstract principal-agent relationship. While some models take account of how various institutional settings affect bureaucratic action (Huber and Shipan 2002), the focus of the recent formal literature has moved away from considering the separation of politics and administration as a question of interest.[3] As noted throughout this chapter, Hayek's claims follow a logic that can be readily formalized. Consequently, his theory provides a blueprint for engagement with a classic and important question in the study of administration in a rigorous formal manner.

CONCLUSION

The purpose of this chapter has been to identify and critically evaluate a theory of administration in Hayek's thought on political institutions. In surveying four decades worth of Hayek's writing on the subject, three claims were identified as constituting the core of Hayek's theory of administration. First, the constitutional separation of legislation and governance is sufficient to bring public administration in line with the requirements of the rule of law, provided that the judiciary is powerful enough to enforce separation of powers. Second, in the absence of separation of powers, democratic control of administration leads to the expansion of the scope and complexity of administration. Third, increasing the scope and complexity of administration makes democratic control over the administrative state impossible. This chapter's broad contribution has been to identify a relatively clear and consistent theory of administration in Hayek's writing on political institutions so that social scientists may revisit and appreciate Hayek as a contributor to the scholarly understanding of the politics of public administration. In particular, Hayek's theory of the administrative state offers contemporary scholars a way of revisiting the classic problem of separating politics from administration.

NOTES

1. Hayek does indeed separate the two in his early analysis of democracy and planning.
2. Meltzer and Richard (1981) make a similar criticism of Hayek.
3. Gailmard and Patty (2007) argue briefly that politics and effective professional administration cannot be supported in their influential model. However, the politics-administration dichotomy is not the focus of their model.

REFERENCES

Agranov, Marina, and Thomas Palfrey. 2015. "Equilibrium Tax Rates and Income Redistribution: A Laboratory Study." *Journal of Public Economics* 130: 45–58.

Alonso, Ricardo, and Niko Matouschek. 2007. "Relational Delegation." *RAND Journal of Economics* 38 (4): 1070–89.

———. 2008. "Optimal Delegation." *Review of Economic Studies* 75 (1): 259–93.

Arnold, R. Douglas. 1979. *Congress and the Bureaucracy*. New Haven, CT: Yale University Press.

Bendor, Jonathan, and Adam Meirowitz. 2004. "Spatial Models of Delegation." *American Political Science Review* 98 (2): 293–310.

Blais, Andre, and Stephane Dion. 1991. *The Budget-Maximizing Bureaucrat: Appraisals and Evidence*. Pittsburgh, PA: University of Pittsburgh Press.

Bolton, Alexander, and Sharece Thrower. 2015. "Legislative Capacity and Executive Unilateralism." *American Journal of Political Science* 60 (3): 649–63.

Brehm, John, and Scott Gates. 1999. *Working, Shirking, and Sabotage: Bureaucratic Response to a Democratic Public*. Ann Arbor: University of Michigan Press.

Buchanan, James, and Gordon Tullock. 1962. *The Calculus of Consent: The Logical Foundations of Constitutional Democracy*. Ann Arbor: University of Michigan Press.

Callander, Steven. 2008. "A Theory of Policy Expertise." *Quarterly Journal of Political Science* 3 (2): 123–40.

Carpenter, Daniel. 2001. *The Forging of Bureaucratic Autonomy: Reputations, Networks, and Policy Innovation in Executive Agencies, 1862–1928*. Princeton, NJ: Princeton University Press.

Crawford, Vincent, and Joel Sobel. 1982. "Strategic Information Transmission." *Econometrica* 50 (6): 1431–51.

Downs, Anthony. 1967. *Inside Bureaucracy*. Boston: Little, Brown.

Epstein, David, and Sharyn O'Halloran. 1999. *Delegating Powers: A Transaction Cost Politics Approach to Policy Making Under Separate Powers*. Cambridge: Cambridge University Press.

Gailmard, Sean. 2009. "Multiple Principals and Oversight of Bureaucratic Policy-Making." *Journal of Theoretical Politics* 21 (2): 161–86.

Gailmard, Sean, and John Patty. 2007. "Slackers and Zealots: Civil Service, Policy Discretion, and Bureaucratic Expertise." *American Journal of Political Science* 51 (4): 873–89.

———. 2012. "Formal Models of Bureaucracy." *Annual Review of Political Science* 15 (1): 353–77.

Goodnow, Frank. 1900. *Politics and Administration*. New York: Russell and Russell.

Hayek, Friedrich. [1939] 1997. "Freedom and the Economic System." In *Socialism and War: Essays, Documents, Reviews*, 189–212. Indianapolis: Liberty Fund.

———. 1973a. *Economic Freedom and Representative Government*. London: Institute of Economic Affairs.

———. 1973b. *Law, Legislation, and Liberty*. Vol. 1: *Rules and Order*. Chicago: University of Chicago Press.

———. 1979. *Law, Legislation, and Liberty*. Vol. 3: *The Political Order of a Free People*. London: Routledge & Kegan Paul.

———. [1994] 2007. *The Road to Serfdom*. Chicago: University of Chicago Press.

———. 2011. *The Constitution of Liberty*. Chicago: University of Chicago Press.

———. 2014. "The Political Ideal of the Rule of Law." In *The Market and Other Orders*, 119–94. Chicago: University of Chicago Press.

Huber, John, and Nolan McCarty. 2004. "Bureaucratic Capacity, Delegation, and Political Reform." *American Political Science Review* 98 (3): 481–94.

Huber, John, and Charles Shipan. 2002. *Deliberate Discretion? The Institutional Foundations of Bureaucratic Autonomy*. Cambridge: Cambridge University Press.

Laver, Michael, and Kenneth Shepsle. 1999. "Government Accountability in Parliamentary Democracy." In *Democracy, Accountability, and Representation*, edited by Adam Przeworski, Susan Stokes, and Bernard Manin, 279–96. Cambridge: Cambridge University Press.

Lewis, David. 2008. *The Politics of Presidential Appointments: Political Control and Bureaucratic Performance*. Princeton, NJ: Princeton University Press.

Lijphart, Arend. 1999. *Patterns of Democracy*. New Haven, CT: Yale University Press.

Linz, Juan. 1994. "Presidential Versus Parliamentary Democracy: Does It Make a Difference?" In *The Failure of Presidential Democracy*, edited by Juan Linz and Arturo Valenzuela, 3–87. Baltimore, MD: Johns Hopkins University Press.

Londregan, John. 2000. *Legislative Institutions and Ideology in Chile*. New York: Cambridge University Press.

McCubbins, Mathew, Roger Noll, and Barry Weingast. 1987. "Administrative Procedures as Instruments of Political Control." *Journal of Law, Economics, and Organization* 3 (2): 243–77.

———. 1989. "Structure and Process, Politics and Policy: Administrative Arrangements and the Political Control of Agencies." *Virginia Law Review* 75 (2): 431–82.

McCubbins, Mathew, and Thomas Schwartz. 1984. "Congressional Oversight Overlooked: Police Patrols versus Fire Alarms." *American Journal of Political Science* 28 (1): 165–79.

Meltzer, Allan, and Scott Richard. 1981. "A Rational Theory of the Size of Government." *Journal of Political Economy* 89 (5): 914–27.

Migue, Jean-Luc, and Gerard Balanger. 1974. "Towards a General Theory of Managerial Discretion." *Public Choice* 17 (1): 27–43.

Mises, Ludwig von. 1962. *Bureaucracy*. Grove City, PA: Libertarian Press.

Moe, Terry. 1989. "The Politics of Bureaucratic Structure." In *Can the Government Govern?*, edited by John E. Chubb and Paul E. Peterson, 267–329. Washington, DC: Brookings Institution Press.

———. 2013. "Delegation, Control, and the Study of Public Bureaucracy." In *The Handbook of Organizational Economics*, edited by Robert Gibbons and John Roberts, 1148–81. Princeton, NJ: Princeton University Press.

Niskanen, William. 1971. *Bureaucracy and Representative Government*. Chicago: Aldine Atherton.

Ostrom, Vincent. 2008. *The Intellectual Crisis in American Public Administration*. Tuscaloosa: University of Alabama Press.

Prendergast, Canice. 2007. "The Motivation and Bias of Bureaucrats." *American Economic Review* 97 (1): 180–96.

Roberts, Kevin. 1977. "Voting over Income Tax Schedules." *Journal of Public Economics* 8 (3): 329–40.

Romer, Thomas. 1975. "Individual Welfare, Majority Voting, and the Properties of a Linear Income Tax." *Journal of Public Economics* 4 (2): 163–85.

Samuels, David. 2009. "Separation of Powers." In *The Oxford Handbook of Comparative Politics*, edited by Carles Boix and Susan Stokes, 703–26. Oxford: Oxford University Press.

Shugart, Matthew, and John Carey. 1992. *Presidents and Assemblies: Constitutional Design and Electoral Dynamics*. Cambridge: Cambridge University Press.

Suleiman, Ezra. 2003. *Dismantling Democratic States*. Princeton, NJ: Princeton University Press.

Tullock, Gordon. 2005. "The Politics of Bureaucracy." In *Bureaucracy*, 3–238. Indianapolis: Liberty Fund.

Weber, Max. 1948. "Bureaucracy." In *From Max Weber: Essays in Sociology*, edited by H. H. Gerth and C. Wright Mills, 196–244. London: Routledge.

Weingast, Barry, and Mark Moran. 1983. "Bureaucratic Discretion or Congressional Control: Regulatory Policymaking by the Federal Trade Commission." *Journal of Political Economy* 91 (5): 765–800.

Widner, Jennifer. 2001. *Building the Rule of Law*. New York: W. W. Norton.

Wilson, James Q. 1989. *Bureaucracy: What Government Agencies Do and Why They Do It*. New York: Basic Books.

Wilson, Woodrow. 1887. "The Study of Administration." *Political Science Quarterly* 2 (2): 197–222.

Part III

SPONTANEOUS ORDER

Chapter 9

Explaining Culture in Hayek's Cultural Evolution

Matthew Martinez

In "Natural Versus Artifactual Man," Hayek stresses the importance of evolutionary thinking for understanding the social world: "With evolutionary selection, however, we are now supplied with a key to a general understanding of the formation of order in life, mind and interpersonal relations" (Hayek 1988). Contemporarily, social and behavioral scientists across multiple disciplines have developed a research program incorporating the principles of evolutionary theory to explain human cognition, behavior, and society. Although Hayek was unable to participate in this research program, pieces of his scholarship are quite similar in trajectory to modern scientific frameworks, specifically cultural group selection and evolutionary psychology (for examples of each framework, see Cosmides and Tooby 2013; Richerson et al. 2016). Past work has highlighted Hayek's similarities to scholars working within the cultural group selection framework (Rubin and Gick 2005; Stone 2010). Evolutionary psychology presents a greater challenge to Hayek's model of cultural evolution, as it works within the framework of methodological individualism and argues that the interaction between biological evolution and human cognition is necessary for understanding social, political, and economic phenomenon. While some scholars have reinterpreted Hayek's work considering modern research, few have directly compared and reinterpreted his work considering the research in the evolutionary psychology approach to studying culture.

In this chapter, I will outline separately Hayek's model of cultural evolution and the contemporary evolutionary psychology approach for studying culture. Hayek's model will then be reassessed and compared to the evolutionary psychology approach. Given Hayek's interests in: (1) evolutionary theorizing; (2) methodological individualism and human psychology; and (3) the fact that contemporary evolutionary psychology is not gene-centric,

I conclude that Hayek would have been interested in the approach presented by contemporary evolutionary psychology. This school of thought helps to explain some of the ambiguities in Hayek's model of cultural evolution, while maintaining the individual as an active agent in generating, transmitting, and refining culture. I will begin by outlining Hayek's motivation for bringing evolutionary theory into his social and political philosophy. After, I will outline his model of cultural evolution. Then I will contrast Hayek's model with the approach to studying culture used by evolutionary psychologists. The chapter is summed up with a postulated response from Hayek on the model of cultural evolution developed using the evolutionary psychology framework.

HAYEK, EVOLUTION, AND COMPLEXITY

Hayek's scholarly work encompasses a diverse set of disciplines and topics. His canon features expansive writings on topics such as monetary policy and political economy to cognitive science and the evolutionary mechanisms by which cultural systems and societies develop and grow. For many other scholars, these topics would not cleanly align into an integrated framework for understanding and explaining the world. However, Hayek connects his principles of liberty, focused mainly in economics and politics, directly to conditions of the mind and the large degree of complexity found in cultural and social systems. For Hayek's study of society, evolutionary modeling is an indispensable tool for understanding the modern world.

At the core of Hayek's understanding of the contemporary social, political, and economic world is complexity. In several writings (e.g., Hayek 1945), Hayek argues that social, political, and economic systems are not easily tractable by individual minds. One individual alone cannot adequately ascertain, assess, and intervene in such a system given its complexity. These systems feature an immeasurable collection of variables with various interdependencies making cause and effect, diagnoses, and interventions not easily or effectively understood, solved, or implemented. This results in a knowledge problem: the true state of the world cannot be comprehended or managed by our cognitive endowment.

The epistemological problem outlined by Hayek is the result of a mind that operates efficiently in tandem with a social and cultural system exhibiting a high degree of complexity. This creates a dilemma. If our species is incapable of designing and controlling the world with a high degree of precision and accuracy, how do stable institutions, societies, and civilizations form and, subsequently, prosper? Hayek proposes that social and cultural systems evolve. Specifically, the formal (e.g., governments) and informal (e.g., customs and traditions) institutions are not rationally designed by man, but are an emergent property of accidents, experiments, and interactions among individuals (Hayek 2013).

CULTURAL EVOLUTION PER HAYEK

The Problems of Biological Evolution

Hayek proposed that societies develop through an evolutionary process, but did not use evolutionary theory rooted in biology to make this case. He believed that biology cannot and should not be used to explain social aspects of an organism. The problem Hayek found was due to biology narrowly focusing on two types of values: values that are genetically determined and values that are "products of rational thought" (Hayek 1979). For Hayek, both aspects are distinct from the emergence of complexity through spontaneous order.

Hayek considered the validity of predictions derived from biological evolution to be insufficient. When outlining the uses and misuses of evolutionary theory, he states the fundamental problem with social scientific inquiry using biological evolution is that

> [e]ven if we tried to apply our explanatory scheme to a single species consisting of a known number of individuals each of which we were able to observe, and assuming that we were able to ascertain and record every single relevant fact, their sheer number would be such that we should never be able to manipulate them, i.e., to insert these data into the appropriate blanks of our theoretical formula and then to solve the "statement equations" thus determined. (Hayek 2014c, 268)

Then, he concludes, "the theoretical understanding of the growth and functioning of organisms can only in the rarest of instances be turned into specific predictions of what will happen in a particular case, because we can hardly ever ascertain all the facts which will contribute to determine the outcome" (Hayek 2014c, 269). Although we can develop a scenario as to why certain outcomes were reached and the variables involved, the large degree of complexity will not allow for a prediction with high confidence to be made.

Hayek's writing on the problems associated with the explanatory power of evolutionary theory was around the time of the development of two fields of research: sociobiology and ethology. Both fields sought to explain human behavior using biological theory, either through genetic evolution (sociobiology) or through observations of other animal species (ethology). Hayek felt that the extension of such frameworks to explaining human behavior and society was too quick, he states, "I have occasionally felt uneasy about an all-too-rapid application of conclusions drawn from the observation of animals to the explanation of human conduct" (Hayek 1979, 153). Relying on animal behavior to explain human behavior is unsatisfying because there is a key component of human life that makes it substantively different from the lives of other animals: culture. Culture, according to Hayek, is the "decisive change from animal to man" (Hayek 1988, 17).

Human culture cannot be dismissed, and it was the missing ingredient in evolutionary models at the time. There are two primary reasons why Hayek believes culture cannot be dismissed. First, biological evolution would provide us with innate instincts that would be disadvantageous in the modern world. Second, a strict reliance on innate instincts would not easily allow the extended order to grow. He states that "forming supraindividual patterns or systems of cooperation required individuals to change their 'natural' or 'instinctual' responses to others, something strongly resisted" (Hayek 1988, 13). Hayek believes that the innate social responses of the human species are not pro-social (at least, outside of a small group of associates) and would not allow the creation of extended orders of cooperation and associations. On top of that, Hayek finds biological evolution to respond too slowly to the changing environment. He states that "there was certainly no justification for some biologists treating evolution as solely a genetic process, and completely forgetting about the similar but much faster process of cultural evolution that now dominates the human scene and presents to our intelligence problems it has not yet learnt to master" (Hayek 1979, 154). The world has changed at a rapid pace in only the past few thousand years of human history. This allotment of time does not allow for the degree of genetic evolution required to account for a social transformation of this scale. This leaves room for the alternative evolutionary process, specifically the selection of cultural features, to provide the stimuli for change.

How would Hayek's evolutionary model that selects on cultural features work? In "The Theory of Complex Phenomena," Hayek presents a brief definition of what an evolutionary mechanism entails: "The basic proposition which has far-reaching implication is that a mechanism of reduplication with transmittable variations and competitive selection of those which prove to have a better chance of survival will in the course of time produce a great variety of structures adapted to continuous adjustment to the environment and to each other" (Hayek 2014c, 267). To best understand the process of cultural evolution, the evolutionary mechanism should be broken down into the three key features found in Hayek's definition: (1) the generation of transmittable cultural variants, (2) how the transmission of cultural variants occurs, and (3) the selection of cultural variants.

Hayek's Cultural Evolution: Generation

Hayek does not offer an explicit theory of the production of cultural information, but he does state that cultural information is not the result of intentional design. According to Hayek, "*Culture is neither natural nor artificial, neither genetically transmitted nor rationally designed.* It is a tradition of learnt rules of conduct which have never been 'invented' and whose functions the acting individuals usually do not understand" (Hayek 1979, 155). Furthermore, culture partially explains the human species cognitive abilities. Hayek claims that, "*It is probably no more justified to claim that thinking man has created his culture than that culture created his reason*" (Hayek 1979, 155). For Hayek, there is a co-evolution of culture and reason. He states that "cultural evolution is not the result of human reason consciously building institutions, but of a process in which culture and reason developed concurrently is, perhaps, beginning to be more widely understood" (Hayek 1979, 155). Culture is produced through accidents and experiments, which then lead to greater understanding, knowledge, and further innovation. We see this throughout history: novel innovation leading to refinement and further innovations (e.g., agriculture).

Hayek's Cultural Evolution: Transmission

Hayek believed that, "All currently civilized groups appear to possess a similar capacity for acquiring civilization by learning certain traditions. Thus, it hardly seems possible that civilization and culture are genetically determined and transmitted. They have to be learnt by all alike through tradition" (Hayek 1988, 16). The mechanism by which cultural information is transmitted is of crucial importance for highly complex social animals, because, as Hayek states, "Unlike genetic properties, cultural properties are not transmitted automatically" (Hayek 1988, 136). For potential cultural information to become widespread among a population, it must first be private information held by an individual and then be transmitted through social learning or imitation of others and stabilize across a widespread network of individuals. This is what drives the distinction between the human species and other animals. Hayek states, "What apparently distinguished him was the capacity to imitate and to pass on what he had learned" (Hayek 1979, 156). Our ability to teach and learn from others allows for the growth and storage of cultural information at a previously unknown degree. The implications are massive: the accumulation of knowledge results in an overall increase in cultural complexity and sophistication. It is directly because of our ability to store knowledge that our species could invest in new endeavors, rather than reinvesting time and energy into learning the same finite ideas developed by previous generations or other populations. In addition, and in some cases more importantly, foolish, poorly designed, and risky ideas could be avoided. This is especially important if one option among a set could result in harm or death (e.g., imagine a trial and error approach to identifying edible foods rather than being taught by others).

Hayek's Cultural Evolution: Selection

Hayek is relatively ambiguous about how cultural traits are selected. He suggests that traits themselves are not selected, but groups with certain traits are selected over other groups without such traits (Hayek 1988). Unfortunately, Hayek does not provide a clear definition of what constitutes a group in his model. This is especially important because of the various collective action problems related to the scale of the group. For example, there are fewer collective action problems associated with a kin-based group compared to a large-scale nation state. Hayek suggests that the first groups that benefitted from cultural evolution were pre-tribal, most likely constituting family or kin-based units. In *The Fatal Conceit*, Hayek states, "Nor should tribes be thought of as the stock from which cultural evolution began; they are, rather, its earliest product. These 'earliest' coherent groups were of common descent and community of practice with other groups an individual with whom they were not necessarily familiar" (Hayek 1988, 31). Non–kin based social collectives, such as a tribe, were unnecessary for the selection of cultural traits to occur. Indeed, Hayek suggests that this is the case: "Hence we can hardly say when tribes first appeared as preservers of shared traditions, and cultural evolution began. Yet somehow, however slowly, however marked by setbacks, orderly cooperation was extended, and common concrete ends were replaced by general, end-independent abstract rules of conduct" (Hayek 1988, 31). Despite the emergence of non–kin based social ties, mutually beneficial and cooperative norms and institutions continued to flourish.

In "The Theory of Complex Phenomena," Hayek is more straightforward about how the process of selection works within cultural evolution. Hayek states that, "For the understanding of animal and human societies the distinction is particularly important because the genetic (and in a great measure also the cultural) *transmission* of rules of conduct takes place from individual to individual, while what may be called the natural *selection* of rules will operate on the basis of the greater or lesser efficiency of the resulting *order of the group*" (Hayek 2014d, 279). The cultural items, such as particular rules of conduct, are passed between individuals. Although the cultural traits are beneficial, this is not enough to guarantee selection. It is plausible that individuals may not fully grasp the benefits that certain cultural practices or behaviors provide. Hayek suggests alternative mechanisms by which cultural traits can be acquired: "Mythical beliefs of some sort may be needed to bring this about, especially where rules of conduct conflicting with instinct are concerned. A merely utilitarian or even functionalist explanation of the different rites or ceremonies will be insufficient, and even implausible" (Hayek 1988, 136). Institutions that seem irrational may provide benefits that are not readily noticed or understood.

The process of selection illustrates how the human species went from living in small-scale societies with low levels of specialization and complexity (i.e., social, political, and economic) to a highly specialized modern world (i.e., "the extended order"). Hayek believes that the resulting modern world is not the product of reason or design: "The structures formed by traditional human practices are neither natural in the sense of being genetically determined, nor artificial in the sense of being the product of intelligent design, but the result of a process of winnowing or sifting, directed by the differential advantages gained by groups from practices adopted for some unknown and perhaps purely accidental reasons" (Hayek 1979, 155). Institutions are developed and then further refined, "because those groups prospered who happened to change them in a way that rendered them increasingly adaptive" (Hayek 1988, 20). A society that allows for experimentation to occur will have a greater chance of seeing good ideas discovered and spread. Thus, societies can only develop and prosper if they are afforded the liberties that allow for experimentation, innovation, and dynamism.

The Product of Cultural Evolution: The Extended Order

Cultural evolution becomes a centerpiece in Hayek's social and political philosophy for the creation of a liberal society. The reason liberty is so vital is because it allows for the mechanism of cultural evolution to sort through computationally vast arrays of variables, select traits that are beneficial on average, without the worry of unintended consequences that may result from human calculation and reason. Hayek states that "the present order of society has largely arisen, not by design, but by the prevailing of more effective institutions in a process of competition" (Hayek 1979, 155). It is because of experiments, accidents, and the spread of good ideas that the mutually beneficial characteristics of the extended order developed and civilization flourished. Accordingly, given the immense complexity and inherent intelligence in social and culture systems, "It is therefore misleading to represent the individual brain or mind as the capping stone of the hierarchy of complex structures produced by evolution, which then designed what we call culture" (Hayek 1979, 157). Thus, many who assume that the human species has designed, built, and managed the modern social order are neglecting what our brain, cognition, and reasoning abilities allow us to do, which according to Hayek is only to absorb culture, not design (Hayek 1979).

Given the discrepancy between the human species' natural biological endowments and the complex built environment we live in, Hayek argues that there is a mismatch. Humans occupy a novel environment, while having the biological adaptations for solving problems we faced in our ancestral environment (i.e., small-scale face-to-face environments with almost no anonymity). Our environmental mismatch produces complications: biologically evolved instinctual drives that resolved problems in small-scale social worlds do not allow for easy cooperation and coordination today. To solve this complication, culture acts as a system of restraints, which allows man to live in a vastly different world from the world he had originally evolved for (Hayek 1979, 1988). Hayek states that "the innate natural longings were appropriate to the condition of life of the small band during which man had developed the neural structure which is still characteristic of Homo sapiens" (Hayek 1979, 160). Our mind's innate computational software is outdated and biological evolution does not provide an upgrade at a quick enough pace. For Hayek, the cultural restraints that emerged spontaneously enable the emergence and expansion of civilization. He states that, "What has made men good is neither nature nor reason but tradition" (Hayek 1979, 160). Moving from small-scale hunting and gathering bands to densely packed, complex, and specialized cities was possible given the tools developed along our cultural evolutionary history, and, subsequently, the transmission and refinement of these tools through the competition and selection.

Many of the mutually beneficial institutions we use today emerged through a process of cultural evolution. Hayek states:

> What is chiefly responsible for having generated this extraordinary order, and the existence of mankind in its present size and structure, are the rules of human conduct that gradually evolved (especially those dealing with several property, honesty, contract, exchange, trade, competition, gain, privacy). These rules are handed on by tradition, teaching and imitation, rather than by instinct. (Hayek 1988, 12)

Several critical features of social interactions and society are the result of unintended cultural evolution. Hayek claims that, "The basic tools of civilization—language, morals, law and money—are all the result of spontaneous growth and not of design, and of the last two organized power has got hold and thoroughly corrupted them" (Hayek 1979, 163). These features and institutions that have emerged through the process of cultural evolution are hallmarks of the modern social order. Without cultural innovations to constrain the natural man, the modern social order would not be feasible.

THE EVOLUTIONARY PSYCHOLOGY APPROACH TO STUDYING CULTURE

Hayek argues that the emergence of the extended order cannot be entirely attributed to genetic predispositions or biological evolution. Sociobiology around the time of Hayek's writing provided reason to be skeptical of the contribution of biology on human behavior and society. Indeed, it is absurd to assume that contemporary socio-political institutions are the direct result of innate biological propensities. It is reasonable to assume that the growth and flourishing of human life, culture, and society is due to the spread of good ideas. History has shown us the ratcheting effect of cumulative cultural evolution. The recent invention of new technologies, such as reading and writing, have drastically shifted social organization and human life.

Given the research at the time, Hayek was unable to take into consideration the full effect that biology and cognition have on the origin, transmission, adoption, and stabilization of specific cultural traits at the population level. Evolutionary psychology argues that biological evolution and the mind profoundly shape culture. It is argued that the organization of the brain and how the mind works will constrain the set of cultural features that can be effectively transmitted and adopted by individuals. The seeming diversity of human culture, traditions, and institutions is not simply due to social learning and transmission of knowledge and ideas, but it is only allowed because of the way the brain and mind are innately organized. There is no master plan or appropriate direction, but human cognition constrains the cultural and social systems that can emerge and stabilize at the population level (Dehaene 2009; Sperber 1996).

An individual-level framework for explaining the evolution of culture argues that the wide-ranging panorama of human culture and institutions, from food preferences and mate preferences to art, morality, and cooperation, are rooted in the brain (for examples, see Baumard, Andre, and Sperber 2013; Gangestad, Haselton, and Buss 2006; Morin 2013). More specifically, the interaction between our evolved mind and social ecology evokes certain behavioral repertoires, cultural features, and social systems. They emerge, stabilize, and spread because they provide great benefits to individuals given the environment and context they are living in (Tooby and Cosmides 1992). This framework agrees with Hayek on one crucial aspect: we cannot rationally and purposefully construct cultural and social systems to serve our needs, if the features of the social system are incongruent with the evolved cognitive features of the mind. Simply put: the mind is not a blank slate (Pinker 2003). Rather, the mind presents robust constraints on the construction and adoption of beliefs, norms, and institutions. For example, the human species did not evolve the capitalism gene or the morality gene, but it does have innate cognitive structures relating to exchange, fairness, and honesty, which easily allow for the adoption of certain cultural beliefs, practices, and institutions (see Cosmides and Tooby 1992).

How the Mind Generates Culture

Hayek argues that cultural traits are not due to biologically determined instincts or the result of reason and rationality (i.e., design). However, he provides little explanation of why certain cultural traits emerge. This issue is not solely confined to Hayek's model of cultural evolution, but much of the cultural evolution literature seems to take for granted the origination of cultural traits, while focusing heavily on how cultural traits are transmitted (see Richerson and Boyd 2005; Richerson et al. 2016). So, where does culture originate? How can we explain human social behavior without relying strictly on rational design and social learning?

The evolutionary psychology approach to explaining culture is a methodological individualist framework that puts individual agents in charge of the creation, transmission, and stabilization of culture (e.g., see Barkow, Cosmides, and Tooby 1992; Hirschfeld and Gelman 1994; Sperber 1996). These scholars argue that while social learning is involved for the acquisition of cultural information, social learning and imitation of others is not enough to explain the origination and stabilization of cultural features at the population level. The transmission and stabilization of cultural information requires high fidelity, which cultural information does not have (Sperber 1996). This complication can be resolved by bringing biological evolution into the framework for explaining the emergence, transmission, and stabilization of culture.

Culture, as defined by Sperber and Claidière (2006, 21) is a set of "relatively stable representations, practices, and artifacts distributed across generations throughout a social group." It is argued that social learning relies on the low-fidelity of cultural information for explaining the stability of culture as this allows for greater generalization and adjustments to individual situations (Claidière and Sperber 2010). This seems paradoxical: culture is stable, yet generalizable enough to allow for fluidity and variation. If biology or imitation are not enough to explain the emergence and stability of cultural systems, how can cultural traits emerge and stabilize at the population level? Explaining cultural evolution must take into consideration the natural (i.e., biological), psychological,-and cultural properties of our species. These three components can be used to explain why cultural information originates, spreads, and remains stable: certain information is inherently more attractive (i.e., informationally rich or relevant), than other information given the domain-specific inferential systems of an evolved mind.

The contrast between the heritability of biological information and cultural information can further illustrate the differences. Biological heritability is robust: a beneficial allele that has been transmitted will be identical to the parental allele. The replication of cultural information is not always as faithful. Cultural information is transmitted in a variety of ways, relying on: (1) imitation, (2) communication, and (3) memory. All three components can generate misunderstandings resulting in slight modifications on the intended information (Sperber and Claidière 2006). Further, imitation presents one major problem: abstract concepts and meanings cannot be acquired through imitation. Acquiring the meanings of words relies on acquiring through inferential knowledge about the world from others, usually with little explicit instruction. This process is entirely indebted to an inferential learning mechanism in the mind (Sperber 2000). This makes human communication nowhere near as robust as the replication of DNA. There are plenty of instances when instructions are given, and only selected pieces are retained for later elicitation. Furthermore, communication is preservative and constructive. For example, memories are not stored in a database to be recalled when convenient; memories are reconstructed based on cues (Schacter 2002). Without robust heritability, there needs to be an additional factor that allows for cultural information to transmit and stabilize.

Cultural attractors are the factors that tend to attract individuals to converge on certain variants of cultural information. These attractors generally fall into two categories: (1) biological and psychological properties of our species and, (2) relevant environmental properties (Claidière, Scott-Phillips, and Sperber 2014). These factors would bias the process of cultural transmission toward representations or practices that are optimal for biologically evolved adaptations that make use of them, or, alternatively, representations and practices that parasitize such evolved adaptations (Claidière and Sperber 2010; for an example in the domain of religious belief, see Boyer 2001). Simply stated, not all cultural information is created equal. Some information is more interesting and relevant to our minds (e.g., social gossip vs. calculus), which thus enables it to be replicated and transmitted more efficiently and accurately. The human mind will constrain the creation and transmission of cultural information.

EXPLAINING THE EXTENDED ORDER

Hayek argues that today's complex societies are the result of thousands of years of cumulative cultural evolution. Much of *The Fatal Conceit* is spent focusing on specific feats of cultural evolution, namely: morality, cooperation, social contracts, and property rights. While these types of institutions today are indebted to cultural innovation and refinement, it is argued by scholars working within the evolutionary psychology framework that their foundations are rooted in our innate cognitive architecture designed and refined through biological evolution. Cognitive intuitiveness would allow for easier adoption of the cultural tools that govern important facets of social life (Boyer and Petersen 2012).

The Evolutionary Psychology Case for Morality, Fairness, and Contracts

Hayek argued that the human species instinctual response must be suppressed by culture so that the extended order could develop. According to Hayek, non-instinctive rules "enabled mankind to expand into an extended order" (Hayek 1988, 12). Presently, researchers from several fields have developed theoretical models and found support for the biological and evolutionary roots of our moral senses. For an individual, exhibiting pro-social tendencies, honesty, and genuineness should be favored as it is welfare enhancing for a member of a social species. Reciprocally, discriminating when selecting social partners based on such characteristics would also provide benefits (Baumard, Andre, and Sperber 2013; Noe and Hammerstein 1994).

The concept of the biological marketplace is used to better understand the evolution of cooperation and our species' intuitive sense and concern for fairness. Biological marketplaces are analogous to how markets for goods and services operate. Among the producers and consumers in the biological marketplace, there is competition to obtain quality goods and services, while minimizing costs (Noe and Hammerstein 1994). A market-like mechanism for explaining cooperation in social exchange would emerge: partner choice. Partner choice models argue that cooperation emerged through a market process whereby non-combative competition between consumers and between consumers and producers results in the emergence and stabilization of mutually beneficial exchanges within a population, even among unrelated and unknown individuals. Partner choice models rely on the ability for individuals to easily switch partners (i.e., an open market of potential cooperators), if their previous partner defects (Andre and Baumard 2011; Noe and Hammerstein 1995). Proponents of partner choice models would argue that cultural tools are not always necessary for explaining the emergence of large-scale mutually beneficial exchange. These types of relations among individuals are not the result of culture constraining natural instincts, but, instead, are deeply rooted, natural, and adaptively relevant instincts.

Partner choice models for explaining cooperation have led researchers to postulate the selection of honest moral dispositions. In an environment where individuals are in competition with one another for being chosen to participate in mutually beneficial cooperative partnerships, certain dispositions and characteristics will be favored. Furthermore, those who are best able to present such a disposition at the lowest cost (i.e., an honest signal of one's character) will be slightly favored, as well. Treating others impartially, while sharing the costs and benefits of cooperative interactions, would be favored among all parties. In a free market of competition, those who do not behave fairly during cooperative interactions would be overlooked when future opportunities arise, while those who are too generous would be exploited (Baumard, Andre, and Sperber 2013). This results in the selection of individuals who can most accurately assess how much he or she should contribute and benefit, while those who cannot do so will, over time, become less represented in the cooperative marketplace.

This model is not isolated to any particular type of society (e.g., market-based societies); concern for fairness in social exchanges is a human universal. It is argued that our species' proclivity to cooperate, share, and engage in social exchange has evolutionary roots. Being cheated in a social contract or collective actions would have been a major adaptive problem we faced throughout our evolutionary history (Tooby, Cosmides, and Price 2006). Due to this, we should find evidence for specialized inferential system in our cognitive architecture that focuses on storing and recalling information related to social contracts. An experiment was designed to test how well we reason about social contracts using a modified Wason Selection Task. The original Wason Selection Task is an experiment measuring deductive reasoning. In this task, participants are asked to identify when the logical proposition, "If P, then Q" has been violated. Over the many iterations of this experiment, only about 25 percent of participants choose the logical and correct answers ("P" and "not-Q") (Cosmides and Tooby 1989). Even the highly educated perform poorly at this task. When the stimulus of the modified Wason Selection Task is framed around social contract violations (i.e., detecting cheaters—those who receive a benefit, without paying the cost), participants perform much better. The frequency of selecting the correct option was significantly higher when the logical proposition was reframed as a social contract compared to all other variants of the task (Cosmides and Tooby 1992). Experimental research on the innate properties of social contract and cheater detection have been replicated cross-culturally (Sugiyama, Tooby, and Cosmides 2002) and extended in a variety of ways (Gigerenzer and Hug 1992). This suggests there is an intuitiveness about social interactions and social contract enforcement that the mind is already prepared for.

Property rights are crucial for the development of prosperous society. Strong institutions for securing property rights bring less uncertainty and greater levels of investment. In *The Fatal Conceit*, Hayek argues that property rights are the product of cultural evolution. This means property rights are not rooted in biology and do not have their basis in the natural man. Although the institutions that govern private property and protect individuals' property may be the result of cultural evolution, it is argued by evolutionary psychologists that the concepts of ownership and property can be understood as innate properties of how the mind understands objects in the world (Boyer 2015). Such dispositions, abilities, and features the human species displays toward ownership of resources may not necessarily require social learning and the osmosis of culture for their development. Furthermore, it is only with the natural intuitions present in our species' evolved minds that the unique characteristics of the modern world, such as institutions that govern the rights to property individuals possess, can stabilize at the population level and thrive (Boyer and Petersen 2012).

In a world of scarcity, who has rights to resources is important. Recently, it is argued that that the cognitive concept of ownership evolved as a coordination mechanism (Boyer 2015). Beyond the evolutionary logic, there are multiple lines of evidence for understanding ownership as an evolved conceptual domain in the mind. Ownership is found among all known cultures, such that all known cultures contain ways of communicating ownership and distinguishing between possessing an object and owning an object. Furthermore, development psychology has revealed that norms and rules regarding ownership are acquired very early and quite readily by young children (Boyer 2015). There is also experimental research examining our species' intuitive sense of rights and ownership. Cross-culturally, it has been found that young children begin accurately and fairly assessing who deserves resources based on merit at a specific developmental period that coincides with increasing social interactions. This occurs despite the society having little market integration, religious life, and no formal policing or institutions for punishment (Liénard et al. 2013). Additionally, it has been demonstrated that coordination on ownership and rights to property may be an adaptive mechanism to avoid costly alternatives, such as fighting (DeScioli and Wilson 2011). Although this is a relatively new domain of study, it is beginning to show the innate conceptual basis for ownership and rights over resources.

HAYEK'S CHALLENGE AND RESPONSE

On the surface, an approach to studying culture that emphasizes human psychology and biological evolution seems incongruent with Hayek's scholarship on cultural evolution. But Hayek wrote extensively on both subjects, with his view of psychology outlined in *The Sensory Order* (1976). He had some objections to the field of psychology, specifically the field of behaviorism, at the time of his work (Caldwell 2004). During this period, the field of psychology narrowly focused on how individuals react to stimuli. In contrast, modern cognitive psychology focuses on how individual minds process information from the external environment, which then elicits a response. With the changes that took place in the field of psychology during the cognitive revolution, a Hayekian interpretation of modern cognitive psychology would be more in line with the proto-cognitive approach he outlined throughout *The Sensory Order*.

In addition to changes in the field of psychology, there are two components of modern evolutionary psychology that Hayek may be particularly interested in. First, it does not suffer the same pitfalls as the gene-centered approach of sociobiology. Instead of determining human behavior, biology and evolution constrain how information is processed in the mind and, thus, the way culture is generated, transmitted, and adopted. Second, this approach does not rely on the use of the social fact as a causal mechanism. Hayek found the emphasis on the objectivity of the collective, institution, or society for scientifically studying society rather than the individual to be "sheer illusion" (Hayek 2014a, 87). The evolutionary psychology approach to studying culture puts the individual agent back into processes of generating culture and does not assume that culture by itself plays the causal role. Culture only has influence because individuals and their minds process cultural information. This is analogous to Hayek's emphasis on the individual and his appreciation for human action as causal.

Digging deeper into Hayek's appreciation of human psychology, there is a particular information processing aspect of the mind that has become increasingly relevant for studying culture: social learning and imitation. Although it was not a topic of discussion among evolutionary biologists, sociobiologists, or proponents of group-selection models at the time of Hayek's writing, the cognitive mechanisms by which cultural information is transmitted and acquired is a major component of contemporary models of cultural evolution (see Sperber 1996). Even if, contemporarily, Hayek did not entertain evolutionary arguments, it seems that his dual interest in the transmission of rules and the human ability to acquire information would lead him, as it did other researchers, to ask why certain information is more valued and what allows this information to be more efficiently transmitted.

In Hayek's paper, "Rules, Perception, and Intelligibility," he highlights the importance of learning and inference through the observation of others. Hayek stumbles onto a dilemma: when observing others, how do we know what some actions mean or what inference to make without being explicitly told? At some point, we must be able to infer actions based on observed patterns that are relevant and informative without explicitly knowing that is what we should be looking for. Hayek begins by stating, "If everything we can express (state, communicate) is intelligible to others only because their mental structure is governed by the same rules as ours, it would seem that these rules themselves can never be communicated" (Hayek 2014a, 251). Similar cognitive structures allow communication and, thus, coordination among individuals. Further, he goes on,

> [t]his seems to imply that in one sense we always know not only more than we can deliberately state but also more than we can be aware of or deliberately test; and that much that we successfully do depends on presuppositions which are outside the range of all conscious thought of what seems obviously true of verbal statements seems to follow from that fact that such thought must, if we are not to be led into an infinite regress, be assumed to be directed by rules which in turn cannot be conscious—by a supra-conscious mechanism which operates upon the contents of consciousness but which cannot itself be conscious. (Hayek 2014a, 251)

Hayek suggests that there as higher-level mechanisms of the mind that cannot be explicitly stated and, thus, not explicitly taught. While he did not hint at the supra-conscious mechanism being an innate cognitive mechanism designed by natural selection, contemporary literature provides support for this. Presently, researchers are debating the conceptual categories of the mind that are potentially innate (see, e.g., Margolis and Laurence 2015). Furthermore, the debate is no longer about whether there are innate concepts in the mind, but precisely what conceptual domains constitute the innate mind (Laurence and Margolis 2015). These innate conceptual categories would be Hayek's supra-conscious mechanism that individuals use for information processing without needing to be aware of their existence.

Hayek argued that precise manipulation of the social world through design and control is not possible without creating unintended consequences. Those working under the evolutionary psychology framework would make a very similar claim: there are constraints and limits on what information is adopted by individuals given our psychology. For example, although it may sound ideal to some, creating a world in which ownership is communal and everyone is treated with utter equality regardless of merit is not plausible. Hayek arrived at a similar conclusion in an example he gave in *The Fatal Conceit*. He suggests that certain types of social orders do not work as well as others because of the individualized heavy costs associated. He states that

> those living within the extended order gain from not treating one another as neighbours, and by applying, in their interactions, rules of the extended order—such as those of several property and contract—instead of the rules of solidarity and altruism. An order in which everyone treated his neighbor as himself would be one where comparatively few could be fruitful and multiple. (Hayek 1988, 13)

Interestingly, this example hints at an individual-level selection mechanism, rather than a group-level selection mechanism: individuals in certain types of institutional settings can either benefit or not benefit. If you are in the correct institutional environment, you will benefit greatly and, thus, "be fruitful and multiple." Further, Hayek goes on to state that, "If we were, say, to respond to all charitable appeals that bombard us through the media, this would exact a heavy cost in distracting us from what we are most competent to do, and likely only make us the tools of particular interest groups or of peculiar views of the relative importance of particular needs" (Hayek 1988, 13). Hayek is suggesting that individuals are selective with what information is most relevant to them. Although we can encourage charity and altruism, these appeals will not be relevant enough to result in a drastic change to the extended order. Not all cultural information can be successful, no matter how forcefully or repeatedly it is taught. Information that is directly against the welfare of the individual, such as extreme charitable giving, would be transmitted frequently, but not adopted by individuals as frequently.

Hayek discusses group-level benefits, but at times, it seems that he falls back into describing what is fundamentally, in an evolutionary sense, an individual-level benefit. This is seen in the previous example, as well as others. In volume 3 of *Law, Legislation, and Liberty*, Hayek states that that traditions are passed down because these traditions have "enhanced the prosperity of certain groups and led to their expansion, perhaps less by more rapid procreation than by the attraction of outsiders" (Hayek 1979, 159). For groups to compete and be selected, there would have to be low levels of inter-group migration, otherwise there is no clearly defined group. At its core, the suggestion that good ideas, institutions, and rules of conduct will attract outsiders to associate themselves is an individual-level argument. This scenario implies that individuals assess their current situation, calculate its relative cost to other possible ways of organizing their life with the information available, and move to wherever their welfare will be enhanced most greatly. It seems as if groups are prospering, especially when societies expand, and other groups adopt the norms of the prosperous group. If you are to examine what individuals within the population are doing, it is clear: they use the information available to determine the best course of action for enhancing their welfare. Individuals are the drivers for group prosperity.

CONCLUSION

In his model of cultural evolution, Hayek dismisses biology and biological evolution for explaining the emergence of the modern social world. In the wake of his writings on cultural evolution, research has advanced Hayek's position on the role of social learning in cultural evolution (i.e., cultural group selection models; see Richerson et al. 2016). The parallels between this school of thought and Hayek's model of cultural evolution have been noted extensively (Rubin and Gick 2005; Stone 2010). Since Hayek's writing, an alternative position fusing evolutionary biology and cognitive science with the social sciences (i.e., evolutionary psychology; see Barkow, Cosmides, and Tooby 1992), has sought to bring a natural understanding to investigating human behavior and culture. The framework offered by evolutionary psychology for studying culture aligns with multiple aspects of Hayek's scholarship. Thus, although speculative, I believe that had Hayek lived longer, he would have at least been willing to engage with researchers who have put together an evolutionary psychology framework for studying culture.

REFERENCES

André, Jean-Baptiste, and Nicholas Baumard. 2011. "The Evolution of Fairness in a Biological Market." *Evolution* 65 (5): 1447–56.

Barkow, Jerome H., Leda Cosmides, and John Tooby. 1992. *The Adapted Mind: Evolutionary Psychology and the Generation of Culture*. Oxford: Oxford University Press.

Baumard, Nicolas, Jean-Baptiste André, and Dan Sperber. 2013. "A Mutualistic Approach to Morality: The Evolution of Fairness by Partner Choice." *Behavioral and Brain Sciences* 36 (1): 59–78.

Baumard, Nicolas, and Coralie Chevallier. 2012. "What Goes Around Comes Around: The Evolutionary Roots of the Belief in Immanent Justice." *Journal of Cognition and Culture* 12 (1–2): 67–80.

Boyer, Pascal. 2001. *Religion Explained: The Evolutionary Origins of Religious Thought*. New York: Basic Books.

_______. 2015. "How Natural Selection Shapes Conceptual Structure: Human Intuitions and Concepts of Ownership." In *The Conceptual Mind: New Directions in the Study of Concepts*, edited by Eric Margolis and Stephen Laurence, 185–200. Cambridge, MA: MIT Press.

Boyer, Pascal, and Michael Bang Petersen. 2012. "The Naturalness of (Many) Social Institutions: Evolved Cognition as Their Foundation." *Journal of Institutional Economics* 8 (1): 1–25.

Caldwell, Bruce. 2004. "Some Reflections on FA Hayek's *The Sensory Order*." *Journal of Bioeconomics* 6 (3): 239–54.

_______. 2010. "Imitation Explains the Propagation, Not the Stability of Animal Culture." *Proceedings of the Royal Society of London B: Biological Sciences* 277 (1681): 651–59.

Claidière, Nicolas, Thomas C. Scott-Phillips, and Dan Sperber. 2014. "How Darwinian Is Cultural Evolution?" *Philosophical Transactions of the Royal Society B* 369 (1642): 20130368.

Cosmides, Leda, and John Tooby. 1989. "Evolutionary Psychology and the Generation of Culture, Part II: Case Study: A Computational Theory of Social Exchange." *Ethology and Sociobiology* 10 (1–3): 51–97.

_______. 1992. "Cognitive Adaptations for Social Exchange." In *The Adapted Mind: Evolutionary Psychology and the Generation of Culture*, edited by Jerome Barkow, Leda Cosmides, and John Tooby, 163–228. Oxford: Oxford University Press.

_______. 2013. "Evolutionary Psychology: New Perspectives on Cognition and Motivation." *Annual Review of Psychology* 64: 201–29.

Dehaene, Stanislas. 2009. *Reading in the Brain: The New Science of How We Read.* London: Penguin Books.

DeScioli, Peter, and Bart J. Wilson. 2011. "The Territorial Foundations of Human Property." *Evolution and Human Behavior* 32 (5): 297–304.

Gangestad, Steven W., Martie G. Haselton, and David M. Buss. 2006. "Evolutionary Foundations of Cultural Variation: Evoked Culture and Mate Preferences." *Psychological Inquiry* 17 (2): 75–95.

Gigerenzer, Gerd, and Klaus Hug. 1992. "Domain-Specific Reasoning: Social Contracts, Cheating, and Perspective Change." *Cognition* 43 (2): 127–71.

Hayek, F. A. 1945. "The Use of Knowledge in Society." *American Economic Review* 35 (4): 519–30.

_______. 1976. *The Sensory Order*. Chicago: University of Chicago Press.

_______. 1979. *Law, Legislation, and Liberty*. Vol. 3: *A New Statement of the Liberal Principles of Justice and Political Economy*. Chicago: University of Chicago Press.

_______. 1988. *The Fatal Conceit: The Errors of Socialism*. Chicago: University of Chicago Press.

_______. 2013. *The Constitution of Liberty: The Definitive Edition*. Chicago: University of Chicago Press.

_______. 2014a. "Rules, Perception, and Intelligibility." In *The Collected Works of F. A. Hayek*. Vol. 15: *The Market and Other Orders*, edited by Bruce Caldwell, 232–53. Chicago: University of Chicago Press.

_______. 2014b. "The Theory of Complex Phenomena." In *The Collected Works of F. A. Hayek*. Vol. 15: *The Market and Other Orders*, edited by Bruce Caldwell, 257–77. Chicago: University of Chicago Press.

_______. 2014c. "The Theory of Complex Phenomena." In *The Collected Works of F. A. Hayek*. Vol. 15: *The Market and Other Orders*, edited by Bruce Caldwell, 257–77. Chicago: University of Chicago Press.

_______. 2014d. "Notes on The Evolution of Systems of Rules of Conduct." In *The Collected Works of F. A. Hayek*. Vol. 15: *The Market and Other Orders*, edited by Bruce Caldwell, 278–92. Chicago: University of Chicago Press.

Hirschfeld, Lawrence A., and Susan A. Gelman. 1994. *Mapping the Mind: Domain Specificity in Cognition and Culture*. Cambridge: Cambridge University Press.

Laurence, Stephen, and Eric Margolis. 2015. "Concept Nativism and Neural Plasticity." In *The Conceptual Mind: New Directions in the Study of Concepts*, edited by Eric Margolis and Stephen Laurence, 117–47. Cambridge, MA: MIT Press.

Liénard, P., C. Chevallier, O. Mascaro, P. Kiura, and N. Baumard. 2013. "Early Understanding of Merit in Turkana Children." *Journal of Cognition and Culture* 13 (1–2): 57–66.

Margolis, Eric, and Stephen Laurence. 2015. *The Conceptual Mind: New Directions in the Study of Concepts*. Cambridge, MA: MIT Press.

Morin, Olivier. 2013. "How Portraits Turned Their Eyes Upon Us: Visual Preferences and Demographic Change in Cultural Evolution." *Evolution and Human Behavior* 34 (3): 222–29.

Noë, Ronald, and Peter Hammerstein. 1994. "Biological Markets: Supply and Demand Determine the Effect of Partner Choice in Cooperation, Mutualism and Mating." *Behavioral Ecology and Sociobiology* 35 (1): 1–11.

_______. 1995. "Biological Markets." *Trends in Ecology & Evolution* 10 (8): 336–39.

Pinker, Steven. 2003. *The Blank Slate: The Modern Denial of Human Nature*. London: Penguin.

Richerson, Peter J., and Robert Boyd. 2005. *Not by Genes Alone*. Chicago: University of Chicago Press.

Richerson, P., R. Baldini, A. V. Bell, K. Demps, K. Frost, V. Hillis, S. Mathew, E. Newton, N. Naar, L. Newson, C. Ross, P. Smaldino, T. Waring, and M. Zefferman. 2016. "Cultural Group Selection Follows Darwin's Classic Syllogism for the Operation of Selection." *Behavioral and Brain Sciences* 39.

Rubin, Paul H., and Evelyn Gick. 2005. "Hayek and Modern Evolutionary Theory." In *Evolutionary Psychology and Economic Theory, Advances in Austrian Economics*, edited by Roger Koppl, 79–100. Bingley, UK: Emerald Group.

Schacter, Daniel L. 2002. *The Seven Sins of Memory: How the Mind Forgets and Remembers*. Boston: Houghton Mifflin Harcourt.

Sperber, Dan. 1996. *Explaining Culture: A Naturalistic Approach*. Oxford: Blackwell.

Sperber, Dan. 2000. "An Objection to the Memetic Approach to Culture." In *Darwinizing Culture: The Status of Memetics as a Science,* edited by Robert Aunger, 163–72. Oxford: Oxford University Press.

Sperber, Dan, and Nicolas Claidière. 2006. "Why Modeling Cultural Evolution Is Still Such a Challenge." *Biological Theory* 1 (1): 20–22.

Stone, Brad Lowell. 2010. "The Current Evidence for Hayek's Cultural Group Selection Theory." *Libertarian Papers* 2 (45): 1–21.

Sugiyama, Lawrence S., John Tooby, and Leda Cosmides. 2002. "Cross-Cultural Evidence of Cognitive Adaptations for Social Exchange Among the Shiwiar of Ecuadorian Amazonia." *Proceedings of the National Academy of Sciences* 99 (17): 11537–42.

Tooby, John, and Leda Cosmides. 1992. "The Psychological Foundations of Culture." In *The Adapted Mind: Evolutionary Psychology and the Generation of Culture*, edited by Jerome Barkow, Leda Cosmides, and John Tooby, 19–136. Oxford: Oxford University Press.

Tooby, John, Leda Cosmides, and Michael E. Price. 2006. "Cognitive Adaptations for N-person Exchange: The Evolutionary Roots of Organizational Behavior." *Managerial and Decision Economics* 27 (2–3): 103–29.

Chapter 10

A Hayekian Perspective on the Domestication of Maize

Crystal A. Dozier

> The misleading effect of the usual approach stands out clearly if we examine the significance of the assertion that man has created his civilization and that he therefore can also change its institutions as he pleases. This assertion would be justified only if man had deliberately created civilization in full understanding of what he was doing or if he at least clearly knew how it was being maintained. In a sense it is true, of course, that man has made his civilization. It is the product of his actions or, rather, of the action of a few hundred generations. This does not mean, however, that civilization is the product of human design, or even that man knows what its functioning or continued existence depends upon. (Hayek [1960] 2011a, 74).

Traditional narratives of human history bookmark the advent of agriculture as the single most important innovation of humankind; that the invention of agriculture allowed for the creation of surplus that fueled all subsequent hallmarks of civilization. This narrative posits that after the invention of this marvelous way of getting food, neighboring groups adopted farming as the preferable mode of subsistence. Those who chose not to take up farming were discounted as uncivilized savages or barbarians, left behind from economic development (Barnard 1999; Bettinger, Garvey, and Tushingham 2015; Lee and Daly 1999).

The above narrative places domestication and farming within a unilinear evolution of human design and action. This is an attractive story for the modern world; it is a tale of human triumph over nature. However, as so many institutions of the modern world, the emergence of this complex phenomenon cannot be understood as a planned and executed human design. While domestication and agriculture are innovations that undeniably allowed for the proliferation of the human species across the globe, the archaeological evidence demonstrates those who first recognized the potential of wild plants likely unwittingly paved the way for these important revolutions.

This is certainly true concerning the domestication of maize (*Zea mays l.*) and the eventual role that it would play in economic, social, religious, and culinary life throughout the Americas and eventually the world. In 2014, maize production across the world reached 717 metric tons (Ranum, Peña-Rosas, and Garcia-Casal 2014). The top three domesticated cereals—rice, maize, and wheat—provide approximately 60 percent of the world's calorie intake; maize alone can account for over 50 percent of dietary calories in areas of Mexico and Latin America (Loftas and Ross 1995). While it is undoubtedly an important food crop, especially in the Americas, maize production has shifted toward other technologies, mostly in the fuel industry. In the United States, approximately 40 percent of maize production is directed toward ethanol production as a bio-fuel (Ranum, Peña-Rosas, and Garcia-Casal 2014). The many uses of maize today would be impossible without its first domestication thousands of years ago in central Mexico.

Guided by Hayekian thought, I first outline theoretical and historical understandings of the domestication process, which I then apply to the archaeological evidence for the domestication of maize. The evidence points to maize's wild ancestor's first exploitation for its sugary stalk, and only later after random mutation did an innovator capitalize on the availability of the kernel for human consumption. I argue that this recognition, like other domestication events of grains like wheat and rice, was likely motivated by the use of maize within competitive feasting socio-economic systems. As Hayek ([1967] 2014b) argued for the emergent, complexity of the market of human action but not of human design, I argue that the advent of domestication and then agriculture of maize is also better understood as unintended consequence, a by-product of a socio-economic system that allowed for individual advancement through innovation and trade.

DOMESTICATION THEORIES

> Although in the study of a particular instance of the evolution of an "institution" like money or language the theoretical problem will frequently be so overlaid by the consideration of the particular circumstances involved (the properly historical task), this does not alter the fact that any explanation of a historical process involves assumptions about the kind of effects—assumptions which, where we have to deal with results which were not directly willed by somebody, can only be stated in the form of a generic scheme, in other words a theory. (Hayek [1952] 2010a, 35)

Domestication is the process by which an organism transforms from a wild form to a form that is exploited by or associated with humans. Almost all foods that people eat today have been drastically transformed from their wild counterparts—wheat, apples, cabbages, cows, peas, plums, rice, goats, strawberries, and so on. Agriculture is the systematic, yearly purposeful planting and harvesting of domesticated plants to meet human demands. The domestication of grains (wheat, barley, rice, sorghum, and maize) and subsequent agricultural patterns set the conditions for the development of more complex human societies. Since the early twentieth century, when archaeological evidence began to coalesce around the idea that agriculture was a technological development that occurred around 10,000 years ago, archaeologists, historians, and other social scientists have endeavored to develop theories to explain why and how this occurred. As Hayek highlights above, these theories involve assumptions which should and can be tested against evidence.

V. Gordon Childe is credited with the first systematic treatment of what is now commonly referred to as the Neolithic Revolution. As one of the very first synthesizers of archaeological patterns in Europe, Childe argued the transition from foraging to agricultural society as one of the most important economic revolutions in human history, one forged out of the evolution of human complexity in stages from barbarism to civilization. His tome, *Man Makes Himself* (1951), relates a Marxist understanding of the transition to agriculture as an inescapable progression of civilization whereas "civilized" peoples created agriculture as a means for progress. In many ways, Childe's perspective has held fast in most popular representations of the Neolithic Revolution, as it reflects the idea that agriculture was a conscious decision of "civilized" people. While Childe was the first to articulate patterns in the spread of agriculture, his treatment did not provide a satisfactory mechanism to explain the "why then" and "how" questions.

K. V. Flannery (1973) articulated the most widely cited and widely understood argument for domestication, which is grounded in environmental change and population density. Flannery argues that climate change in conjunction with population density growth encouraged increased exploitation of cereals, especially in the Middle East context. A more sophisticated form of this argument was posited by Binford (1968), who argued that human population versus animal/plant density would determine subsistence patterns. As paleoclimatic reconstructions have improved, it has become clear that the Pleistocene, commonly referred to as the Ice Age from approximately 200,000–13,000 years ago, is characterized by fluctuations in temperature that would have made cultivation an incredibly risky or impossible venture. However, even the earliest agricultural production began thousands of years after the end of the Pleistocene—if climate was the only restricting factor, why did people not start the domestication or agricultural transition process earlier? Paleoclimatic reconstructions for the timing of Mediterranean vegetation communities have also argued that an acidification of the region made stands of wild cereals more prevalent on the landscape (Combourieu Nebout et al. 2009; Rossignol-Strick 1999; Suc 1984), but again this does not explain how or why domestication took place. While geography and climate are certainly limiting factors on the possibility of domestication and agricultural practice, there is not a close enough correlation between climatic changes and domestication events to warrant it as the explanatory mechanism.

With a similar emphasis on productivity as the driving force for domestication, Douglass North (1981) articulated the now predominate historical economic perspective on the Neolithic Revolution. He also acknowledges the shortfalls in the narratives of Childe, Flannery, and Binford but maintains that productivity is the major factor contributing to agricultural transition. North argues that the foraging productivity will decrease with time (similar to Binford and Flannery) and that subsequent increases in labor force will require a transition to agriculture to maintain the population. However, the important innovation, North maintains, is not of the agricultural practice itself, but in the creation of private property that agriculture requires. While agriculture requires private property, the creation and maintenance of private property is seen with a variety of subsistence strategies (Arnold et al. 2015). I have argued elsewhere (Dozier 2017) that the conception of property rights can be traced much further into the past, with pre- or non-agricultural feasting societies. Also, while North has appropriate faith in humans to be innately familiar with their environment, he assumes that the transition from wild to domesticated plants is simple selective breeding, that domestication can be assumed, and that private property, which allows for individualized productivity, is the primary key to understanding the right conditions for domestication.

Flannery and colleagues (Beadle 1972; Flannery 1973; Flannery and Ford 1972) did a series of experiments in wild maize (teosinte) kernel productivity to try and explain how maize might have been domesticated. Their experiments indicate that productivity of teosinte cultivation could range from 80 to 152 kilograms per hectare of cultivation. However, mesquite bean shrubs (*Prosopis spp.*), another common indigenous food that does *not* require cultivation and is common in most parts of central America, produces 160–180 kilograms per hectare in dense wild stands. Zapotec opportunistic farmers of central Mexico, who only farm when the conditions are good and otherwise forage for their subsistence, do not bother even with modern maize cultivation for less than 200–250 kilograms per hectare (Kirkby 1973); this makes the theory that teosinte was domesticated as a form of intensifying productivity incredibly questionable. As Flannery notes, "disregarding for the moment any nutritional differences between *Prosopis* [mesquite] and *Zea* [teosinte], it would hardly seem worth clearing the native mesquite from the floodplains unless a yield higher than 180 kg per hectare could be expected" (1973, 298). As will be explained in detail below, even if the production of teosinte could be manipulated to create a high crop, humans were unlikely to be exploiting the kernels, as they are covered in a tough, inedible shell! Caloric productivity explanations for exploitation of teosinte, then, fail to explain human involvement in the domestication process of maize.

A HAYEKIAN THEORY OF DOMESTICATION

If we are to understand domestication as innovation, Hayek provides a theoretical framework to investigate the elements necessary to and promoting innovation. Hayek follows within the methodological individualistic paradigm of Mises and colleagues to describe information as held within the individual, rather than as information held within a supposed collective mind or culture ([1952] 2010a). The kinds of practices and knowledge development that individuals follow, however, will be determined by the rules of the society in which an individual takes part. Some arrangements or practices will encourage experimentation and innovation, while others do not. Experimentation and innovation can be incredibly risky ventures, with failure common. Hayek argues that such creative endeavors are best supported within societies that are free, a term that in "The Creative Powers of a Free Civilization" ([1960] 2011b) he means primarily as freedom of thought and economic action.

Freedom of economic action, at least, is fairly regulated at both ends of the spectrum of socio-political complexity. Within complex state-level societies, economic processes are often regulated to certain spaces, goods, and actors; however, egalitarian small-scale societies also tend to have strict social rules about how, when, and by whom trade, commerce, and invention can commence. Indeed, marketplace and market interactions work within the structure of cultural institutions, and those frameworks are important to understand in order to compare and understand different economic systems (Storr 2010, 2013). It is within those cultural institutions, Hayek and his protégés recognize, that economic innovations can either be promoted or suppressed, depending on the institutional frameworks that (dis)incentive entrepreneurial action. With such an important and life-way altering innovation as domestication, especially due to the rather conservative nature of cultural change (Boyd and Richerson 1996), then, it is important to look at the institutional and incentive frameworks in which those innovations occurred.

In a Hayekian perspective, for an innovation such as domestication to occur, the societal rules must have allowed for some kind of interaction with the wild plant by an alert entrepreneur to recognize potential alternative uses. Such innovations are enhanced or motivated by feedback mechanisms that allow for the advancements of individuals (and therefore societies) that adopt useful inventions. While the archaeological record cannot provide a complete understanding of the societal rules that occurred during the domestication of cereals, it is associated with the emergence of feasting, throwing large consumption events that promote the advancement of individuals within a society (Dozier 2017). Feasting societies provide prestige, as well as material advancement, to individuals who are able to coordinate the accumulation and trade/redistribution of various goods. Within this framework, individuals are incentivized to innovate new and desired material goods, especially within cooking regimes, which is the hallmark activity within feasts. This shift toward individual advancement with technological innovation is aligned with what a Hayekian perspective would predict.

In the more popular works of Hayek's oeuvre, he argues that the economic structures and institutions of a particular set of rules, socialism, are fatally flawed, as the governmental distribution of the economy lacks the ability to properly assess the material needs of a market, like the price system does (Hayek [1945] 2014d, [1944] 2007a, [1944] 2007b). This narrative has borne out in the collapse of most socialist economic systems (see Boettke 1995). At the core, this argument emphasizes the crucial role that feedback mechanisms play in economic systems and that innovation is reliant on systems that allow for individual advancement in a free society; a Hayekian perspective emphasizes that entrepreneurship is reliant on a socio-economic system that both promotes individual advancement and has a system of feedback for the adoption of that innovation (Hayek [1945] 2014d, [1968] 2014b, [1967] 2014a, [1960] 2011b). While Hayek was focused on state-level society, mechanisms of individual advancement also vary within non- or pre-state societies; therefore, this focus on the cultural institutions that motivate individual action can provide a useful perspective for understanding technological innovation seen throughout human history.

As will be elaborated below, the archaeological evidence for the domestication of maize indicates a long use of the plant as a special product, with innovation into large-scale use of the plant as a staple only following substantial population increase in areas that already had territoriality or non-formal forms of property rights. As such, agricultural practice may be seen as an unintended consequence of entrepreneurial innovation within maize. I argue, congruent with a Hayekian perspective, that the recognition of domestication was an act of entrepreneurial innovation, only made possible within a society that promoted individual advancement, that allowed for this plant to transform into a staple crop around the world.

MAIZE

> If we think, for example, of the problem of the archaeologist trying to determine whether what looks like a stone implement is in truth an "artefact," made by man, or merely a chance product of nature. There is no way of deciding this but by trying to understand the working of the mind of pre-historic man, of attempting to understand how he would have made such an implement. If we are not more aware that this is what we actually do in such cases and that we necessarily rely on our own knowledge of the working of a human mind, this is so mainly because of the impossibility of conceiving of an observer who does not possess a human mind and interprets what he sees in terms of the working of his own mind. (Hayek [1945] 2010b, 91)

Archaeological inquiry, as Hayek highlights above, is reliant on the ability to extend analogies and inferences concerning human action into the past (Binford 1967; Fogelin 2007). The biology and archaeology concerning the domestication of maize, however, is robust and in agreement: humans could not and would not have selectively bred domesticated maize from its wild ancestor, teosinte, for exploitation of the kernel (grain).

Genetic Evidence

While it was clear that maize was a descendant of a tropical grass, the exact wild progenitor was widely debated in the latter half of the twentieth century. A suite of ancient DNA and modern maize DNA sequencing efforts have confirmed that teosinte is the wild ancestor to maize and have provided further insights into the domestication sequence (Doebley and Stec 1991, 1993; Goloubinoff, Paabo, and Wilson 1993; Hufford et al. 2012; Iltis 2000; Jaenicke-Despres and Smith 2010; Matsuoka et al. 2002; Staller and Thompson 2002; Wang et al. 2005; Wang et al. 1999; Whitt et al. 2002; Zeder et al. 2006). Teosinte looks remarkably different than maize (see Figure 10.1). There are five areas within the genome of teosinte that have been significantly modified in the creation of maize. These areas control for the two major functional differences of maize from teosinte for human use: the casings that surround the kernel (teosinte has a hard casing around the kernel while maize does not) and the branch patterns of the plant (teosinte has many branches while maize has a single stalk). The variation in cob size, kernel number, kernel starch production, color, ecological adaptations, and other such distinctions that are important in the human use of the plant are genetically quite limited and directly related to selective breeding practices following the two major functional differences (Hufford et al. 2012; Wang et al. 1999).

Of primary importance is the removal of the kernel casings of teosinte in the domestication process of corn. Several genetic studies have shown that this important change is due to a single-point mutation (Matsuoka et al. 2002; Wang et al. 2005; Wang et al. 1999). This mutation is not a type of alteration that is possible due to selective breeding; rather, the mutation must have occurred naturally/randomly and have been propagated/promoted by humans. The removal of the hard casing makes the plant more vulnerable to attack by predators: it is a disadvantage to the plant because the kernels are much more susceptible to being destroyed when being eaten or transported. However, it is the removal of the casing that is crucial to human use of the cob—as explained in more detail further on, humans cannot and did not exploit teosinte for the cob as the casing makes the kernels indigestible.

With this genetic evidence in mind, how and why, then, were humans interacting with teosinte, a plant that they could not eat the kernels of, in such a way to recognize the potential for domestication and horticultural use when the mutation did arise? This evidence of the important transformation indicates that while humans are not directly responsible for the mutation that occurred, an individual must have promoted the spread of this mutation through harvest and either increased usage or even horticulture. The earliest evidence for maize in Mexico around 8,000 years ago is not well correlated with any climatic fluctuations (Piperno et al. 2009). The genetic evidence does not match the self-determined, climatic, and productivity theories of Childe, Flannery, and North; rather, the archaeological evidence points to a sweeter motivational relationship between humans, teosinte, and eventually maize.

Debunking Productivity Theory: The Sweet Stalk Hypothesis

Teosinte kernels are not suitable for human exploitation, and there is little evidence that they ever have been. Smalley and Blake (2003) have most clearly outlined the so-called sweet stalk hypothesis, which was first broadly suggested by Iltis (2000); their investigation revealed that very few teosinte kernels have been recovered at central Mexican archaeological sites. However, teosinte was evidently used by humans for their sugar-rich sap—Smalley and Blake compile an impressive inventory of teosinte quids (human-chewed stalks) excavated from dry cave environments, where plant remains are well preserved. In these contexts, where teosinte kernels would also be well preserved, there was a deficit of the kernels or cobs—it seems that people were not exploiting teosinte for the kernel.

Instead, people in the distant past were likely exploiting teosinte for the stalk, which has a substantial concentration of sugar, a feature that was preserved and strengthened in maize as the branches consolidated into a single stalk. Sources of pure sucrose (sugar) are relatively rare in the pre-industrial world and ethnographic and historic sources abound with the dire lengths that people will go to acquire highly prized, and metabolically rewarding, sources of sucrose. Sugar has been found to have addictive properties to mice and men (Avena, Rada, and Hoebel 2008; Fortuna 2010; Hoebel et al. 2009).

Beyond chewing on the branches of teosinte, Smalley and Blake (2003) suggest that teosinte stalks may have been ground to extract the maximum sugary sap. A variety of ethnographic sources indicate that maize stalks were and continue to be processed for their sap to be fermented into a simple wine (Beals 1932; Bruman 2000; Feest 1983; Smalley and Blake 2003). The fermentation process transforms the simple sugars from the sap into ethanol alcohol, which is especially well digested in humans for maximum calorie absorption, as well as the familiar and pleasant psychological effects. Teosinte contains a similar concentration of sucrose in the stalk at a concentration suitable for fermentation (albeit in smaller branches). The indigenous peoples of Mexico had full access to the technological suite necessary for teosinte sap wine production well before 5,000 years ago. No direct archaeological evidence of teosinte sap wine residue has been found, but there are also no current methods that could evidence the practice; such an ephemeral product would leave little or no trace in the archaeological record.

The sweet stalk hypothesis is consistent with the archaeological evidence, and moreover provides a context to understand why humans would interact with a plant when they could not eat the kernels, at least not yet. Moreover, only occasional exploitation is inconsistent with the process of domestication—there are many plants that are exploited by humans but not used intensively or dramatically changed by the human-plant interaction. Rather, the intensive process of altering the genetic code within a substantial enough proportion of a species to incite change indicate a systematic and intensive exploitation. The desire for sugary (and likely alcoholic products) is consistent with the demands of domestication; an alcoholic motivation for the domestication of other cereals (such as wheat and rice) has also been posited and well supported (Braidwood et al. 1953; Hayden 1995, 2009; Hayden, Canuel, and Shanse 2013; Joffe 1998; Wadley and Hayden 2015).

The recognition of the kernel as an additional product for innovation was a crucial action that must have motivated the subsequent selective breeding. Access to the complex carbohydrates of the kernel allows for a variety of cooking processes and further extraction of calories from the plant. The social and economic situations from which maize was bred and expanded point to the important socio-economic conditions that promote such innovation.

COMPETITIVE SYSTEMS

> The competition on which the process of selection rests . . . involves competition between organized and unorganized groups no less than competition between individuals. (Hayek [1960] 2011b, 88)

In market economies, it is well understood that competition fuels innovation. However, the market economy is a relatively recent human institution, and yet much innovation and invention have taken humans from chipped stone technologies and wild animals to the sophisticated irrigation and agricultural schemes of the Neolithic Revolution. As I have argued in detail elsewhere (Dozier 2017), the social mechanisms necessary for small-band, mobile hunter-gatherers promote social cohesion and equality *within* the group, which often is communicated in the downplaying of individual status; for example, among the modern (recently foraging) San, boasting about a large kill is considered taboo (Lee 1969). Within the archaeological record, this phenomenon is characterized by little difference in nutrition and burial status and little long-distance trade. It is not until the period immediately preceding Neolithic-like revolutions that patterns in intergroup interaction and trade are found.

Feasts, large inter-group meetings of trade and festivities, are the first indication in the archaeological record of changing hierarchies and social mobility. While feasting behavior can be seen in a variety of social situations, of interest here is the tradition of competitive feasting. Competitive feasting is a tradition of holding elaborate events between different socio-ethnic groups (Hayden [1968] 2014b); this tradition allows for peaceful trade, collaboration, and marriage between groups that are in contact on the landscape.

As counter-intuitive as it may seem, the hosts of feasts gain both social and material benefits from the competitive feasting system, including access to higher quality goods (Coupland 2006; Martindale 2006; Samuels 2006; Sahlins 1963) and reproductive advantages (Hayden 2014b, 17). The competitive nature of feasting, however, is of primary consideration for the discussion here. As individuals vie for the social prestige (and material well-being) of hosting the most elaborate feasts, there is an incentive for increasing quantity and quality of goods.

The intensified extraction of foodstuff from the landscape and the increased incentive for long-distance exotic trade from competitive feasting regimes is seen across the globe (Dozier 2017; Hayden 2014b). Indeed, it is the process of feasting that aligns personal and social advancements: a host must provide for his or her guests and the host benefits from such service to the guests. The incentive for exotic and high-cost foodstuffs has been well connected to domestication events, as some of the earliest evidence for the exploitation of pre-domesticates is found within feasting archaeological remains (Fuller, Allaby, and Stevens 2010; Hayden 1995, 2009, 2014a).

Unfortunately, the archaeological period surrounding the domestication of maize is poorly understood in Mexico. However, studies of the pre-Classic periods attest to the importance of feasting in the emergence of complex (ranked) societies within the region (Rosenswig 2000, 2007). In the conclusion for *Histories of Maize in Mesoamerica*, Benz and Staller (2009, 271) recognize that with the current information about maize cultivation and domestication that "a strong possibility exists that in its early stages, maize was primarily a ritual plant used to make fermented beer or *chicha* that was consumed in the context of gift giving, ritual *feasts* and religious ceremonies" (emphasis added). Feasting societies provide the individual incentive to innovate on prestige goods, which is aligned with a Hayekian focus on the cultural incentive and feedback structures to economic development. In the case of teosinte, a product that was likely being used for its highly valued sugar, a feasting society would have incentives to further exploit this elite good.

Increased investment into teosinte under these conditions likely allowed for an alert entrepreneur to take advantage of a mutant strain of teosinte that could be used for the kernel in addition to the stalk. With such individual action promoted under the rules of a feasting society, further innovation and experimentation could take place. While individuals may have only sought to increase the grandeur of their feasts, the unintended consequences allowed for a domesticated strain that could be used within an agricultural regime. This narrative of maize domestication fits well within Hayek's theoretical understanding of the importance of individual advancement and freedom to technological and societal innovation. Exploration of the spread and diversification of maize agriculture following domestication is beyond the scope of this current endeavor, but the practice spread across elite trade networks to dominate food production in both North and South America.

> The successful combination of knowledge and aptitude is not selected by common deliberation, by people seeking a solution to their problems through a joint effort; it is the product of individuals imitating those who have been more successful and from their being guided by signs and symbols . . . in short their using the results of the experiences of others. (Hayek [1960] 2011a, 80)

CONCLUSIONS

> Humiliating to human pride as it may be, we must recognize that the advance and even the preservation of civilization are dependent upon a maximum of opportunity for accidents to happen. (Hayek [1960] 2011b, 81)

In the modern era, history records the many innovations and inventions that manifested as accident. In prehistory, the names and dates and exact locations of such accidental inventions are lost, yet the importance of these innovations are not. Maize is a particularly powerful example of this trend.

While the mutation that allowed for the hard casing around the kernel of teosinte could not be controlled by human action, it was the interaction between human and plant that ensured that the plant survived and could be transformed into a useful product. In this period, the plant was likely exploited as a luxury good, which it continued to be reserved as until full agricultural transition. It was the opportunity for innovation in a competitive society where some individuals were alerted to the potential of this elite good for further exploitation. Among the mobile hunting and gathering groups that would have first cultivated this plant, it seems incredibly unlikely that settled agriculture was the desired outcome.

In short, the domestication of maize and its development as an agricultural staple was the result of human action, but not necessarily human design.

Like many other technological advancements, this innovation was reserved primarily for elite use and consumption (Hayden 1998). The innovation of larger and increased number of kernels allowed for the production of new foods, especially in the form of corn meal or gruel that can be eaten by the most vulnerable populations, those without teeth: infants and the elderly. The proliferation of cereal innovations have been linked to a decrease in birth spacing as women do not need to breastfeed for as long and thereby can have more children within a lifetime (Armelagos, Goodman, and Jacobs 1991). However, increased reliance on cereal crops is also correlated with general health decline in a population, and it is in this period that the first indices of inequality are distinctly marked, as diets between men and women and elite versus non-elite differ. Hierarchies are well-established trademarks of agricultural societies, and the Neolithic marks the transition to increasingly complex and hierarchical forms of society (Frangipane 2007; Wright 2014). While reliance on grains has some negative consequences for individual health, agriculture allowed for the expansion of complex human societies across the globe.

Hayekian perspectives allow for understandings of how complex phenomenon, such as agriculture, could arise from human innovation without planning (Ciote 2012; Hayek [1964] 2014c, [1967] 2014b; Kilpatrick 2001). The domestication and spread of maize is a complex story, many aspects of which have only been available with recent archaeological and genetic technologies and inquiry. The facts of maize domestication, however, challenge traditional narratives of domestication. Rather than directed enhancement, the initial domestication of maize was likely the accidental by-product of interaction with the parent plant, teosinte, for an alternative use. Consequent to the initial domestication event, the adoption and spread of maize is consistent with societies that allow for competition and trade. While geographic and climatic conditions certainly frame the opportunity for agriculture, it is the demographic and institutional frameworks that determine when and how such innovations take hold in society. A Hayekian perspective highlights the importance of individual freedom and incentivization for technological innovation to occur. As such, the story of maize domestication, an accident taken advantage of by an alert entrepreneur, changed the course of human history across the Americas.

APPENDIX

Figure 10.1 Comparison of teosinte (top), maize-teosinte hybrid (middle), and modern maize (bottom). Note the hard casing surrounding the kernels of teosinte. Image: John Doebley, 2015. https://commons.wikimedia.org/wiki/File:Maize-teosinte.jpg.

NOTE

I would like to thank the Mercatus Center at George Mason University for providing this opportunity for truly interdisciplinary work. Primary thanks go to our thoughtful editors, Pete, Jayme, and Virgil: thank y'all so much for the thoughtful comments and suggestions to improve this argument. I would also like to thank my colleagues in this volume for your helpful suggestions and critiques. All errors and omissions are of my own ignorance.

REFERENCES

Armelagos, George J., Alan H. Goodman, and Kenneth H. Jacobs. 1991. "The Origins of Agriculture: Population Growth during a Period of Declining Health." *Population and Environment* 13 (1): 9–22.

Arnold, Jean E., S. Sunell, K. J. Bishop, B. T. Nigra, T. Jones, and J. Bongers. 2015. "Entrenched Disbelief: Complex Hunter-Gatherers and the Case for Inclusive Cultural Evolutionary Thinking." *Journal of Archaeological Method and Theory* 23 (2): 448–99. https://doi.org/10.1007/s10816-015-9246-y.

Avena, Nicole M., Pedro Rada, and Bartley G. Hoebel. 2008. "Evidence for Sugar Addiction: Behavioral and Neurochemical Effects of Intermittent, Excessive Sugar Intake." *Neuroscience & Biobehavioral Reviews* 32 (1): 20–39. https://doi.org/10.1016/j.neubiorev.2007.04.019.

Barnard, Alan. 1999. "Images of Hunter-Gatherers in European Social Thought." In *Cambridge Encyclopedia of Hunters and Gatherers*, edited by Richard B. Lee and Richard Daly, 375–83. Cambridge: Cambridge University Press.

Beadle, George W. 1972. "Mystery of Maize." *Field Museum of Natural History Bulletin* 43 (10): 2–11.

Beals, Ralph Leon. 1932. *The Comparative Ethnology of Northern Mexico before 1750*. Ibero-Americana 2. Berkeley: University of California Press.

Benz, Bruce F., and John E. Staller. 2009. "The Antiquity, Biogeography and Culture History of Maize in Mesoamerica." In *Histories of Maize in Mesoamerica: Multidisciplinary Approaches*, edited by John E. Staller, Robert H. Tykot, and Bruce F. Benz, 267–75. Walnut Creek, CA: Left Coast Press.

Bettinger, Robert L., Raven Garvey, and Shannon Tushingham. 2015. *Hunter-Gatherers: Archaeological and Evolutionary Theory*. 2nd ed. Interdisciplinary Contributions to Archaeology. New York: Springer.

Binford, Lewis R. 1967. "Smudge Pits and Hide Smoking: The Use of Analogy in Archaeological Reasoning." *American Antiquity* 32 (1): 1–12. https://doi.org/10.2307/278774.

_______. 1968. "Post-Pleistocene Adaptations. " In *New Perspectives in Archeology*, edited by L. R. Binford and S. R. Binford, 313–42. Chicago: Aldine.

Boettke, Peter J. 1995. "Hayek's *The Road to Serfdom* Revisited: Government Failure in the Argument against Socialism." *Eastern Economic Journal* 21 (1): 7–26.

Boyd, Robert, and Peter J. Richerson. 1996. "Why Culture Is Common, but Cultural Evolution Is Rare." *Proceedings of British Academy* 88: 77–94.

Braidwood, Robert J., Jonathan D. Sauer, Hans Helbaek, Paul C. Mangelsdorf, Hugh C. Cutler, Carleton S. Coon, Ralph Linton, Julian Steward, and A. Leo Oppenheim. 1953. "Symposium: Did Man Once Live by Beer Alone?" *American Anthropologist* 55 (4): 515–26.

Bruman, H. J. 2000. *Alcohol in Ancient Mexico*. Salt Lake City: University of Utah Press.

Childe, V. Gordon. 1951. *Man Makes Himself*. New York: Mentor Books.

Ciote, Cristina Steliana. 2012. "Complexity Theory and Hayekian Natural Order." *Economics, Management and Financial Markets* 7 (4): 459–65.

Combourieu Nebout, Nathalie, Odile Peyron, Isabelle Dormoy, Stéphanie Desprat, Célia Beaudouin, Ulrich Kotthoff, and Fabienne Marret. 2009. "Rapid Climatic Variability in the West Mediterranean during the Last 25,000 Years from High Resolution Pollen Data." *Climate of the Past* 5 (3): 503–21.

Coupland, Gary. 2006. "A Chief's House Speaks: Communicating Power on the Northern Northwest Coast." In *Household Archaeology on the Northwest Coast*, edited by E. Sobel, A. Gahr, and K. Ames, 80–96. Ann Arbor, MI: International Monographs in Prehistory.

Doebley, John F., and Adrian Stec. 1991. "Genetic Analysis of the Morphological Differences between Maize and Teosinte." *Genetics* 129 (1): 285–95.

_______. 1993. "Inheritance of the Morphological Differences between Maize and Teosinte: Comparison of Results for Two F2 Populations." *Genetics* 134 (2): 559–70.

Dozier, Crystal A. 2017. "The Origins of Entrepreneurship and the Market Process: An Archaeological Assessment of Competitive Feasting, Trade, and Social Cooperation." In *Interdisciplinary Studies of the Market Order: New Applications of Market Process Theory*, edited by Peter J. Boettke, Virgil Henry Storr, and Christopher J. Coyne, 113–37. London: Rowman & Littlefield International.

Feest, Christian F. 1983. "New Wines and Beers of Native North America." *Journal of Ethnopharmacology* 9 (2): 329–35. https://doi.org/10.1016/0378-8741(83)90041-7.

Flannery, Kent V. 1973. "The Origins of Agriculture." *Annual Review of Anthropology* 2 (January): 271–310. https://doi.org/10.2307/2949273.

Flannery, Kent V., and R. I. Ford. 1972. "A Productivity Study of Teosinte (Zea Mexicana), Nov. 22–25, 1971." *University of Michigan Museum of Anthropological Archeology* 1 (8).

Fogelin, Lars. 2007. "Inference to the Best Explanation: A Common and Effective Form of Archaeological Reasoning." *American Antiquity* 72 (4): 603–25. https://doi.org/10.2307/25470436.

Fortuna, Jeffrey L. 2010. "Sweet Preference, Sugar Addiction and the Familial History of Alcohol Dependence: Shared Neural Pathways and Genes." *Journal of Psychoactive Drugs* 42 (2): 147–51. https://doi.org/10.1080/02791072.2010.10400687.

Frangipane, Marcella. 2007. "Different Types of Egalitarian Societies and the Development of Inequality in Early Mesopotamia." *World Archaeology* 39 (2): 151–76. https://doi.org/10.1080/00438240701249504.

Fuller, Dorian Q., Robin G. Allaby, and Chris Stevens. 2010. "Domestication as Innovation: The Entanglement of Techniques, Technology and Chance in the Domestication of Cereal Crops." *World Archaeology* 42 (1): 13–28. https://doi.org/10.1080/00438240903429680.

Goloubinoff, Pierre, Svante Paabo, and Allan C. Wilson. 1993. "Evolution of Maize Inferred from Sequence Diversity of an Adh2 Gene Segment from Archaeological Specimens." *Proceedings of the National Academy of Sciences of the United States of America* 90 (5): 1997–2001. https://doi.org/10.2307/2361445.

Hayden, Brian. 1995. "A New Overview of Domestication." In *Last Hunters, First Farmers: New Perspectives on the Prehistoric Transition to Agriculture*, 273–99.

School of American Research Advanced Seminar Series. Santa Fe, NM: School of American Research Press.
_______. 1998. "Practical and Prestige Technologies: The Evolution of Material Systems." *Journal of Archaeological Method and Theory* 5 (1): 1–55. https://doi.org/10.1007/BF02428415.
_______. 2009. "The Proof Is in the Pudding." *Current Anthropology* 50 (5): 597–601.
_______. [1968] 2014a. "Competitive Feasting before Cultivation?" *Current Anthropology* 55 (2): 230–31.
_______. 2014b. *The Power of Feasts*. Cambridge: Cambridge University Press.
Hayden, Brian, Neil Canuel, and Jennifer Shanse. 2013. "What Was Brewing in the Natufian? An Archaeological Assessment of Brewing Technology in the Epipaleolithic." *Journal of Archaeological Method & Theory* 20 (1): 102–50.
Hayek, F. A. [1944] 2007a. "The 'Inevitability' of Planning." In *The Collected Works of F. A. Hayek*, Volume 2: *The Road to Serfdom: Texts and Documents,* edited by Bruce Caldwell, 91–99. Chicago: University of Chicago Press.
_______. [1944] 2007b. "Planning and Democracy." In *The Collected Works of F. A. Hayek.* Volume 2: *The Road to Serfdom: Texts and Documents,* edited by Bruce Caldwell, 100–11. Chicago: University of Chicago Press.
_______. [1952] 2010a. "The Individualist and 'Compositive' Method of the Social Sciences." In *The Collected Works of F. A. Hayek.* Volume 13: *Studies on the Abuse and Decline of Reason,* edited by Bruce Caldwell, 99–107. Chicago: University of Chicago Press.
_______. [1945] 2010b. "The Subjective Character of the Data of the Social Sciences." In *The Collected Works of F. A. Hayek.* Volume 13: *Studies on the Abuse and Decline of Reason*, edited by Bruce Caldwell, 88–98. Chicago: University of Chicago Press.
_______. [1960] 2011a. *The Collected Works of F. A. Hayek.* Volume 17: *The Constitution of Liberty.* Edited by Ronald Hamowy. Chicago: University of Chicago Press.
_______. [1960] 2011b. "The Creative Powers of a Free Civilization." In *The Collected Works of F. A. Hayek.* Volume 17: *The Constitution of Liberty*, edited by Ronald Hamowy, 73–90. Chicago: University of Chicago Press.
_______. [1967] 2014a. "Competition as a Discovery Procedure." In *The Collected Works of F. A. Hayek.* Volume 15: *The Market and Other Orders*, edited by Bruce Caldwell, 304–13. Chicago: University of Chicago Press.
_______. [1967] 2014b. "The Results of Human Action but Not of Human Design." In *The Collected Works of F. A. Hayek.* Volume 15: *The Market and Other Orders*, edited by Bruce Caldwell, 293–303. Chicago: University of Chicago Press.
_______. [1964] 2014c. "The Theory of Complex Phenomena." In *The Collected Works of F. A. Hayek.* Volume 15: *The Market and Other Orders*, edited by Bruce Caldwell, 257–77. Chicago: University of Chicago Press.
_______. [1945] 2014d. "The Use of Knowledge in Society." In *The Collected Works of F. A. Hayek.* Volume 15: *The Market and Other Orders*, edited by Bruce Caldwell, 93–104. Chicago: University of Chicago Press.
Hoebel, Bartley G., Nicole M. Avena, Miriam E. Bocarsly, and Pedro Rada. 2009. "A Behavioral and Circuit Model Based on Sugar Addiction in Rats." *Journal of Addiction Medicine* 3 (1): 33–41. https://doi.org/10.1097/ADM.0b013e31819aa621.

Hufford, Matthew B., Xun Xu, Joost van Heerwaarden, Tanja Pyhajarvi, Jer-Ming Chia, Reed A. Cartwright, Robert J. Elshire, et al. 2012. "Comparative Population Genomics of Maize Domestication and Improvement." *Nature Genetics* 44 (7): 808–11. https://doi.org/10.1038/ng.2309.

Iltis, Hugh H. 2000. "Homeotic Sexual Translocations and the Origin of Maize (Zea Mays, Poaceae): A New Look at an Old Problem." *Economic Botany* 54 (1): 7–42. https://doi.org/10.1007/BF02866598.

Jaenicke-Despres, Viviane, and Bruce D. Smith. 2010. "Ancient DNA and the Integration of Archaeological and Genetic Approaches to the Study of Maize Domestication." In *Histories of Maize: Multidisciplinary Approaches*, edited by John Staller, Robert Tykot, and Bruce Benz, 32–44. Walnut Creek, CA: Left Coast Press.

Joffe, Alexander H. 1998. "Alcohol and Social Complexity in Ancient Western Asia." *Current Anthropology* 39 (3): 297–322. https://doi.org/10.1086/204736.

Kilpatrick, Henry E. 2001. "Complexity, Spontaneous Order, and Friedrich Hayek: Are Spontaneous Order and Complexity Essentially the Same Thing?" *Complexity* 6 (4): 16–20.

Kirkby, Anne V. T. 1973. "Use of Land and Water Resources in the Past and Present Valley of Oaxaca, Mexico." *Memoirs of the Michigan Museum of Anthropology* 5 (Prehistory and Human Ecology of the Valley of Oaxaca).

Lee, Richard B. 1969. "Eating Christmas in the Kalahari." *Natural History* (December): 60–64.

Lee, Richard B., and Richard Daly. 1999. "Foragers and Others." In *Cambridge Encyclopedia of Hunters and Gatherers*, edited by Richard B. Lee and Richard Daly, 1–19. Cambridge: Cambridge University Press.

Loftas, Tony, and Jane Ross. 1995. *Dimensions of Need: An Atlas of Food and Agriculture*. Rome, Italy: Food and Agriculture Organization of the United Nations.

Martindale, A. 2006. "Tsimshian Houses and Households through the Contact Period." In *Household Archaeology on the Northwest Coast*, edited by E. Sobel, A. Gahr, and K. Ames, 140–58. Ann Arbor, MI: International Monographs in Prehistory.

Matsuoka, Yoshihiro, Yves Vigouroux, Major M. Goodman, Jesus Sanchez G., Edward Buckler, and John F. Doebley. 2002. "A Single Domestication for Maize Shown by Multilocus Microsatellite Genotyping." *Proceedings of the National Academy of Sciences of the United States of America* 99 (9): 6080–84. https://doi.org/10.1073/pnas.052125199.

North, Douglass C. 1981. *Structure and Change in Economic History*. New York: W. W. Norton.

Piperno, Dolores R., Anthony J. Ranere, Irene Holst, Jose Iriarte, and Ruth Dickau. 2009. "Starch Grain and Phytolith Evidence for Early Ninth Millennium BP Maize from the Central Balsas River Valley, Mexico." *Proceedings of the National Academy of Sciences* 106 (13): 5019–24.

Ranum, Peter, Juan Pablo Peña-Rosas, and Maria Nieves Garcia-Casal. 2014. "Global Maize Production, Utilization, and Consumption." *Annals of the New York Academy of Sciences* 1312 (1): 105–12. https://doi.org/10.1111/nyas.12396.

Rosenswig, Robert M. 2000. "Some Political Processes of Ranked Societies." *Journal of Anthropological Archaeology* 19 (4): 413–60. https://doi.org/10.1006/jaar.2000.0360.

———. 2007. "Beyond Identifying Elites: Feasting as a Means to Understand Early Middle Formative Society on the Pacific Coast of Mexico." *Journal of Anthropological Archaeology* 26 (1): 1–27. https://doi.org/10.1016/j.jaa.2006.02.002.

Rossignol-Strick, Martine. 1999. "The Holocene Climatic Optimum and Pollen Records of Sapropel 1 in the Eastern Mediterranean, 9000–6000BP." *Quaternary Science Reviews* 18 (4): 515–30.

Sahlins, Marshall D. 1963. "Poor Man, Rich Man, Big-Man, Chief: Political Types in Melanesia and Polynesia." *Comparative Studies in Society and History* 5 (3): 285–303.

Samuels, S. 2006. "Households at Ozette." In *Household Archaeology on the Northwest Coast*, edited by E. Sobel, A. Gahr, and K. Ames, 200–32. Ann Arbor, MI: International Monographs in Prehistory.

Smalley, John, and Michael Blake. 2003. "Sweet Beginnings." *Current Anthropology* 44 (5): 675–703.

Staller, John E., and Robert G. Thompson. 2002. "A Multidisciplinary Approach to Understanding the Initial Introduction of Maize into Coastal Ecuador." *Journal of Archaeological Science* 29 (1): 33–50. https://doi.org/10.1006/jasc.2001.0750.

Storr, Virgil Henry. 2010. "The Social Construction of the Market." *Society* 47 (3): 200–6.

———. 2013. *Understanding the Culture of Markets*. Routledge Foundations of the Market Economy 31. New York: Routledge.

Suc, Jean Pierre. 1984. "Origin and Evolution of the Mediterranean Vegetation and Climate in Europe." *Nature* 307 (5950): 429–32.

Wadley, Greg, and Brian Hayden. 2015. "Pharmacological Influences on the Neolithic Transition." *Journal of Ethnobiology* 35 (3): 566–84. https://doi.org/10.2993/etbi-35-03-566-584.1.

Wang, Huai, Tina Nussbaum-Wagler, Bailin Li, Qiong Zhao, Yves Vigouroux, Marianna Faller, Kirsten Bomblies-Yant, Lewis Lukens, and John F. Doebley. 2005. "The Origin of the Naked Grains of Maize." *Nature* 436 (7051): 714–19. https://doi.org/10.1038/nature03863.

Wang, Rong-Lin, Adrian Stec, Jody Hey, Lewis Lukens, and John F. Doebley. 1999. "The Limits of Selection during Maize Domestication." *Nature* 398 (6724): 236–39. https://doi.org/10.1038/18435.

Whitt, Sherry R., Larissa M. Wilson, Maud I. Tenaillon, Brandon S. Gaut, and Edward S. Buckler. 2002. "Genetic Diversity and Selection in the Maize Starch Pathway." *Proceedings of the National Academy of Sciences* 99 (20): 12959–62. https://doi.org/10.1073/pnas.202476999.

Wright, Katherine I. 2014. "Domestication and Inequality? Households, Corporate Groups and Food Processing Tools at Neolithic Çatalhöyük." *Journal of Anthropological Archaeology* 33 (March): 1–33. https://doi.org/10.1016/j.jaa.2013.09.007.

Zeder, Melinda A., Eve Emshwiller, Bruce D. Smith, and Daniel G. Bradley. 2006. "Documenting Domestication: The Intersection of Genetics and Archaeology." *Trends in Genetics* 22 (3): 139–55. https://doi.org/10.1016/j.tig.2006.01.007.

Chapter 11

Bad Spontaneous Orders

Trust, Ignorance, and White Supremacy

Caleb Harrison

In introducing the notion of a spontaneous order, F. A. Hayek introduced a powerful tool for social scientists to use in order to analyze social phenomena, shifting the analysis of social phenomena from those orders that could be explained solely by appeal to the intentional actions of the humans involved, to those that could be explained even in cases where no human intentionally acted to effect the design. Hayek notes that we can distinguish between two kinds of social orders: those that are the product of human design, and those that are the product of intentional human action, but not of intentional human design. Hayek calls the first kind of order *organizations*, meaning such social phenomena as "the family, the farm, the plant, the firm, the corporation and the various associations, and all the public institutions including government" (Hayek 1973, 46). The second kind of orders he calls *spontaneous orders*, meaning the order that we can find in the integration of all such organizations with all of the individuals that might also make up such organizations (Hayek 1973, 47).

While acknowledging that an order is a spontaneous order is neutral with respect to the goodness of the order, Hayek, and the spontaneous order theorists following in his stead, have tended to focus on the positive aspects of spontaneous orders. Some spontaneous order theorists do make note of the fact that not everything that is a spontaneous order is going to be beneficial. Nozick (1974, 20–21), for instance, provides a list of spontaneous orders, some of which are beneficial and some of which are not. Martin and Storr (2008) examine both negative belief systems and mobs as instances of what they call *perverse spontaneous orders*, identifying the nature of such orders, the feedback mechanisms that sustain them, and the conditions under which they emerge. While Nozick, Martin, and Storr give examples of spontaneous orders that are not beneficial, they do not offer a means of assessing whether or not a spontaneous order is a *good* or *bad* order.[1] In fact, I am not sure that anybody has offered criteria for evaluating spontaneous orders.

In this chapter, I suggest a standard of assessment for spontaneous orders. In particular, I argue that a spontaneous order that undermines trust is a bad spontaneous order.[2] I will examine what I take to be a particular and pressing instance of a spontaneous order that undermines trust, namely that of contemporary American white supremacy. In arguing for this standard as a valuable way of assessing spontaneous orders, I aim to accomplish two tasks.

First, I would like to bring into conversation two groups of people who, at least in the literature with which I am familiar, have yet to be in direct conversation with each other, despite a common interest in a particular phenomenon. The first of these groups, whom I will call the Spontaneous Order Theorists, would recognize this phenomenon as a spontaneous order, about which they have theorized a great deal.[3] The second of these groups, whom I will call the Critical Race Theorists, would recognize this phenomenon as the contemporary system of white supremacy about which they have theorized. Putting these two traditions into conversation with one another does two things. First, it provides Spontaneous Order Theorists the opportunity to analyze perverse spontaneous orders, an acknowledged but under-explored phenomenon.[4] Second, it provides Critical Race Theorists with an underutilized tool for theorizing about the structure of white supremacy, the mechanisms that reproduce white supremacy, and the implications such an analysis has for dismantling white supremacy.[5]

These implications are the focus of the second, normative aim of this chapter, which is to explore what normative implications we might draw from such an analysis. A spontaneous order analysis lends itself to three considerations that bear on the normative implications of the analysis. First, it helps to identify the relevant underlying features from which the order emerges. This tells us which aspects of society would need to change, if we were to want to change the nature of the order.[6] Second, it tells us what is practically available as a target for change: namely, aspects of the process that generate particular (unknown and unknowable) outcomes, and not any particular outcome itself. Finally, it tells us that that which is practically available as a target for change is also that which is available for normative assessment. This tells us where to look in assessing whether an order is good or bad. To anticipate, I aim to show that contemporary America's white supremacist order is a *bad* spontaneous order and, as such, one that we should aim to change.

The argument will proceed as follows. First, I offer a more detailed description of spontaneous orders (good and bad). This positions us to see how the aspects of the order may interact with the order itself in a way that could be undermining of trust. Next, I explain the conception of trust that

I have in mind, and defend it as a value that is worth securing. I then explain how contemporary American white supremacy is adequately described as a spontaneous order. This positions us to see why trust would be relevant to assessments of contemporary American white supremacy. Finally, I explore the role that ignorance plays in maintaining and reproducing American white supremacy, and in undermining trust. This gives us an example of a feature that is partially constitutive of the spontaneous order, and that also makes the spontaneous order a bad one. I conclude with observations about the limits of spontaneous order analysis, as well as our own practical limits in effecting change in light of the adequacy of a spontaneous order analysis of American white supremacy.

SPONTANEOUS ORDERS, GOOD AND BAD

Theorists of various ideological stripes disagree as to whether or not *contemporary* America is a white supremacist state. While it is clear that America began as an explicitly white supremacist state, and it is generally agreed that America continued to operate as a white supremacist state at least through the Civil Rights Movement, scholars differ on exactly what to make of the racial order of the country after that point. I don't intend in this chapter to provide an argument for the claim that contemporary America *is* a white supremacist state, but will proceed with my argument under the assumption that this is the case.[7] We might next ask what *can* be done about America's white supremacist social order, and what *should* be done about it.[8] With respect to the first question, Hayekian analyses of spontaneous orders provide one way to go about determining what *can* (or more likely, what cannot) be done about America's social order. To see this, we should get clear on what a spontaneous order is.

A social order is a spontaneous order when it can be characterized as emerging from (i) actions of large numbers of individuals (ii) in an environment of a determinate nature, which (iii) includes the actions of others, all of whom (iv) respond to local knowledge of that environment (v) from a potentially wide variety of motives (vi) within the limits defined by the system of rules in force in the relevant population.[9] We see first that spontaneous orders tend to be—though they need not be—complex orders that emerge from the actions of a large number of individuals (Hayek 1973, 38, 41). Part of what distinguishes spontaneous orders from "made" orders (*organizations*) is the fact that spontaneous orders are (typically) of a complexity that defies the purposive designs of human agents; the very structure of an order that is grown rather than made is such that the order could not have been intentionally designed by human agents.[10] Second, we see that such orders exist in an environment of a determinate nature. By this, Hayek means simply to highlight the fact that human beings *act* only in response to the world as it is represented by them. As such, it is their immediate environment in which they act, as this environment is determinately represented by them. Though there may be a story to tell about why an agent's environment is as it is represented to him or her, the details of this story may be invisible to the agent, and so his or her action may not be in response to any of these details. For instance, a restaurant owner who adopts a particular way of speaking to cater to wealthy diners need not know anything about the historical reasons that contribute to the development of such patterns of speech between those in the service industry and those with money; she need merely be responding to the mannerisms of the clients as they are represented to her in her immediate environment.[11]

Included in the environment within which the agent acts are the actions of others in the environment, each of whom is also responding to local knowledge of their immediate environment, from a potentially wide variety of motives, within the limits defined by the system of rules in force in the group. Returning to our restaurant owner, her immediate environment may include restaurant patrons as well as employees of local regulatory bodies. All of these other actors may act in their more-or-less shared immediate environments, in response to their own local knowledge of their more-or-less shared immediate environments: patrons will go to some restaurants and not others on the basis of their knowledge of, for instance, the relative merits of competing restaurants, their plans for the evening, and various competing interests; some employees of regulatory agencies will be motivated by a desire to protect customers from shady business practices, others perhaps to make it difficult for disfavored businesses to compete; and all of these agents will act within the limits of the system of rules in force in the group.[12]

Hayek's conception of "rules" and their role in creating and maintaining spontaneous orders is very specific. By "rules," Hayek means to identify those patterns of thought and action that guide subjects in their attempts to achieve their aims. Rules have several characteristic features (Postema 2009, 2–4). First, subjects need not be consciously aware of the rules that they follow, though rules *do* only exist in the minds (so to speak) of subjects (Hayek 1973, 30). Our restaurant owner will be acting in accordance with a rule when she switches her speaking patterns upon encountering wealthy patrons, though she need not do so because she grasped, intellectually, that obsequious speech conduces to her end of drawing in the wealthy patrons. Second, the rules are abstractions, or patterns resulting from the selective ordering and relation of some elements of experience at the expense of others. Our restaurant owner may respond in action, thought, or judgment to the abstract combination of factors that are instantiated in the wealthy patron's presence outside of her restaurant. Third, the rules *determine*, and do not merely guide, the thoughts and actions of the subjects who follow them. It will be true of our restaurant owner that she recognizes a certain rule if and only if her recognition of a pattern determines a disposition to respond in a particular way. Finally, rules determine *dispositions* to respond, which are not themselves fully determinative of the subject's *responses*, and rules can combine in unpredictable ways. Given the complexity of the environments that we find ourselves in, such a distinction can help explain the extent to which human action is *un*determined. Rules that generate dispositions to act in one way may, when combined with different rules, generate dispositions to act in another way. And this combinatorial feature of rules can operate at greater and greater degrees of complexity.

Taken together, we see that a spontaneous order is an order that emerges from the interactions of an often complex array of rule-following agents, an order with features that are identifiable but not themselves the target of the intentional design of these agents, and one that persists and is reproduced by these interactions. As has been noted, such a picture does not itself say anything about the normative status of such an order; a given order may well be either a good order or a bad one. How might we understand the suggestion that a spontaneous order is itself *bad*?

Understood one way, the question is ill-formed. The aim of spontaneous order theory is purely to describe an order as such, and so spontaneous order theory is simply not in the business of offering up normative evaluations of particular spontaneous orders. So a better question is whether it is good or bad that such a spontaneous order be. This question can be posed in a number of ways. We could ask whether or not such an order is *socially beneficial* or *socially harmful*. We could ask whether or not such an order *secures certain rights*, or *observes procedural constraints* we think it good to observe. We could also be asking whether or not such an order *makes possible certain goods* that we think are required for any minimally decent order.[13] I will proceed by exploring a version of this latter question, namely whether or not white supremacy makes possible a fundamental good. The good that I will consider is the warranted holding of *trusting attitudes*. I will focus on one kind of trusting attitude in particular—thin trust—the warranted holding of which both depends on the degree and content of one's knowledge and ignorance, and ought to be made available in any minimally decent social order.

The failure of any spontaneous order to produce this good makes it a bad order, and gives us a strong, prima facie reason to endeavor to change the order. Knowing that a social order is a spontaneous order tells us that to change the order, we must change its underlying rules.[14] I will argue that the failure of American white supremacy to make possible the warranted holding of this attitude suggests that we ought to endeavor to change the underlying rules of the order. First, however, I will motivate the claim that the holding of thin trust *is* a fundamental good.

TRUST

Philosophers have said a great deal about interpersonal trust and its role in our moral lives over the years, and their discussions of trusting attitudes have tended to characterize one of two kinds of trust.[15] First, there are discussions of a relatively minimal notion of trust (call it "thin trust"). Second, there are discussions of a relatively thick notion of trust (call it "thick trust"). I will focus on thin trust, as much of what can be said about thin trust, with respect to knowledge and ignorance, will also apply to thick trust.

The two features offered as central to a trusting attitude, whether thin or thick, are expectations and a sense of vulnerability. To trust another person is to have particular expectations regarding, and to willingly be vulnerable to, that person. We can distinguish between *predictive* and *normative* expectations.[16] Predictive expectations are expectations that predict how someone *will* be, or what they will do, on the basis of past regularities or general assumptions. Normative expectations are expectations that someone *should* be some way, or do some thing. To trust another person is to have normative and predictive expectations that he or she will do some thing or be some way, and to be willingly vulnerable to him or her. We can distinguish among such trust-related attitudes as trust, mere reliance, neither trust nor distrust, and distrust, by attending to the various ways in which our different expectations and our vulnerability combine. As we will see, justifiably trusting others is good for one's well-being, and the flourishing of a community depends on the existence of conditions that foster trust.

As an example of the difference between trust and such attitudes as mere reliance, consider the following case. My morning routine consists in letting my dog, Alfie, into our fenced-in yard before I drink coffee and read the news. Around 7:20 every morning, my neighbors, along with their dog, pass by our house as they walk their kids to school. When they walk by, Alfie begins to bark and growl at their dog. I should usually be getting a move on by 7:20 if I want to get to campus on time, and so I have come to associate Alfie's barking with my needing to get ready. This has led me to form particular expectations with respect to my neighbors. I predictively expect that they will walk by around this time because they have consistently done so in the past. However, I do not normatively expect them to do so. When 8:00 comes around, and I realize that my growing unease is the result of Alfie's unusual morning silence, I do not think that my neighbors have done something that they should not have, even if they have done something that I did not expect. In this case, my attitude toward them is one of mere reliance.

It might also be the case that I *do* have normative expectations. I may, for instance, expect of my neighbors that they observe certain constraints against harming me, across a number of contexts (Preston-Roedder 2017). Predictively, I may expect that they *will not* observe such constraints, in which case my attitude toward them is likely to be one of distrust; if I have other options, I may avoid interacting with them at all. I might also not have any predictive expectations whatsoever about whether they will or will not observe constraints against harming me, in which case it is best to characterize my attitude as neither distrusting nor trusting. This may be the attitude that I hold toward neighbors in unfamiliar countries, for instance, particularly in countries that I believe to be unsafe. It may be the case, though, that I predictively expect of my neighbors that they *will* observe the constraints against harming me that I normatively expect them to observe. Here, it seems that my attitude is much more plausibly characterized as one of trust.

Whether or not my attitude *is* a trusting attitude depends on the extent to which I accept my vulnerability to the other people in my neighborhood. If I clutch my bag to my chest when they are near, or make it difficult for them to be near me, then despite the coherence of my normative and predictive expectations, the attitude that I hold toward my neighbors is not a trusting attitude. If my normative and predictive expectations regarding others cohere, and if I make myself vulnerable to them, however, then my attitude is a trusting attitude. I call this minimal notion of trust *thin trust*.[17]

Later in the chapter I discuss one of the outcomes of the combination of the "rules" that underlie white supremacy, which is the construction of a dominant race whose members tend to, and are expected to, be ignorant of important social and historical facts.[18] I argue that this ignorance undermines the possibility of thin trust, which gives us, prima facie, strong reason to rid ourselves of the rules generating the order. First, however, I should explain the relevance of knowledge to trust. Because vulnerability and expectations are required for thin trust, thin trust is only possible in epistemic environments of imperfect knowledge. Consider how perfect knowledge affects trust. Recall that you must be vulnerable to another for your attitude toward him or her to be one of trust. If I always know when my neighbors will walk, for instance, I can't be vulnerable to the whims of their decisions. Nor would I expect them to walk. Rather, I would simply know that they will or will not walk, much the same as I know that two plus two is four. Trust is incompatible with perfect knowledge. Trust is also incompatible with perfect ignorance. Recall also that your vulnerability to another must be *accepted*; it is not enough that one merely *be* vulnerable, one must also (correctly) *recognize* that one is vulnerable, and accept that vulnerability. If I fail to recognize the presence of a person outside my unlocked vehicle upon exiting, and subsequently do not lock my car, this is not an indication that I trust that person; it is merely an indication that I did not know someone was nearby. So I at least need to know that I am vulnerable to another person for it to be the case that I trust that person.[19]

There is value and use in being able to justifiably hold such a trusting attitude toward others. This value exists both for any given member of a community composed of members who are worthy of such trusting attitudes (call this the *agent-neutral* value of thin trust), and for the particular members of the community who can justifiably hold such an attitude toward other members of the community (call this the *agent-relative* value of thin trust) (Preston-Roedder 2017, 11–13). The prevalence of justified thin trust in a community makes life in such a community a life worth living. Life in such a community is a life where one can live and work with others, free from the kind of dominating fear that can draw our attention away from goods we might enjoy and toward possible harms or losses (Preston-Roedder 2017, 12). We avoid the stress that comes from feeling a constant need to protect that which tends to be both most valuable to us, and most vulnerable to the arbitrary power of others—namely our bodies, our minds, and our autonomy (Jones 2004, 10–11). The fact that these goods are available to all members of a community in which thin trust is prevalent makes thin trust something that all members of a community have reason to value.

Scholars have defended markets by proposing that they promote conditions that, it turns out, are conducive to building trust. In particular, free markets incentivize people to comport themselves such that others find them worthy of cooperation, and by way of these cooperative interactions, market participants form normative and predictive expectations warranting their making themselves vulnerable to others by engaging in exchange (Herzog 2017).[20] When the appropriate conditions are in place, and markets do facilitate trust-building relationships, then we see an example of a good spontaneous order: both one that benefits members of the community who can participate in such an order (by facilitating mutual gains from exchange), and one that benefits members of the community in virtue of their being justified in holding thin trust toward others in the first place.

Consider the agent-relative value of justifiably holding thin trust. In the first place, many of one's goals are only achievable in cooperation with others. Though it may not be the case that trust is required for cooperation—we often must make do with hope or the existence of sufficient external incentives—few would doubt that it does not make cooperation more likely. The importance of trust to the achievement of one's goals is particularly evident when it comes to the protection of fundamental vulnerabilities; few of us in contemporary society can survive for long without food, water, and shelter, and the attainment of these goods depends in large part on other people believing that one is safe to cooperate with. Aside from the securing of these basic necessities, however, a life in which others feel free to be vulnerable around one is a life in which one is likelier to have and to maintain the intimate and familial relationships that make life worth living.[21]

We can also see the value in being able to justifiably direct a trusting attitude toward others by looking to what is lost for those for whom such trust is not available. Psychologists who work on betrayal trauma theory note the lifelong damage that can follow from serious betrayals of trust that was thought to be there, including experiencing "visceral, intense, and protracted negative feelings," an "unrelenting anger," and a sense of the world as a disordered place (Koehler and Gershoff 2003, 245). Karen Jones discusses the negative effects that can accompany one's sense that trust is inappropriate in the first place. She explores the effects of terrorism on what she calls *basal security*, or the underlying, affectively laden state that explains our willingness to enter into particular trusting relations with others (Jones 2004, 8). One's assessment of the risk of harm in particular encounters is inversely related to the strength of one's sense of basal security. When one's basal security is low, one assesses the risk of harm from one's being vulnerable to others to be higher than it objectively is (Jones 2004, 9–11).[22] Survivors of sexual or racial trauma, for instance, may assess their vulnerability to members of other sexes or races as being riskier than it in fact is.[23] Not only will a damaged sense of basal security prevent one from enjoying the good of potential relationships and instrumentally valuable cooperation with those to whom they perceive themselves to be highly vulnerable, but it may prevent them from enjoying the good of a sense of integrity and agency that is a basic component of human flourishing.[24] There is, then, much of value at stake in being able to live in a society in which justified thin trust is possible, which makes the possibility of thin trust an appropriate criterion for the normative evaluation of spontaneous orders.

WHITE SUPREMACY AS SPONTANEOUS ORDER

Before explaining how white supremacy is undermining of the possibility of warranted trust, I will first explain what I mean by "white supremacy," such that it is recognizable by Critical Race Theorists *as* white supremacy, and by Hayekians as a spontaneous order. There are a number of conceptions one might have in mind when discussing white supremacy, though most conceptions identify the domination of whites over non-whites as a central feature of the social order. I will proceed with a conception of white supremacy according to which the term denotes any society in which whites dominate over non-whites, whether that be through juridical or non-juridical means. Frances Lee Ansley provides a helpful description of such a conception, suggesting that we conceive of white supremacy as "a political, economic, and cultural system in which whites overwhelmingly control power and material resources, conscious and unconscious ideas of white superiority and entitlement are widespread, and relations of white dominance and non-white subordination are daily reenacted across a broad array of institutions and social settings" (Ansley 1989, 1024, fn. 9). I will focus in particular on the widespread ideas, conscious and unconscious, of white superiority and entitlement.

A conception of white supremacy as a system of white domination over non-whites also requires something to be said about the underlying conception of race; we need to know who is "white" and who is not, if we are to know whether or not the social order that we are examining is a white supremacist social order. Here, I will assume an account of race according to which race is a social construction, rather than a natural or biological kind. According to such an account of race, racial categories are social-political categories that are brought into existence by social-political orders. Racial categories do not refer to natural kinds, nor do they track a biological essence. A social order will be a white supremacist social order, then, when the structure of the order is such that some members of the order are constructed as being "white" while some are not, and when those who are constructed as white "overwhelmingly control power and material resources, conscious and unconscious ideas of [their] superiority and entitlement are widespread, and relations of [their] dominance and [non-members'] subordination are daily reenacted across a broad array of institutions and social settings" (Ansley 1989, 1024, fn. 9).

It seems clear that American white supremacy meets Hayek's description of a spontaneous order. First, American white supremacy emerges from the actions of large numbers of individuals in an environment of a determinate nature. One way to understand an order as an environment of a "determinate nature" is to understand the order as being a "state of affairs in which . . . we may learn from our acquaintance with some spatial or temporal part of the whole to form correct expectations concerning the rest" (Hayek 1973, 36). With regard to American white supremacy, we may learn from our acquaintance with some part of the whole—with racial categories, for instance—to form correct expectations concerning other parts of the order—distributions of and access to resources, for instance. Second, American white supremacy emerges from the actions of those who comprise the order, each of whom is responding to local knowledge of the environment from a potentially wide variety of motives within the limits defined by the system of rules in force in the group. White supremacy emerges from individual actors' coordinated and uncoordinated daily pursuits of their interests. American white supremacy does not depend for its maintenance on the presumption that these actors have particular motivations, but is compatible with the daily pursuit of interests from a variety of motives. It is true that America was, by design, founded as an explicitly racist, white supremacist political order, but explaining the persisting domination of non-whites by whites today by appeal to the intentional coordination of whites would require "conspiracy of the first order"; conceived of as a spontaneous order, we need make no such appeal to explain the persistence of white supremacy (Lebron 2013, 38). Third, the people from whom American white supremacy emerges act within the limits defined by the system of rules in force in America. It is worth emphasizing that rules, for Hayek, can be tacit or explicit, but they always involve dispositions to respond—to see, feel, or possibly judge something—in a patterned way (Postema 2009, 4). Widespread ideas of white entitlement and superiority in America, whether they are consciously endorsed or unconsciously acted on, dispose Americans to respond in a patterned way.[25]

This is a particularly important point that will be expanded on in the next section. One consequence of American white supremacy is the construction of racial categories that are *normative* in nature. In addition to describing category membership, racial categories serve to prescribe thoughts and actions of those who are described as fitting into particular racial categories.[26] The fact that white supremacy constructs these prescriptive racial categories helps to explain the final feature of white supremacy that is consistent with its being described as a spontaneous order. This final feature is the self-reinforcing nature of American white supremacy—it has proven itself adaptive to exogenous and endogenous shocks to the order. Such exogenous shocks to the order as the various historical changes in demographics, which threatened the coherence and dominance of the "white" race, have led to the white racialization of such formerly excluded groups as the Irish, Slavs, Mediterraneans, and Jews (Mills 1997, 88). The resilience of American white supremacy in the face of endogenous shocks—changes to the rules of the order, which direct the actions of the individuals from which the order emerges—is exemplified by the persistence of extreme levels of racial inequality in contemporary America, despite the fact that it is generally considered unacceptable for individuals to hold explicitly racist beliefs, or to explicitly pursue racist ends and implement racist policies.

Supposing, then, that contemporary American white supremacy *is* a spontaneous order, we can now look to see how it is that white supremacy undermines the possibility of holding justified thin trust. I will do so by focusing in on particular Hayekian rules that perpetuate the order—namely, norms promoting historical and perceptual ignorance in those categorized as "white."

WHITENESS AND IGNORANCE

We see, from the previous sections, that thin trust is a value worth securing, and that for thin trust to be possible, some minimum degree of relevant knowledge must be available.[27] Whether or not American white supremacy can secure thin trust will depend on whether or not it makes possible this minimum degree of relevant knowledge; I argue that it does not. More specifically, I argue that white supremacy constructs racial categories that prescribe a degree of ignorance that undermines the possibility of justified thin trust between whites and non-whites.

Recent work on the epistemology of ignorance helps to shed light on the role that ignorance plays in the production and maintenance of contemporary American white supremacy. I will focus on two ways in which white supremacy and ignorance mutually reinforce each other—namely, in the historical misunderstandings required by whiteness, and in the distorted perceptions of non-whites that are encouraged in whites—where the persistence of ignorance in each case functions so as to maintain an order that undermines the possibility of thin trust. Such ignorance is an important part of the system of rules from which American white supremacy emerges, and mitigating such ignorance could provide the sort of shock that would destabilize white supremacy.

James Baldwin, in his powerful essay *The Fire Next Time*, argues that white Americans "do not know . . . and do not want to know" that they have destroyed, and continue to destroy, countless millions of lives (Baldwin 1998a). Nor do they wish to believe that "Black America's grievances are real," because that would require them to do what they cannot do, which is to "face what [the truth of such grievances] says about themselves and their country." Rather, he imagines, white folk must "merely make reassuring sounds" in their conversations with one another (Baldwin 1998a, 1998b). Of course, there is ignoring and there is ignoring, and it is important to clarify what Baldwin might mean by suggesting that white Americans "do not know" their history (Spelman 2007). On the one hand, to say that one is ignorant of some thing may be to say that one has no knowledge of that thing, nor any knowledge that may be related to that thing. Here I can give no example from experience, in virtue of the fact that any example I could come up with would be something that I have at least *some* knowledge of. On the other hand, to say that one is ignorant of some thing may be to say that one merely *ignores* that thing. I, for instance, am ignorant of the elemental composition of Jupiter's atmosphere. I know that Jupiter has an atmosphere, and I know that it must have some elemental composition, but I just don't know, or desire to find out, any such facts.[28]

In discussing the ignorance of white America, Baldwin has in mind the latter kind of ignorance.[29] We have good data that such ignorance is prevalent.

Black Americans are disproportionately stopped by police, arrested, tried, and convicted for crimes, and they tend to receive longer sentences than whites do for similar crimes (Starr and Rehavi 2013). Black Americans know this, and report unfair encounters with the police at three times the rate of white Americans (30% vs. 13%) (Peffley and Hurwitz 2010, 189). Still, despite the clear evidence that Black Americans tend to be treated unfairly by law enforcement and the criminal justice system, there is a severe discrepancy between Black and white attitudes regarding both. Black Americans on average are nearly four times as likely as whites to rate as a "serious problem" in their neighborhood, the stopping of Black people by police officers, the relative unconcern police officers show for Black people who are victims of crimes compared to whites, and the harsher sentencing by courts of Black persons (70% vs. 18%). Further, Black Americans were twice as likely as whites to respond affirmatively to the claim that African Americans were treated less fairly than white Americans in police dealings in their neighborhoods (77% vs. 35%). Such an ignorance is psychologically understandable; the intolerable thought of living in an unjust world—what psychologists call *system justification bias*—inclines people to interpret their social world as just, and attending to the historical record is not conducive to such an interpretation (Jost 2001, 90). In light of this, the popular history of America is a (distorted) history of an America in which the cooperative relations of Squanto, Pocahontas, Sacajawea, and American "settlers" are elevated over the (near-)genocide of America's indigenous inhabitants (Sterba 1996, 430–31; Stiffarm and Lane Jr. 1992, 35)[30]; in which the portrayal of slavery as a "peculiar institution" of the Southern states is elevated over the centrality of slavery to the entire nation's economics and politics[31]; in which the successful unification of the North and the South is elevated over the extreme domestic terrorism and lynching campaigns of Reconstruction, the Black Codes, and Jim Crow[32]; and in which the portrayal of white American wealth as the result of hard work is elevated over a record of state-sanctioned discrimination.[33] How we understand the world to have been, and how we understand the world to be, affects how we act and think in the world *now*. If white supremacy encourages whites to be ignorant of history, and if our understandings of the causes of the patterns we perceive in the world are shaped by our understandings of history, then the patterns that whites perceive in the world will be shaped by their distorted understanding of history. To the extent that white people respond to these perceived patterns, whether or not they are aware of the cause of their responses, these patterns of historical ignorance can be understood to be part of the system of rules that define the limit of individual actions in the white supremacist order.

In addition to an ignorance of history, whiteness is produced and maintained by a kind of *perceptual* ignorance. Elizabeth Anderson offers a compelling account of the mutually reinforcing relationship between interracial group representations and practices of segregation that helps reproduce categorical inequalities (Anderson 2010). Human stereotyping processes, which are largely automatic, universal cognitive processes, generate simple schemas about classes of objects that, once generated, can be used to make inferences about particular objects that are recognized as belonging to the general class (Anderson 2010, 45). When stereotypes result in public narratives or interpretive frames that explain perceived group differences in demeaning ways, these stereotypes serve to stigmatize members of the stereotyped groups. By attributing negative stereotypes to dispositional features of group members, rather than to features of the situation in which group members find themselves, a lack of goodwill toward group members is thereby rationalized.

The discussion of historical ignorance suggests that whites are encouraged to ignore historical explanations for their enjoying the privileges that they enjoy as members of the dominant social and political group.[34] Even were we to set aside the influence of history, however, whites would face perceptual challenges that arise from the confluence of stigma-reinforcing cognitive biases and segregation, for instance. In-group favoritism, the shared reality bias, and the illusory correlation bias link the spatial and social segregation of races to Black stigmatization. Spatial segregation is likely to lead whites to belong to few groups with many Black members, reducing the opportunity to extend in-group favoritism to Blacks, to build shared realities that incorporate Black experience, and to mitigate the effect of deviant encounters with Blacks (Anderson 2010, 47). Whites are thereby encouraged to form false (and damaging) stereotypes of Blacks—as essentially criminal,[35] for instance—which may impede the ability of whites to empathize with Blacks, or to give Black testimony its appropriate uptake (Fricker 1998).

When historical ignorance is combined with perceptual ignorance, the situation looks much worse. If whites needed only to overcome historical ignorance, the perception of the world around them should suffice to demonstrate that a history from which they escape unblemished is a history that ought to be discarded. Alternatively, if whites needed only to overcome perceptual ignorance, the history of the world around them should suffice to demonstrate that there are clear historical reasons for the perceived state of group inequalities today. The simultaneous operation of both forms of ignorance, however, serves to bolster belief-forming practices that make epistemic escape difficult. White supremacy constructs a dominant social-political group whose members are encouraged *not* to be motivated to critique their relative power, *not* to be aware of the prevalence of certain experiences as a result of their relative social location, and are encouraged *to* take up belief-forming practices that distort their historical and perceptual understanding of the world (Alcoff 2007, 47–49).

How does this ignorance affect Americans' ability to justifiably trust one another? To trust another, one must predictively expect that the other will not take advantage of whatever power he or she may have over one's vulnerabilities. By prescribing perceptual and historical ignorance in the construction of whiteness, white supremacy encourages those who are constructed as white to be untrustworthy to those who aren't. When whites are encouraged to discount non-white testimony, then non-whites cannot expect that whites will take up their grievances.[36] When whites are encouraged to ignore the harms that may befall non-whites when pursuing seemingly morally neutral interests—as when they lobby for zoning restrictions keeping multifamily homes out of their neighborhoods—then non-whites cannot expect that whites will prioritize the protection of non-white vulnerability over the pursuit of white interests (Shelby 2016, 44). And when whites are encouraged to promote social stability and the security of their property, then non-whites cannot expect that whites will respect their lives (Wills 2016). The prevalence of such distrust plays out in political psychology surveys.

In one survey, more than half of Blacks believe that whites harbor negative stereotypes about blacks as a racial group (Sigelman and Tuch 1997). Shayla Nunnally found, in the 2007 National Politics and Socialization Survey, that Blacks view Asians and Latinx folk as more trustworthy than whites, and whites as less trustworthy than "people in general" (Nunnally 2012, 102–4); whites are perceived as being more likely to lie than other racial groups (Nunnally 2012, 105); and whites and "people in general" are believed to be most likely to racially discriminate, with Blacks, Asians, and Latinx believed to be least likely to (Nunnally 2012, 119). Of particular interest is the fact that an increased feeling of interconnection to the fates of other Blacks—subscribing to a nationalist racial ideology, for example—is associated with an increased likelihood of reporting experiences of racial discrimination, and to express race-based uncertainty about others (Sellers and Shelton 2003; Dawson 1994).[37] To rephrase this in my terms, an increase in the feeling among Black Americans that their individual life outcomes are partly determined by their being constructed as non-white is associated with an increase in the likelihood that they predictively expect whites to take their race into account in interactions.

Other surveys suggest a mutuality of negative interracial attitudes. According to several, nearly half of whites view Blacks as less intelligent than whites (Massey 2007, 69). These negative interracial attitudes, when situated in a society featuring severe racial and socioeconomic inequalities, facilitate the segregation of important resources and opportunities (Anderson 2010, chap.

3). Though intraracial trust may increase in response to de facto and de jure discrimination, helping to enhance Black social networks as "counterpublics," and to provide important institutions for Blacks' sociopolitical advancement, these networks and institutions are marginalized and insular, locked out from the resources needed to address (rather than merely ameliorate) structural barriers to reducing inequality (Anderson 2010; Massey 2007; Nunnally 2012; Orr 1999).

To be sure, there are benefits to a world in which intraracial trust increases in response to systemic racial inequality; better still, however, would be a world in which such trust was not required in the first place. As a reason for thinking that the benefits of intraracial trust do not outweigh the costs of interracial distrust, consider recent findings on the link between trust and individual well-being.[38] One study shows that trust in others is associated with a general sense of belonging, and that people report a higher subjective sense of well-being when they feel this sense of belonging in their communities (Helliwell, Huang, and Wang 2014). People also experience a premium when they feel that they belong at both local levels (i.e., within their local communities) and global levels (i.e., within their state or nation); such a premium is likely to be lacking for members of racial groups who report trusting whites less than "people in general," particularly when these racial groups are minorities relative to both whites and "people in general" (Helliwell, Huang, and Wang 2017; Wilkes and Wu 2017). Not only are there benefits to living in an environment where you feel you can trust others, but the costs to *not* living in such an environment are substantial: those who generally think that other people can be trusted experience significantly reduced well-being effects of a discriminatory environment, ill-health, and unemployment (Helliwell, Huang, and Wang 2017). Living in an environment where you feel unwarranted in trusting other people is costly to general well-being; all the more so for those who, thanks to the segregating effects of white supremacy, are more likely to experience such effects. In a social order that is perpetuated through the division of the populace into a dominant and subordinate group, the undermining of the possibility of thin trust between group members constitutes a devastating loss of something of fundamental value.

CONCLUSION

> It's likely that should white supremacy fall, the means by which that happens might be unthinkable to those of us bound by present realities and politics.
>
> —*Ta-Nehisi Coates*

American white supremacy seems adequately described as a spontaneous order, and the construction of white ignorance seems to undermine the possibility of thin trust between whites and non-whites. Given this, we ought to reject our white supremacist order. This would be relatively simple if white supremacy were a *made* order; we need merely design a new one. But the fact, if it is a fact, that contemporary American white supremacy is a spontaneous order suggests that rejecting the order will not be so easy. First, that white supremacy is a spontaneous order tells us that we will not, by addressing some subset of the rules from which the order emerges, be able to target a specific outcome. Hayek notes that "we can know at most the rules observed by the elements of various kinds of which the structures are made up, but not all the individual elements and never all the particular circumstances in which each of them is placed" (Hayek 1973, 41). Not being able to know all of the relevant features of the order prevents us from identifying and arranging said features toward a particular desired end. Second, that white supremacy is a spontaneous order helps to explain Coates' quote above—we may not be able to know for sure which rule changes will be sufficient to change the overall character of the order. Hayek notes that "we shall often not be able to foresee the particular changes by which the necessary adaptation to altered external circumstances will be brought about, and sometimes perhaps not even be able to conceive in what manner the restoration of a disturbed "equilibrium" or "balance" can be accomplished" (Hayek 1973, 63).

Conceiving of American white supremacy as a spontaneous order may be unappealing in its implication that our available responses are limited. Still, doing so can be helpful in that by knowing the limits of what can be accomplished, we are better positioned to evaluate what should be done. While noting that we may not be able to determine all of the rules and elements (and the relations that obtain between them) of an order, Hayek *does* note that we "may be in a position to alter *at least some* of the rules of conduct which the elements obey, [and] we shall thereby be able to influence . . . the general character . . . of the resulting order" (Hayek 1973; emphasis added). Hayek is primarily worried that we understand what follows from the fact that an order is spontaneous. First, we should understand that we may not effect an order of a particular character or design by trying to design the underlying details in accordance with our interests. And if we do try to, there's no guarantee that we won't affect the general character of the order, possibly disintegrating the order altogether. If our concern with white supremacy was, for instance, over the benefits of the distribution of wealth under a white supremacist order as compared to candidate alternative orders, Hayek's concerns may be applicable. He would remind us that in attempting to redistribute the wealth in accordance with our desires, we may ultimately undermine the order itself, losing what little benefits that the order provides in the process.

Alternatively, if the order were to survive our intervention, he might remind us that we would be unable to control the final distribution of harms and benefits, and would, in electing to benefit one group, inevitably harm some other group. In our case, however, we are not concerned with the *distribution* of a particular good among members of the order. Rather, we are concerned with the existence of a fundamental good within the order. Given that the general character of the order is such that this good is not provided, we ought to do what we can to "alter at least some of the rules of conduct" thereby influencing "the general character . . . of the resulting order" (Hayek 1973).

The rules amounting to the prescribed historical and perceptual ignorance among whites are good places to start. Some efforts have been made, and are being made, to bring to light overlooked aspects of American history. The recently opened National Museum of African American History & Culture in Washington, DC, and the Equal Justice Initiative's soon-to-be-opened national memorial to victims of lynching, and museum exploring African American history from enslavement to mass incarceration, are important first steps in an effort to undermine the prescribed white historical ignorance. In addition to general education interventions, more targeted interventions may be needed. Christopher Lebron suggests that "reasonable propaganda" could be supported by what he calls the "Just Trojan Horse Principle." Reasonable propaganda might require, for instance, that news and other trusted public media be monitored to ensure fair racial representations, or that reports of crime be accompanied by statistics regarding housing and employment opportunities, and past policies of public spending, in the neighborhoods (Lebron 2013, 147–48).

Such a recommendation may seem tongue-in-cheek, but similar recommendations for intervention tend to find support when it comes to altering undesirable norms in other countries. Cristina Bicchieri, for instance, favorably cites "information campaigns, edutainment (ranging from soap operas to video games), and other more modest forms of collective entertainment, such as village theater," as interventions that have proven successful in changing cultural norms encouraging female genital mutilation and child marriage (Bicchieri 2017, 147). It stands to reason that if interventions like these are successful in changing undesirable norms, then interventions like these could be used to target the norms prescribing white historical and perceptual ignorance in America. Hayek was clearly no fan of government intervention—particularly government intervention into the operations of the market—but note again that what is at stake is not the optimal operations of a market, but the provision of a fundamental good. Thin trust is valuable, and ought to be possible for and between all members of society. Contemporary American white supremacy undermines the possibility of such trust. What can we do about it?

Critical Race Theorists have done a marvelous job demystifying contemporary white supremacy. They have also been charged with leaning too heavily on a conception of white supremacy that is "overly blunt" and that "lacks analytic nuance" (Lebron 2013, 16, 19). Conceiving of white supremacy as a spontaneous order may provide for a more nuanced analysis. Spontaneous Order Theorists have identified features of spontaneous orders, and the relation that these features bear to possible changes to the order. We can't design for specific outcomes, for instance, as spontaneous orders are by nature undesigned. We can't undo spontaneous orders solely through legislation, as they are reproduced through the combined interaction of underlying rules, some (if not most) of which are informal social norms. Though Spontaneous Order Theorists have done much to analyze spontaneous orders, they have neglected bad spontaneous orders. Conceiving of white supremacy as a spontaneous order provides Spontaneous Order Theorists with an opportunity to explore bad spontaneous orders, and to think through possible standards for distinguishing between good and bad orders. I have suggested that one criterion for a good order is its ability to make possible thin trust between members of the order. When an order fails along this criterion—and white supremacy fails abysmally—then we have good reason to endeavor to change the order. The way to do so is by altering the underlying rules. I have suggested that the prescribed white historical and perceptual ignorance is as good a place as any to start. What the other rules are, and what the best means of addressing them is, should be determined through the combined efforts of Spontaneous Order and Critical Race Theorists across the social sciences and humanities. If contemporary American white supremacy is a spontaneous order, we know the path forward will be a fog-covered, uphill journey, with no clear end in sight, nor with any knowledge of what the end will be. Still, it's a path we should gladly take.

NOTES

I would like to thank Virgil Storr, Jayme Lemke, and Peter Boettke, for their helpful comments and suggestions for revision; the Mercatus Center for its support; and Peter Lipsey, Lane Conaway, Lauren Dieckhaus, Courtney Dunn, and the rest of the Mercatus staff for the work they do to keep things going. Finally, thanks to my Smith Fellows, whose conversation and company kept *me* going.

1. There are benefits to market economies, for instance, but Marxists are happy to question whether or not market economies are good.
2. I will spend a great deal of what remains in this chapter explaining what I mean by trust.
3. This name is in some ways a misnomer, as I do not intend for it to pick out those who themselves subscribe to the tenets of Hayek's thought (except, perhaps,

for Hayek himself). Rather, I intend for the name to pick out those theorists who take seriously the idea of a spontaneous order, and who find it an analytically useful tool for understanding and explaining our social world.

4. Martin and Storr (2008) is one notable exception.

5. White supremacy theorists may welcome the emphasis that spontaneous order theory places on the generation of particular orders without the intentional design of human agents, given the vexing linguistic challenge of describing how white dominance can persist in light of the (apparent) excision of explicitly white supremacist policies and norms.

6. Though, given the nature of spontaneous orders, this does not tell us what will be the outcome of changing these features.

7. Philosophers endorsing America as a white supremacist order include Charles Mills, Lucius T. Outlaw Jr., Patricia Hill Collins, and Linda Martín Alcoff. See Collins (2002); Outlaw (2005); Mills (2017); Alcoff (2015). Philosophers who take issue with the critical notion of white supremacy, but who nonetheless find it important to conceptualize white dominance include Anderson (2010); Lebron (2013); and Shelby (2016).

8. It may be easier to discuss white supremacy in the less-contested historical past, but it is also less clear what is gained by applying spontaneous order theory to intended, designed orders. The proffered normative evaluation for spontaneous orders should prove valuable to those who are unconvinced that contemporary America is a white supremacist state.

9. I will largely follow Gerald Postema's characterization in what follows. See Postema (2009). Other theorists offer alternative characterizations that are also helpful. Robert Sugden and Gerald Gaus suggest that spontaneous orders, as Hayek conceives of them, (1) are path-dependent, (2) approximate equilibrium, (3) are to some degree self-maintaining, and (4) their spontaneity is a matter of degree; see Gaus (2006). Nona Martin and Virgil Storr characterize spontaneous orders toward the end of explaining perverse spontaneous orders, noting that spontaneous orders, perverse or not, have the following characteristics: (a) they can be meaningfully described as orders; (b) they are the result of human action; (c) they are not the result of human design; (d) the elements of the order follow rules of conduct; and (e) they are self-reinforcing. See Martin and Storr (2008).

10. Hayek is clear that this is not *necessarily* true of every order that is correctly described as a spontaneous order, but that it is one of the features of such orders that makes it useful to have a separate category of orders available for us to theorize about.

11. This case also helps illustrate why, despite having originated as a designed order, a spontaneous order may nonetheless persist long after the conditions that helped form the original order disappear. Supposing that the communicative practice she is taking up originated in an explicitly classist system, she need not be aware of that fact to perpetuate the practice; she need only be responding to her environment.

12. What is important here is the thought that human action is partly in response to rules that are *in force* in the group. This is not to say that action is constrained by laws or purported moral norms, however. Rather, it is to say that the action is in response to the rules that people are represented as *in fact* following in the environment in which

agents act. Compare with what Cristina Bicchieri calls operative "social norms." See Bicchieri 2006, chap. 1.

13. We might also speak in terms of "fundamental goods," where a fundamental good is a good, the absence of which in a spontaneous order gives us good reason to reject the order.

14. It also tells us (1) that we can't successfully target a particular outcome, and (2) that we can't know for sure which rule changes will be sufficient for changing the order itself.

15. Baier (1986); Govier (1992); Jones (1996); Hardin (2002); O'Neill (2002); Potter (2002); Preston-Roedder (2017). In addition to providing accounts of trust, many of these philosophers defend a version of the claim that trust is fundamental to a good life. I will assume without argument that such claims are true.

16. For more on this difference in kinds of expectations, see Woozley (1973); Hollis (1998); Walker (2006). Bicchieri's work on the nature of moral, personal, and social norms is also helpful in thinking through the many ways in which expectations shape the trusting attitudes we may (or may not) hold toward others.

17. Discussions of civic trust, and the background conditions required for holding it, include Jones (2004); Preston-Roedder (2017); Welch (2013).

18. I am understanding "rules" in Hayekian terms, here, as those patterns of thought or action that guide one in one's pursuit of one's ends.

19. Recall also that as trust requires expectations of and about the trusted, it is minimally required that I have sufficient knowledge to form relevant expectations.

20. Proponents of the trust-building capacity of markets are, I think, identifying a willingness to cooperate, and not a trusting attitude. The account given here, of the relationship of the market to the fostering of thin trust, borrows from the consequential defenses of the market noted by Lisa Herzog (2017).

21. We will see what the effects on well-being are for one's being justified in holding trust toward others in their community.

22. The converse holds when one's basal security is high.

23. This, too, after accounting for the fact that they may *in fact* be at higher risk of harm from said groups.

24. For a compelling firsthand account of the effect of sexual trauma on one's sense of self, see Brison (1993).

25. For more on cognitive mechanisms underlying racial stigmatization of Blacks in America, see Anderson (2010, chap. 3).

26. Note that this is not to suggest that racial categories determine thoughts or actions.

27. It would be false to suggest that trust of *any* kind could not obtain between any two persons in contemporary America, so long as one of them was white and the other was not; my suggestion is not that no kind of trust is ever possible. (While I haven't characterized "thick trust" in this chapter, I take it to be a kind of trust that arises when one has a sense of the other's character. Such a sense can develop over time, even if it was circumstantial necessity, rather than thin trust, that brought people together in the first place.) Rather, my suggestion is that American white supremacy makes impossible warranted thin trust between those who are constructed as non-white and

those who are constructed as white, because of the ignorance that it inculcates in those who are constructed as white.

28. This is not entirely true; Jupiter is amazing, and I would love to know the elemental composition of its atmosphere.

29. He notes: "A great deal of one's energy is expended in reassuring white Americans that they do not see what they see. This is utterly futile, of course, since they *do* see what they see. And what they see is an appallingly oppressive and bloody history known all over the world. What they see is a disastrous, continuing, present condition which menaces them, and for which they bear an inescapable responsibility. But since in the main they seem to lack the energy to change this condition they would rather not be reminded of it." See Baldwin (1998b).

30. James P. Sterba points out that it is only true that colonial treatment of indigenous Americans fell short of genocide if we consider Native Americans as one big undifferentiated group. He cites Lenore A. Stiffarm, noting that "The 1890 U.S. Census found that the once populous Karankawans, Akokisa, Bidui, Tejas, and Coahuiltecans were entirely extinct."

31. While historians and economists debate the precise nature of the role that slavery played in the development of the US and global economy, few can deny the centrality of slavery as a cause of the Civil War, given Alexander H. Stephens's 1861 declaration that the cornerstone of the Confederacy rests "upon that great truth that the negro is not equal to the white man; that slavery, subordination to the superior race is his natural and normal condition. This, our new government, is the first, in the history of the world, based upon this great physical, philosophical, and moral truth." Despite this, there is only one museum in the country dedicated to slavery (Schott 1996, 334). For discussion of the role of slavery in US economy and politics, see Williams 2014; Baptist 2016.

32. Abraham Lincoln is one of the most celebrated presidents of all time, with calls for a memorial coming within years of his death. (See Rottinghaus and Vaughn 2015.) The first museum dedicated to African American history—the Smithsonian's National Museum of African American History and Culture—did not open until 2016 (https://nmaahc.si.edu/about/museum). The first museum dedicated to Reconstruction's failures and the terrors of the Jim Crow–era lynching campaigns—the Equal Justice Initiative's museum, From Enslavement to Mass Incarceration—is not slated to open until 2018. (See Equal Justice Initiative n.d.)

33. For a thorough run-down of the role that selective memory plays in maintaining white ignorance, see Mills (2007). For a detailed account of the role that state-sanctioned redlining and housing discrimination played in generating intergenerational wealth disparities between Black and white families in twentieth-century Chicago, see Coates (2014).

34. Given that the production and maintenance of ignorance is a result of structural forces, such structures as class and patriarchy are likely to inculcate a degree of ignorance in the respective dominant groups (e.g., members of the upper class, and men).

35. "There are any number of ways in which African Americans are represented disproportionately in crime coverage, most blatantly by portraying them as violent offenders far more frequently than Whites are so portrayed (e.g., Peffley et al. 1996;

Dixon and Linz 2000; Gilliam and Iyengar 2000; Entman and Rojecki 2001). But there are more subtle practices that have the same effect. Oliver (1994) has found that Blacks are substantially more often shown resisting arrest and/or assaulting police officers, and are also more likely to be shown in a mug shot (Chiricos and Eschholz 2002). Entman and Rojecki (2001), moreover, have also argued that African Americans are more often shown in the grip of police officers than are Whites, who are often shielded by attorneys, and that White officers speak of Black offenders while the reverse is virtually never portrayed in the media." See Peffley and Hurwitz (2010, 149).

36. Consider Kant, regarding the views of a "Negro carpenter": "And it might be, that there were something in this which perhaps deserved to be considered; but in short, this fellow was *quite black* from head to foot, a clear proof that what he said was stupid" (Kant and Goldthwait 1960).

37. Note that this is consistent with both the claim that an increased focus on race is associated with overestimations of the prevalence of racial discrimination, and with the claim that an increased focus on race is associated with *more accurate* estimations of the prevalence of racial discrimination. Given that the empirical data is clear that racial inequality in America is drastic, and that stigmatizing stereotypes about Blacks are quite common, the latter claim finds more support.

38. I do want to note that I am very skeptical that the data reported in studies of "social trust" and "political trust" are really capturing *trust*; they seem like much better metrics of "expected cooperation" or "expected non-ill-will." Still, I think they are capturing something in the ballpark of trust, and so are illustrative of the effects we might expect to see for the trust with which we are here concerned.

REFERENCES

Alcoff, Linda Martín. 2007. "Epistemologies of Ignorance: Three Types." In *Race and Epistemologies of Ignorance*, edited by Shannon Sullivan and Nancy Tuana, 39–57. Albany: State University of New York Press.

———. 2015. *The Future of Whiteness*. Cambridge, UK: Polity Press.

Anderson, Elizabeth. 2010. *The Imperative of Integration*. Princeton, NJ: Princeton University Press.

Ansley, Frances Lee. 1989. "Stirring the Ashes: Race, Class and the Future of Civil Rights Scholarship." *Cornell Law Review* 74 (6): 993–1077.

Baier, Annette C. 1986. "Trust and Antitrust." *Ethics* 96 (2): 231–60.

Baldwin, James, ed. 1998a. *James Baldwin: Collected Essays*. New York: Library of America.

———. 1998b. "White Man's Guilt." In *James Baldwin: Collected Essays*, edited by Toni Morrison, 722–27. New York: Library of America.

Baptist, Edward E. 2016. *The Half Has Never Been Told*. New York: Basic Books.

Bicchieri, Cristina. 2006. *The Grammar of Society: The Emergence and Dynamics of Social Norms*. Cambridge, MA: Cambridge University Press.

———. 2017. *Norms in the Wild: How to Diagnose, Measure, and Change Social Norms*. Oxford, UK: Oxford University Press.

Brison, Susan T. 1993. "Surviving Sexual Violence: A Philosophical Perspective." *Journal of Social Philosophy* 24 (1): 5–22.

Coates, Ta-Nehisi. 2014. "The Case for Reparations." *The Atlantic*, June. https://www.theatlantic.com/magazine/archive/2014/06/the-case-for-reparations/361631/.

Collins, Patricia Hill. 2002. *Black Feminist Thought: Knowledge, Consciousness, and the Politics of Empowerment*. New York: Routledge.

Dawson, Michael. 1994. *Behind the Mule: Race and Class in African American Politics*. Princeton, NJ: Princeton University Press.

Equal Justice Initiative. "From Enslavement to Mass Incarceration Museum." https://eji.org/enslavement-to-mass-incarceration-museum.

Fricker, Miranda. 1998. "Rational Authority and Social Power: Towards a Truly Social Epistemology." *Proceedings of the Aristotelian Society* 98 (2): 159–77.

Gaus, Gerald F. 2006. *Hayek on the Evolution of Society and Mind*. Cambridge, UK: Cambridge University Press.

Govier, Trudy. 1992. "Trust, Distrust, and Feminist Theory." *Hypatia* 7 (1): 16–33.

Hardin, Russell. 2002. *Trust and Trustworthiness*. New York: Russell Sage Foundation.

Hayek, F. A. 1973. *Law, Legislation and Liberty: Rules and Order*. Chicago: University of Chicago Press.

Helliwell, John F., Haifang Huang, and Shun Wang. 2014. "Social Capital and Well-Being in Times of Crisis." *Journal of Happiness Studies* 15 (1): 145–62.

———. 2017. "New Evidence on Trust and Well-Being." Edited by Eric M. Uslaner. Oxford, UK: Oxford University Press.

Herzog, Lisa. 2017. "Markets." In *The Stanford Encyclopedia of Philosophy*, edited by Edward N. Zalta. Stanford, CA: Metaphysics Research Lab, Stanford University. https://plato.stanford.edu/archives/fall2017/entries/markets/.

Hollis, Martin. 1998. *Trust Within Reason*. Cambridge, UK: Cambridge University Press.

Jones, Karen. 1996. "Trust as an Affective Attitude." *Ethics* 107 (1): 4–25.

———. 2004. "Trust and Terror." In *Moral Psychology: Feminist Ethics and Social Theory*, edited by Peggy DesAutels, and Margaret Urban Walker, 3–18. Lanham, MD: Rowman & Littlefield.

Jost, John T. 2001. "Outgroup Favoritism and the Theory of System Justification: A Paradigm for Investigating the Effects of Socioeconomic Success on Stereotype Content." In *Cognitive Social Psychology: The Princeton Symposium on the Legacy and Future of Social Cognition*, edited by Gordon B. Moskowitz, 89–102. Abingdon, UK: Taylor and Francis.

Kant, Immanuel, and John T. Goldthwait. 1960. *Observations on the Feeling of the Beautiful and Sublime*. Berkeley: University of California Press.

Koehler, Jonathan J., and Andrew D. Gershoff. 2003. "Betrayal Aversion: When Agents of Protection Become Agents of Harm." *Organizational Behavior and Human Decision Processes* 90 (2): 244–61.

Lebron, Christopher J. 2013. *The Color of Our Shame: Race and Justice in Our Time*. Oxford, UK: Oxford University Press.

Martin, Nona, and Virgil Henry Storr. 2008. "On Perverse Emergent Orders." *Studies in Emergent Order* 1 (1): 73–91.

Massey, Douglas S. 2007. *Categorically Unequal: The American Stratification System*. New York: Russell Sage Foundation.

Mills, Charles W. 1997. *The Racial Contract*. Ithaca, NY: Cornell University Press.

Mills, Charles W. 2007. "White Ignorance." In *Race and Epistemologies of Ignorance*, edited by Shannon Sullivan and Nancy Tuana, 11–38. Albany: State University of New York Press.

Mills, Charles W. 2017. *Black Rights/White Wrongs: The Critique of Racial Liberalism*. New York: Oxford University Press.

Nozick, Robert. 1974. *Anarchy, State, and Utopia*. New York: Basic Books.

Nunnally, Shayla C. 2012. *Trust in Black America: Race, Discrimination, and Politics*. New York: New York University Press.

O'Neill, Onora. 2002. *A Question of Trust: The BBS Reith Lectures 2002*. Cambridge, UK: Cambridge University Press.

Orr, Marion. 1999. *Black Social Capital: The Politics of School Reform in Baltimore, 1986–1998. Studies in Government and Public Policy*. Lawrence: University Press of Kansas.

Outlaw, Lucius T., Jr. 2005. *Critical Social Theory in the Interests of Black Folks*. Lanham, MD: Rowman & Littlefield.

Peffley, Mark, and Jon Hurwitz. 2010. *Justice in America: The Separate Realities of Blacks and Whites*. Cambridge, UK: Cambridge University Press.

Postema, Gerald J. 2009. "Nature as First Custom: Hayek on the Evolution of Social Rules." UNC Legal Studies Research Paper No. 1505430.

Potter, Nancy Nyquist. 2002. *How Can I Be Trusted? A Virtue Theory of Trustworthiness*. Lanham, MD: Rowman & Littlefield.

Preston-Roedder, Ryan. 2017. "Civic Trust." *Philosophers' Imprint* 17 (4): 1–22.

Rottinghaus, Brandon, and Justin S. Vaughn. 2015. "Measuring Obama Against the Great Presidents." https://www.brookings.edu/blog/fixgov/2015/02/13/measuring-obama-against-the-great-presidents/.

Schott, T. E. 1996. *Alexander H. Stephens of Georgia: A Biography*. Baton Rouge: Louisiana State University Press.

Sellers, Robert M., and J. Nicole Shelton. 2003. "The Role of Racial Identity in Perceived Racial Discrimination." *Journal of Personality and Social Psychology* 84 (5): 1079–92.

Shelby, Tommie. 2016. *Dark Ghettos: Injustice, Dissent, and Reform*. Cambridge, MA: Harvard University Press.

Sigelman, Lee, and Steven A. Tuch. 1997. "Metastereotypes: Blacks' Perceptions of Whites' Stereotypes of Blacks." *Public Opinion Quarterly* 61 (1): 87–101.

Spelman, Elizabeth V. 2007. "Managing Ignorance." In *Race and Epistemologies of Ignorance*, edited by Shannon Sullivan, and Nancy Tuana, 119–31. Albany: State University of New York Press.

Starr, Sonja B., and M. Marit Rehavi. 2013. "Mandatory Sentencing and Racial Disparity: Assessing the Role of Prosecutors and the Effects of Booker." *Yale Law Journal* 123: 2–80.

Sterba, James P. 1996. "Review: Understanding Evil: American Slavery, the Holocaust, and the Conquest of the American Indians: Vessels of Evil: American

Slavery and the Holocaust. By Laurence Mordekhai Thomas." *Ethics* 106 (2): 424–48.

Stiffarm, Lenore A., and Phil Lane Jr. 1992. "The Demography of Native North America: A Question of American Indian Survival." In *The State of Native America: Genocide, Colonization, and Resistance*, edited by M. A. Jaimes. Boston: South End Press.

Walker, Margaret Urban. 2006. *Moral Repair: Reconstructing Moral Relations after Wrongdoing*. Cambridge, UK: Cambridge University Press.

Welch, Shay. 2013. "Transparent Trust and Oppression." *Critical Review of International Social and Political Philosophy* 16 (1): 45–64.

Wilkes, Rima, and Cary Wu. 2017. "Trust and Minority Groups." In *The Oxford Handbook of Social and Political Trust*, edited by Eric M. Uslaner. Oxford, UK: Oxford University Press.

Williams, Eric. 2014. *Capitalism and Slavery*. Chapel Hill, NC: UNC Press Books.

Wills, Vanessa. 2016. "Bad Guys and Dirty Hands: 'Ethical Policing' in the Presence of Racial Injustice." *The Critique* May/June 2016.

Woozley, Anthony D. 1973. "Injustice." *American Philosophical Quarterly Monograph Series: Studies in Ethics* 7.

Index

About the Contributors

Mr. Mikołaj Barczentewicz, lecturer, University of Surrey, The School of Law, and research associate, University of Oxford Programme for the Foundation of Law and Constitutional Government.

Dr. Peter J. Boettke, university professor of Economics and Philosophy, George Mason University, and director, F. A. Hayek Program for Advanced Study in Philosophy, Politics and Economics, Mercatus Center at George Mason University.

Dr. Crystal A. Dozier, assistant professor, Wichita State University, Department of Anthropology.

Mr. Adam Frost, PhD student, Harvard University.

Mr. Daniel Gibbs, PhD student, Princeton University.

Ms. Samantha Godwin, resident fellow, Information Society Project, Yale University.

Mr. Caleb Harrison, PhD student, University of North Carolina-Chapel Hill.

Ms. Liz Hemsley, PhD student, The University of Hong Kong.

Dr. Brian Kogelmann, assistant professor, University of Maryland; faculty affiliate, Ed Snider Center for Enterprise and Markets; and affiliated fellow,

F. A. Hayek Program for Advanced Study in Philosophy, Politics, and Economics, Mercatus Center at George Mason University.

Dr. Jayme S. Lemke, senior fellow, F. A. Hayek Program for Advanced Study in Philosophy, Politics and Economics, and senior research fellow, Mercatus Center at George Mason University.

Mr. Matthew Martinez, PhD student, University of Nevada–Las Vegas.

Mr. Gregory Robson, PhD student, University of Arizona.

Dr. Virgil Henry Storr, research associate professor of Economics, George Mason University, and Don C. Lavoie Senior Fellow, F. A. Hayek Program for Advanced Study in Philosophy, Politics and Economics, Mercatus Center at George Mason University.

Dr. Brianne Wolf, assistant professor, Ashland University, Department of History and Political Science, and director, Political Economy Program, Ashland University.

www.ingramcontent.com/pod-product-compliance
Lightning Source LLC
LaVergne TN
LVHW101445200926
848483LV00001B/56
* 9 7 8 1 7 8 6 6 0 5 6 3 4 *